Performing the Queer Past

Methuen Drama Agitations: Text, Politics and Performances

Theater has always offered immediate responses to political, social, economic and cultural crisis events that are local, national, and global in dimension, establishing itself as a prime medium of engagement. Methuen Drama Agitations interrogates these manifold intersections between theater and the contemporary: What is the relationship between theater and reality? Which functions does the theater perform in public life? Where does the radical potential of the theater reside and how is it untapped?

Methuen Drama Agitations addresses issues from across a number of spectrums, including contemporary politics, environmental concerns, issues of gender and race, and the challenges of globalization. The series focuses on text as much as performance, on theory as much as practice. It investigates the lively dialogues between theater and contemporary lived experience.

Series Editors
William C. Boles (Rollins College, USA)
Anja Hartl (University of Innsbruck, Austria)

Advisory Board
Lynnette Goddard (Royal Holloway, University of London, UK)
Anton Krueger (Rhodes University, South Africa)
Marcus Tan (Nanyang Technological University, Singapore)
Sarah J. Townsend (Penn State University, USA)
Denise Varney (University of Melbourne, Australia)

Theater of Lockdown: Digital and Distanced Performance in a Time of Pandemic
Barbara Fuchs

Theater in a Post-Truth World: Texts, Politics, and Performance
Edited by William C. Boles

Performing Statecraft: The Postdiplomatic Theatre of Sovereigns, Citizens, and States
Edited by James R. Ball III

Contemporary Black Theatre and Performance: Acts of Rebellion, Activism, and Solidarity
Edited by DeRon S. Williams, Khalid Y. Long and Martine Kei Green-Rogers

Performing Left Populism: Performance, Politics and the People
Edited by Goran Petrović Lotina and Théo Aiolfi

Forthcoming Titles

Theatre and its Audiences: Reimagining the Relationship in Times of Crisis
Kate Craddock and Helen Freshwater

Theatres of Disruption in 21st-Century Britain: Plays and Performances in Turbulent Times
Ellen Redling

Performing the Queer Past

Public Possessions

Fintan Walsh

methuen | drama
LONDON • NEW YORK • OXFORD • NEW DELHI • SYDNEY

METHUEN DRAMA
Bloomsbury Publishing Plc
50 Bedford Square, London, WC1B 3DP, UK
1385 Broadway, New York, NY 10018, USA
29 Earlsfort Terrace, Dublin 2, Ireland

BLOOMSBURY, METHUEN DRAMA and the Methuen Drama logo are trademarks of Bloomsbury Publishing Plc

First published in Great Britain 2023
Paperback edition published 2025

Copyright © Fintan Walsh, 2023

Fintan Walsh has asserted his right under the Copyright, Designs and Patents Act, 1988, to be identified as Author of this work.

For legal purposes the Acknowledgements on pp. xii–xiii constitute an extension of this copyright page.

Series design by Ben Anslow
Cover image: Gardenia (Photograph © Luk Monsaert / laGeste)

All rights reserved. No part of this publication may be reproduced or transmitted in any form or by any means, electronic or mechanical, including photocopying, recording, or any information storage or retrieval system, without prior permission in writing from the publishers.

Bloomsbury Publishing Plc does not have any control over, or responsibility for, any third-party websites referred to or in this book. All internet addresses given in this book were correct at the time of going to press. The author and publisher regret any inconvenience caused if addresses have changed or sites have ceased to exist, but can accept no responsibility for any such changes.

A catalogue record for this book is available from the British Library.

A catalog record for this book is available from the Library of Congress.

ISBN: HB: 978-1-3502-9796-8
PB: 978-1-3502-9800-2
ePDF: 978-1-3502-9798-2
eBook: 978-1-3502-9797-5

Series: Methuen Drama Agitations: Text, Politics and Performances

Typeset by Newgen KnowledgeWorks Pvt. Ltd., Chennai, India

To find out more about our authors and books visit www.bloomsbury.com and sign up for our newsletters.

For George

Contents

List of Figures x
Acknowledgements xii

Introduction: Performing queer possession 1
1 Channelling ghosts: The haunted present 31
2 Muscle memories: Exe(o)rcising history 59
3 Re-enacting violence: Sharing responsibility 85
4 Arresting objects: Transforming matters 107
5 Wilde spirits: Occupation and commemoration 131
6 Grief's ricochet: Intermedial returns 161
7 Epilogue: Shorelines of the dispossessed 185

Notes 193
References 203
Index 221

Figures

0.1 The deceased former cast member, Andrea de Laet, is remembered with an empty chair bearing her dress in *Gardenia – 10 Years Later,* NTGent, Ghent, Belgium (2021).   2
1.1 Dickie Beau lip-synchs the voices of the absent and dead, on stage and via digital screens, in *Re-Member Me*, Almeida Theatre, London, UK (2017).   40
1.2 Karen Finley performing in *Written in Sand*, The Pit, Barbican, London, UK (2015).   49
2.1 Franko B fights with a milk-filled golden boxing bag, which leaks across the floor, in *Milk & Blood*, Toynbee Studios, London, UK (2015).   67
2.2 Cassils is captured mounting clay in *Becoming an Image,* Perth Institute of Contemporary Arts, Australia (2019).   72
3.1 Tom Adjibi, who plays Ihsane Jarfi, is interviewed as part of the staged casting process in *La Reprise: Histoire(s) du théâtre (I)*, Théâtre National, Wallonie-Bruxelles, Belgium (2018).   89
3.2 Travis Alabanza performing in *Burgerz*, Hackney Showroom, London, UK (2018).   98
4.1 Franklin (Terique Jarrett), surrounded by the dolls he has made representing his mother Zora (left) and partner Andre (right) in *'Daddy': A Melodrama*, Almeida Theatre, London, UK (2022).   113
4.2 Rachel Mars welding in *Forge*, Testbed, Leeds, UK (2022).   120

5.1	Artangel's *Inside: Artists and Writers in Reading Prison* featuring Oscar Wilde's cell door in Jean-Michel Pancin's installation *In Memoriam*, Reading, UK (2016).	141
5.2	Artangel's *Inside: Artists and Writers in Reading Prison* featuring Marlene Dumas's painting *Oscar Wilde*, Reading, UK (2016).	142
5.3	McDermott & McGough's *The Oscar Wilde Temple*, Studio Voltaire, London, UK (2018).	146
5.4	Francis Fay kisses a cell wall in Kilmainham Gaol, Dublin, Ireland, as part of his durational performance *Marking Time/A Love Letter* (2010).	153
6.1	Belfast Ensemble's digital production of *Ten Plagues* (2022) featuring Matthew Cavan.	166
6.2	Peggy Shaw (left) and Lois Weaver (right) in *Last Gasp: A Recalibration*, The Pit, Barbican, London, UK (2021).	173
7.1	Théodore Géricault, *Le Radeau de la Méduse* (1818–19), Musée du Louvre, Paris, France.	187
7.2	David Hoyle speaking from a pulpit in *Ten Commandments*, Soho Theatre, London, UK (2022).	189

Acknowledgements

In the Department of English, Theatre and Creative Writing at Birkbeck, University of London, I am indebted to all those who have helped make it such a supportive and stimulating environment in which to conduct this research. I am especially grateful to those with whom I have worked most closely in recent years, including Anthony Bale, Heike Bauer, Emma Bennett, Carolyn Burdett, Luisa Calè, Lewis Church, Isabel Davis, Molly Flynn, Seda Ilter, Caoimhe Mader McGuinness, Flora Pitrolo, Rob Swain, Sue Wiseman and Gillian Woods. Louise Owen deserves special mention, for my work and life benefit enormously from our professional and personal relationship. Some of this project, especially Chapter 1, was thankfully supported by Birkbeck Wellcome Trust Institutional Strategic Support Fund.

Birkbeck's endlessly inspiring students joined me in exploring some of these ideas in embryonic form, and my thinking certainly benefitted from those conversations. Early drafts of some chapters were first shared with colleagues in the Queer Futures working group of the International Federation for Theatre Research, and I invariably appreciate the encouraging and cordial environment that this forum provides.

Portions of this book have already been published in different forms. Chapter 1 contains some material previously published as 'Viral Hamlet: History, Memory, Kinship', in *Theatres of Contagion: Transmitting Early Modern to Contemporary Performance*, ed. Fintan Walsh (London: Methuen Drama, 2020); a version of Chapter 2 was published as 'Pugilistic Queer Performance: Working Through and Working Out', *GLQ: A Journal of Gay and Lesbian Studies*, 26(4) (2020), and most of Chapter 5 has appeared as 'ReWild(e)ing Queer Performance', *Contemporary Theatre Review*, 31(3) (2021). I am grateful to those who helped bring these publications to print, and to the publishers for granting me permission to reproduce them in revised form.

I am thankful to those artists who have discussed their work with me, in particular Dickie Beau and Rachel Mars. I am indebted to Dickie and Rachel for generously sharing production materials with me, alongside Artangel, Cassils, Francis Fay, Karen Finley, les ballet C de la B, McDermott & McGough and Lois Weaver. Thanks also to the photographers who allowed me to include their images. I am grateful to all those at Bloomsbury and Methuen Drama who helped bring this book to publication, including the series editors William C. Boles and Anja Hartl, Senior Publisher Mark Dudgeon, Editorial Assistant Ella Wilson, copyeditors and reviewers.

Finally, my deepest gratitude and love to friends, for time spent inside and outside galleries and theatres, including Áine, Aoife, Barry, Brian, David, Fiona, George, Graham, Joseph, Laurence, Louise, Luigi, Phillip, Teo, Thomas and Willy.

Introduction: Performing queer possession

A vacant chair, reserved for the dead, takes centre stage at the opening of the 2021 revival of *Gardenia* at Sadler's Wells Theatre, London. Strewn over its wooden shoulders, the sequined gown of Andrea De Laet, one of the production's original performers who died in 2016, ensures that the past persists in the memories and materials of the present (Figure 0.1). The chair to my right is also free, having been stood up by a friend who suddenly fell ill. From the first circle, I spy empty seats punctuate the auditorium too, perhaps reflecting a broad reluctance to return to live events after months of covid-19 lockdowns. As each cast member is introduced by compere Vanessa Van Durme, the audience is invited to remember all those who cannot be with us on this crisp November night, by acknowledging the absence that they leave behind and the space that they continue to take up.

Directed by Frank Van Laecke and Alain Platel for Ghent-based les ballets C de la B, *Gardenia* has enjoyed over a decade of touring, commentary and documentation since its premiere in 2010.[1] Underscoring its surprise longevity, this pandemic production has arrived under the revised title *Gardenia – 10 Years Later*. Devised with older drag queens and transgender performers, the conceit of the show is that we are watching the last performance of the Gardenia cabaret. This structuring narrative is inspired by Sonia Herman Dolz's documentary film *Yo Soy Asi* (2000), which captures the final days of Barcelona's variety club La Bodega Bohemia. The small but legendary venue began its life as a grocery store in the 1920s, with a backdoor leading to a performance space, which survived most of the century until the city's aggressive gentrification schemes of the 1990s conspired to shut it down for good.

Figure 0.1 The deceased former cast member, Andrea de Laet, is remembered with an empty chair bearing her dress in *Gardenia – 10 Years Later*, NTGent, Ghent, Belgium (2021). Photographer: Luk Monsaert.

Gardenia unfolds as the performers throw off their everyday clothes and slip into lavish cabaret costumes, while delivering speeches, lip-synch routines and subtly choreographed sequences. Initially, I am struck by how the pacing is much slower than I had expected. Perhaps, I surmise, we are all moving more cautiously since 2010. Opening with a crackling rendition of 'Somewhere Over the Rainbow,' whose riffs reverberate throughout the show, it is never entirely clear whether this production deems the bluebird-flying good times to be above us or below us, behind us or ahead of us, or right here in the busy junction of live performance. For despite being a show about theatrical closure, in its eleven-year run to date, this production seems rather hesitant to end itself. In its internal dramaturgy and production history, a cabaret's ending only precipitates this show's beginning, another chance to perform again.

Since its premiere, *Gardenia*'s meaning and significance have inevitably changed. The show can no longer be received as solely about the former lives of its performers, but what has happened to the original cast and the world in the intervening period. In the Western milieu of its circulation, this was a time defined by the legal recognition of same-sex partnerships and marriages across many countries, but also assaults on the hard-won rights of LGBTQ+ people. Most recently, in 2022, this includes the introduction of the so-called 'Don't Say Gay Bill' (HB 1557) in Florida, which supports 'prohibiting a school district from encouraging classroom discussion about sexual orientation or gender identity in primary grade levels' (2022: 1),[2] and which recalls Britain's former Section 28 of the Local Government Act 1988 that banned the 'promotion' of homosexuality in schools (1988: 27).[3] It was a period also characterized by the broad social acceptance of LGBTQ+ people, as well as a rise in homophobic and transphobic attacks across Europe and the United States,[4] and a threat to bodily autonomy as a result of the overturning of Roe *v* Wade in 2022.[5] It was a period during which the increased visibility of LGBTQ+ people and culture was matched by the shutting down of queer venues across most of the main metropolitan centres, sometimes as an outcome of strategic vandalism.⁶ It was a time dominated by a proliferation of debate concerning trans identities and rights, as well as concurrent attempts to ferociously control and curtail them via manufacturing panic surrounding bathroom usage and gender self-identification, resembling a resurgence of 1990s style culture wars. It was an era during which the German Bundestag passed the Act on the Criminal Rehabilitation of Persons Sentenced for Consensual Homosexual Acts after 8 May 1945 (2017), which pardoned all men who had been convicted by German courts of consensual homosexual acts after the end of the Nazi regime, quickly chased by reported spikes in hate crimes against LGBTI+ people, especially on the grounds of gender identity.⁷ In the UK, the period produced the momentous pardoning of all men charged with gross indecency under Section 11 of the Criminal Law Amendment Act 1885, with the passing of the Policing and Crime Act 2017, or so-called Turing Law, while subsequent administrations chewed over the merits of conversion therapy.⁸ A decade that began in the shadow of a global recession ended with a coronavirus pandemic, which recalled the peak of the AIDS crisis as it affected queer communities in the 1980s and 1990s, and wreaked havoc on our personal, social, medical and economic lives.

While this list is by no means an exhaustive account of the recent lurches forwards and backwards affecting LGBTQ+ people, some of the most damaging sabotage appeared to happen internally. What was, ten years ago, taken for granted as the natural alliance among all the letters in the LGBTQ+ initialism, has also become a particularly fraught relationship, often to the detriment of the trans community. This is perhaps best evidenced in the UK, where anti-trans discourse became especially virulent, led by the establishment of the LGB Alliance in 2019, to oppose the LGBT rights charity Stonewall's more inclusive policies on transgender individuals. For more reasons than one, *Gardenia* in 2021 could not simply be read as about the closure of a queer venue, as it may have been in 2010, but of queer culture's capacity to absorb, resist, remember and survive extraordinary personal, social, political and economic adversity.

Although the world has changed since *Gardenia* first opened, in the tradition of cabaret, the production has unapologetically returned loss with extravagance, grief with joy, death with regeneration. When I attended the revival, the stakes for this exchange felt particularly high. Not only was *Gardenia* the first show I saw in person after intermittent lockdowns, but it had also taken me ten years to rebook the ticket I had first purchased in 2011, when the production played as part of Dublin Theatre Festival. On that occasion, a move from Dublin to London spoiled my theatre-going plans. A decade later, and we have both lived a bit more, grown a bit older, flipped fresh layers of experience onto the bank we call 'the past'.

When I began writing this book, I had not intended for its temporal parameters to align so neatly with my efforts to attend *Gardenia*. Initially spurred by an essay I wrote on the sense of psychical and theatrical possession in the work of Dickie Beau (Walsh 2020, in part reproduced in Chapter 1), my original aim was to examine how the queer past seemed to possess contemporary theatre and performance as a kind of haunting. It was only when I finally saw *Gardenia* did I realize that not only had I been writing about a specific time of cultural production, and associated social and legal transformation, but also about personal experience, and the encounters and opportunities that my time living and working in the UK had made possible. I had been writing about my own recent past, and the histories nested within it, which opened like stacking dolls into a pool of time that I did not immediately recognize as my own. If queer theatre and performance are possessed by the past, as I came to realize in writing this book, it is only because we are too.

Temporal tensions

Social and political progress are often accompanied by coercive presentism, which seeks to minimize or deny prior complicity in violence. But as the period between 2010 and 2023, which this book focuses on, makes clear: whatever progress LGBTQ+ culture makes does not happen in straight lines, but in the swerves, escalations and reversions of time that show every generation, every apparent step forward, to be possessed by the past that produced it, and which it endeavours to supersede. Indeed, even what seems like one culture's or person's past, is often another's present or imminent reality: time ticks unevenly locally, globally and personally. It may be true that *it gets better* for some queer people, as the celebrity-endorsed slogan proposes, but not for all, and rarely without also getting worse.[9]

This pattern of uneven progress is also reflected in some of the debates and initiatives that have dominated queer culture in recent years. One significant example includes concern surrounding the need to commemorate AIDS history via public monuments and gardens, recently exemplified by the opening of the AIDS Garden Chicago in 2022, while London, and other urban centres, still fight for similar sites. Similarly, this has been evidenced in cultural programming, which has indicated that the past must be continuously kept alive to interrogate, support, supplement and contest social and legal transformations. For instance, the exhibition *Out and About! Archiving LGBTQ+ history at Bishopsgate Institute* at the Barbican's The Curve in 2022, featured installation, objects, ephemera and media to document the social, cultural and political history of LGBTQ+ Londoners. In the same year, Queer Britain, the country's first LGBTQ+ museum opened in London, with the aim of ensuring the past remains a vital guide in how we navigate the present, following other institutions such as Schwules Museum, Berlin or GLBT Historical Society Museum, San Francisco.

Retrospectives sought to foreground the transformative contributions of queer people and culture in recent history, while signposting their legacy and ongoing relevance. Such was the effect of numerous exhibitions, including Leigh Bowery's costumes (*Tell Them I've Gone to Papua New Guinea*, The Fitzrovia Chapel, London, 2022); Michael Clarke's dance and choreography (*Michael Clarke: Cosmic Dancer*, Barbican, London, 2022); Derek Jarman's protest art (*Derek*

Jarman Protest!, Manchester Art Gallery, 2021 and IMMA [Irish Museum of Modern Art], Dublin, 2019), and Keith Haring's visual corpus (*Keith Haring*, Tate Liverpool, 2019). In these retrospectives, we were offered a vivid glimpse into how queer lives and art have interacted with and shaped broader social movements, political debates and cultural production since the latter part of the twentieth century, while continuing to enrich and pressure the present.

While these particular retrospectives are not analysed in depth in this book, the study is committed to exploring the kinds of temporal overlaps, juxtapositions and tensions they signal in the context of contemporary theatre and performance. I am not interested in containing and packaging the past as neat and complete, but in exploring how it makes itself felt in the present – its immaterial and material hauntings, occupations and claims. To this end, in this book I ask: how do contemporary theatre and performance appear to be possessed by the queer past? What aesthetic practices and dramaturgical devices are deployed to invoke these possessions in the public spaces of theatre and performance? What histories of loss, hurt and grief does possessed performance deliver? What tactics are mobilized to remodel the past's possession of the present, and the present's possession of the past? How might the experience of theatre and performance work to relieve the present of its most arduous burdens?

This book primarily focuses on cultural production since 2010, drawing on examples that emerged from or circulated within Western Europe and North America. While I often encountered this work in the UK, I do not aim to tell a single national or even cultural story, let alone to write a history. In fact, the book is premised on the assumption that such methodologies belie the extent to which queer theatre and performance confound neat orderings of time and place, not only in their eclectic influences and production routes, but in the ways they are possessed by pasts that are not obviously their own. Rather, the study foregrounds the diverse means by which the past's hold on the present is enacted, by analysing a range of innovative forms deployed by contemporary theatre and performance, including digital theatre, experimental performance, installation, live art and site-specific interventions. In endeavouring to understand this body of work, I explore possession via the sometimes overlapping domains of haunting, holding, occupying and owning, and develop a theory of queer possession as both the occupation of the present by the past, and the present's attempt to take control of these occupations. Theatre and performance, viewed from this perspective, are deemed to have the capacity to hold history, materially and immaterially, and to share (or withhold) it in the present.

My critical approach advances that minds, bodies, sites, archives, objects and narratives are often haunted, claimed or imprinted by troubled or unsettled pasts, and it looks to theatre and performance practices that stage a reckoning with these occupations. Situated at the intersection of psychic experience and material conditions, this model of queer possession plays out in theatre and performance via strategies of channelling and haunting, working through and working out, recollection and replay, reproduction and transformation, occupation and commemoration, intermedial recontextualization and dissemination. These modes not only insist on the difficult past's place in the present, but also offer new ways for understanding queer history and culture, the locus of violence and trauma, the power of representational and narrative control, and theatre and performance's shared role in shaping civic and political life. While the theory of queer possession developed here is mobilized across specific case studies, I offer it as a conceptual framework that might enjoy wider application beyond the specific parameters of this book, to help understand the many ways in which the past haunts and occupies the present.

In researching this project, I must admit there have been times when I felt unsure what the word 'queer' even meant anymore, or what political value it might still hold. My initial interest in queer theory was its facility to disturb and thwart singular identity claims rather than to affirm them, in order to make room for those who would benefit from such a space-making gesture. In recent years, however, the term has shifted from being an umbrella descriptor that signalled the shared interests of a plethora of non-normative identities, to naming a singular identity, to describing a vague style or feeling of difference. Certainly, the current social and political flavour of queer discourse seems unable to absorb the kind of non-identitarian rhetoric espoused by 1990s high queer theory, which arguably peaked with Lee Edelman's *No Future* (2004).

Across the various chapters that comprise this book, I ground queerness in specific instances of sexual and cultural politics that also disrupt simple and singular constructions of identity, while also allowing it to drift towards new conceptual borders that help us to better understand the operations of aesthetic and dramaturgical form in mining and representing history. Despite my occasional frustrations with such a protean concept, my approach to queerness is nonetheless informed by a belief that the term still has something to offer us in trying to navigate and politicize the ambiguous interstices between mind and body, subjectivity and identity, identity and sociality, enactment and representation and the often unpredictable interactions and interruptions of time and/in space. Queerness, as an heuristic, is an invitation to attend to all the impulses, feelings and experiences that more rigidly regulated social formations, such as identity and history, cannot readily account for. In this formulation, queerness operates as a structuring temporal and spatial metaphor for all that cannot be neatly kept apart. As a set of aesthetic practices or dramaturgical devices, queer possession allows us to apprehend in tacit, diffuse and material form the past that we unwittingly inherit and contain, and our efforts to hold these histories in place and to pass them on; that is, to make them meaningful and bearable.

Queer time

The temporal tensions that define the period explored in this book are reflected in some of the conceptual frameworks and vocabularies to have emerged within queer theory in the surrounding period. Historically, queer cultural production has often been inclined towards death, informed by the presumed incapacity of queer people to reproduce, the moral danger associated with their sexuality, and the risk of death linked to AIDS. Legislation for same-sex marriage and adoption, however, and advancements in HIV treatment and prevention – in particular the availability of PrEP (pre-exposure prophylaxis) medication for some since 2012 – have disrupted this morbid association. In queer theory, this temporal shift has been at least implicitly reflected in the fact that some of the most influential theoretical contributions in the past two decades have focused on queerness's relationship to the future. For instance, while Edelman figured queerness as that which opposes reproductive futurism, which he elaborates as 'the bar to every realization of futurity, the resistance, internal to the social, to every social structure or form' (2004: 4), José Esteban Muñoz imagined a utopian future from the artistic imprints of the past, proposing that we 'animate our critical faculties by bringing the past to bear on the present and the future' (2009: 27).

In the bleak presentism of Edelman, and the warmer Messianism of Muñoz, I find no easy comfort nor convincing guidance on how to manage the terrors of time past, passing or dawning. While seemingly opposed, both positions are premised on an idea of self-sacrifice, in which the present must be endured, either as an ethical stand against the future (Edelman), or in anticipation of something better (Muñoz). Not everyone can afford to endure the present, and turn their sacrifice into something of value – this a privilege that cuts across gendered, class and racial lines. But without rejecting the future or desperately holding out for a better one, we might at minimum acknowledge the ways in which we are already possessed by pasts that we must live with, own and share – that is, histories that we must possess and dispossess, including via the aesthetic and dramaturgical structures of artistic practice.

The futural investments of Edelman and Muñoz are tempered by Elizabeth Freeman's focus on queer historiography. Freeman critiques a chrononormative model of time, which she takes to be causal, sequential, linear and progressive, to explore the manifold ways via which we are bound to the past. This queer temporality, as Freeman describes it, can be discerned in instances of temporal drag, or 'the pull of the past on the present' (2010: 62), such as 'moments of asynchrony, anachronism, anastrophe, belatedness, compression, delay, ellipsis, flashback, hysteron-proteron, pause, prolepsis, repetition, reversal, surprise, and other ways of breaking apart what Walter Benjamin calls "homogeneous empty time"' (ibid.: xxii).

These queer temporalities, Freeman advances, are 'points of resistance to this temporal order that, in turn, propose other possibilities for living in relation to indeterminately past, present, and future others: that is, of living historically' (ibid.). For Freeman, this drag is 'a *productive* obstacle to progress, a usefully distorting pull backward, and a necessary pressure on the present tense' (ibid.: 64). In Rebecca Schneider's conceptualization, temporal drag equates to 'temporal play as cross-generational negotiation' (2011: 14). Describing her own method as erotohistoriographical, Freeman asserts that it 'does not write the lost object into the present so much as encounters it already in the present, by treating the present itself as hybrid. And it uses the body as a tool to effect, figure or perform that encounter' (2010: 95).

Freeman's work absorbs and refashions the postcolonial critiques of Homi K. Bhabha. For Bhabha, postcolonial modernity is neither teleological nor all slippage, but can be characterized by a time-lag, which slows down the 'progressive time of modernity' to reveal its gaps and stresses. Bhabha holds up Bertolt Brecht's epic theatre as an example of how this operates, 'by damming the stream of real life, by bringing the flow to a standstill in a reflux of astonishment' (1991: 214). 'When the dialectic of modernity is brought to a standstill', Bhabha continues, 'then the temporal action of modernity – its progressive, future drive – is *staged*, revealing "everything that is involved in the act of staging *per se*"' (ibid.). This slowing down, or lagging of time, which Bhabha associates with Brecht, 'keeps alive the making of the past' (ibid.: 215).

Political theatre has evolved since Brecht, of course, although his influence can still be felt in the disruptive gestures, temporal layering and historical reordering of some queer theatre and performance. Aspects of these devices, for instance, can be discerned in Jacyln I. Pryor's conceptualization of the slipperiness of time in the experience of watching queer performance. Pryor's interpretative approach shares more vocabulary with Freeman than Brecht, but with a focus on the subjective experience of spectatorship in the context of 'trauma and survivorship' (2017: 4). The term 'time slips' is advanced by Pryor to denote moments in which they, as a spectator (or maker), 'experienced time queerly'; that is, felt it 'move backward, lunge forward, loop, jump, stack, stop, pause, linger, elongate, pulsate, slip', allowing them to 'feel the violence of linear time and historical "progress"' (ibid.: 9). Focusing on moments in contemporary Black art and performance, in which subversions of sexual and gender conformity prove 'excessive, disorderly, or simply unintelligible to an external gaze', Tavia Nyong'o submits that this work has the capacity to distort our sense of linear time, rearranging our perceptions of chronology, time and temporality' (2019: 4).

Striking a different note, which resonates with Peggy Phelan's early claims on the ontology of performance (1993), Joshua Chambers-Letson argues that performance, like communism, like the party, 'is an ephemeral, temporary happening in which singular beings crash into each other for a time to become a being singular plural' (2018: xxi). When the performance and the party end, Chambers-Letson suggests, 'they slip away from each other, falling back into the void' (ibid.). We may feel a sense of ephemerality and voiding at the end of a performance, as with the end of a party, but as the chapters in this book seek to illustrate, that which appears to slip away never quite disappears, when imprinted in the memories, bodies, sites, archives, objects and narratives of the present.

Scenes of possession are a feature of the theatrical avant-garde, James M. Harding has suggested, confirming that its spirit lives on past any claims to its singular origin or death. Harding identifies the 'state of possession' which Dadaist pioneer Hugo Ball effected at the Cabaret Voltaire in Zurich, Switzerland, in July 1916, while incantating the non-sensical verse 'Gadji Beri Bimba', as the start of one particularly influential avant-garde. The sounds that Ball performed on the night in question, Harding claims, ironized political doublespeak and war lust, and 'functioned as an exorcism of sorts, a battle to expel the forces that prey upon the vulnerability of words to cynical political appropriation' (Harding 2013: 6).

The kinds of possession at play in this book could be seen as regressive, insofar as they perform attachments to the past that might hold queer culture back from a brighter present, and because they seem not quite compatible with the idea of a clean break with tradition that has dominated interpretations of the artistic avant-garde. As I endeavour to demonstrate, however, we can also detect in this possessiveness the vanguardism of queer history's ghosts and legacies, whose transformative power resides in their capacity to double, haunt, shadow, fade and disappear, within a culture that privileges clear and clean narratives, and in particular traumatic resolution and historical closure.

With each of these aforementioned thinkers, I share a sense of time's pliant morphology, which theatre and performance, as temporal and spatial practices, are uniquely placed to expose and explore. The experience of time *as queer*, however, is not reserved for those who identify as such. Yet, because of the specificities of queer history, which have been largely defined by erasure, loss and death, queer cultural production allows us to access something of the *queer feeling* that the experience of all historical time can produce, especially troubled pasts. When I talk about queer time, therefore, I do not mean a category of time that only queer-identifying people can access and experience, but in a more broadly figurative sense, the queerness of all time; that is, the uncanny way it never charges forward, without looping backwards; how it never stays in the past, without seeming to flow into the future.

While the title of this book refers to the 'queer past' to help define the temporal coordinates of the project, the *back thereness* of the past it evokes is itself illusory. Certainly, the past cannot be stored in containers that separate it from the present, rather the past is always *of* the present. As Michel-Rolph Trouillot argues, the past can only exist because we have the present, although both are imaginary constructs – there is no past *there* about which we can speak, no present *here* from which we might do so. Rather, as Trouillot puts it, 'The past – or, more accurately, pastness – is a position' (1995: 15). In a similar spirit, in this book I approach the queer past – or *pastness* – less as a destination that we can visit, than as a position within the present from where we can look, to observe and understand what has transpired and is burgeoning, and the ways in which these modes of eventing are invariably interwoven.

Returns of the dis/possessed

This book strives to understand the ways and means by which the past appears in the public spaces of theatre and performance via ideas of possession. The *Merriam-Webster Dictionary* defines possession in multiple ways, including: 'the act of having or taking into control'; 'something owned, occupied, or controlled'; 'domination by something (such as an evil spirit, a passion, or an idea)'.[10] Drawing at various stages on each of these explanations, my guiding definition of possession is the act, feeling or thought of haunting, holding, occupying or owning a person, idea or thing. We might make the additional distinction between that which we are *possessed by*, and that which takes *possession of* us. Yet, as we will discover over the course of this book, these divisions frequently blur, and the balance of power between both poles often sways back and forth.

In this study I explore possession in psychic and physical dimensions, that is as both an immaterial and material phenomenon, and how it operates within and among the minds, bodies, sites, archives, objects and narratives that comprise the book. I analyse how the past possesses the present psychically, emotionally and materially, and how the present endeavours to take ownership and control of the past. The idea of 'public possession', central to the book, takes on number of meanings and functions. In one sense, it refers to the means by which the past haunts the public spaces of culture, via memory, fantasy, commemorative objects and gestures, and the psychic life and communications of artists and audiences. In another way, it indexes how queer people and their spaces are objectified and commodified in the public sphere, through violation or commemoration, and the ways they take charge of how history is recorded and communicated via artistic production. Shaped by the sometimes competing pressures of deliberate actions and unconscious impulses, in the spaces of public possession we try to grapple what it is in history that haunts us – the ghosts we need to keep or just occasionally remember, and those we need to exorcise for good.

A constellation of philosophical, sociological and psychoanalytic thought on possession and haunting guides my approach. Jacques Derrida coined the word 'hauntology', as a portmanteau of haunting and ontology, to describe how the past returns in the present, like a ghost, and how the spectre's materialization is (forever) anticipated. In *Specters of Marx*, Derrida considers the figure of the spectre in Marxism, starting with the opening lines of *The Communist Manifesto* – 'A specter is haunting Europe – the specter of communism' (Marx and Engels [1848] 1955: 8). Derrida reads this spectral invocation, alongside other immaterial allusions in Marx, next to the arrival of the ghost at the start of *Hamlet*. For Derrida, the experience of spectrality is defined by anticipation for the thing that is 'going to come' ([1993] 2006: 2) – like the ghost of Hamlet's father, or the ghost of Marx 'that goes on speaking' (ibid.: 38), or the promise of communism 'which has always been and will remain spectral' (ibid.: 123). If, as in *Hamlet*, time is out of joint, it is because the past, present and future cannot be neatly divided, as exemplified by the figure of the ghost. For the ghost, like the apparent past, 'never dies, it remains always to come and to come-back' (ibid.: 123).

Taking a more sociological approach, Avery F. Gordon contends that the word 'haunting' has broader application than ghostly apparition or occupation, and can be used to describe 'those singular yet repetitive instances when home becomes unfamiliar, when your bearings on the world lose direction, when the over-and-done-with comes alive, when what's been in your blind spot comes into view' ([1997] 2008: xvi). What haunts us is immaterial and material, Gordon proposes, and it can alter 'the experience of being in time, the way we separate the past, the present, and the future' (ibid.).

Echoing Gordon, Stephen Frosh asserts that to be haunted 'is to be influenced by a kind of inner voice that will not stop speaking and cannot be excised, that keeps cropping up to trouble us and stop us going peaceably on our way' (2013: 2–3). Frosh likens it to an embodied presence that we might be quietly aware of, or even overwhelmed by, that contains 'elements of past experience and future anxiety and hope, and *that will not let us be*' (ibid.: 3). For Frosh, reading Gordon, this makes haunting *real*, insofar as its ghostly presences 'are manifestations of actually existing, present-tense losses, resistances and suppressed wishes' (ibid.). These hauntings transpire, Frosh continues, because 'there are people who are made ghostly by the silencing of their voices; and even if these people belong to the past, the effects of their silencing, of their writing out from history, can be felt today' (ibid.: 4). Those things that haunt us cannot be released by being spoken about alone, according to Frosh, rather 'they can only be set free by some kind of action to bring them the justice they deserve. Haunting therefore demands a liberatory practice' (ibid.).

Frosh and Gordon focus on haunting as a broad category to account for experiences of encountering the past and its dead. In my own thinking, haunting operates as a sub-category of possession, which capaciously signifies how minds, bodies, sites, archives, objects and narratives in the present appear to be materially or structurally attached to or fixed in the past. When I refer to haunting, I am mostly describing the way the past, and its ghosts, seem to shadow the feelings and atmospheres of the present in often intangible, diffuse ways.

In order to understand our powerful attachment to possession – the desire to possess and to be possessed – it is instructive to turn to the founding conditions of subjectivity as mapped by psychoanalysis. Sigmund Freud offers us a model in which selfhood is always a composite of the identification with or unconscious repression of others – of being *filled with* and *emptied of* the other – and the flame of desire set in motion by these dynamics. As part of his neurological training, working under Jean-Martin Charcot at the Pitié-Salpêtrière, Paris (1885–6), Freud was influenced by Charcot's work that suggested links between spiritual possession and what was being termed medically as hysteria (e.g. Charcot and Richer 1987). Josef Breuer, with whom Freud later worked, tried explaining demonic possession as the more medically legitimate hysteria. For Breuer, the 'split-off mind' produced a demonic effect that led some individuals to believe that such patients were 'possessed' ([1893–1895] 2001: 250). However, according to Breuer, the possessive spirit was not an alien one, but part of the individual's own mind. Influenced by both Charcot and Breuer, Freud radically shifted the religious interpretation of possession as arising from the occupation of a body by a spirit, to being rooted in pathogenic ideas or traumas. Although influenced by Charcot's study of possession, Freud's work largely secularizes this terminology, prioritizing ideas of identification, incorporation and projection throughout his writing to account for how the other enters, marks and exits the subject via fantasy and desire. As Carl Jung wrote, the key features of possession did not change, even as

Freud sought to rehabilitate the concept: 'Possession, though old-fashioned, has by no means become obsolete; only the name has changed. Formerly they spoke of "evil spirits", now we call them "neuroses" or "unconscious complexes"' ([1945] 1976: 599).

We see this transition being mapped out in 'Totem and Taboo', for instance, in which Freud offers a psychoanalytic reading of taboo prohibitions and totemic objects in what he refers to as 'primitive' societies. Here, Freud insists that taboos protect against the 'contagious power' of some objects, which might be transmitted via close contact or touch ([1913] 2001: 34). Sometimes this power is understood to be a soul, capable of entering and exiting bodies. Crucially, Freud likens the belief that the soul can leave the body and hide in another to his understanding of consciousness and unconsciousness: 'Its volatile and mobile quality, its power of leaving the body and of taking possession, temporarily or permanently, of another body – these are characteristics which remind us unmistakably of the nature of consciousness. But the way in which it remains concealed behind the manifest personality is reminiscent of the unconscious' ([1919] 2001: 94).

Freud's Oedipus complex offers us an inherently possessive model of desire, premised on the incorporation of or defence against the other, supported by rivalry (e.g. *The Interpretation of Dreams*, 1900; 'Three Essays on the Theory of Sexuality', 1905; 'The Ego and the Id', 1923; 'The Dissolution of the Oedipus Complex', 1924). Becoming a subject, in the Freudian schema, involves a process of trying to master the other at the level of fantasy – that is, to possess it even as it possesses us. As Diana Fuss puts it, '*every* identification involves a degree of symbolic violence, a measure of temporary mastery and possession' (1995: 9). The presence of these organizing others is often most powerfully felt in the dispossessing experiences of loss, grief and trauma, and how they continue to possess us, unpredictably, into the future.

For Freud, this model does not just shape us subjectively, but also culturally. The process of becoming a subject of culture, as outlined in 'Civilization and its Discontents', is dependent on our capacity to control these others via the repression and sublimation of instincts and impulses. As Freud describes it: 'civilization is built up upon a renunciation of instinct ... the non-satisfaction (by suppression, repression or some other means?) of powerful instincts' ([1930] 2001: 97). An always incomplete process, these forces invariably threaten to agitate consciousness, disrupting a sense of coherent subjectivity and culture.

Frosh aligns the interruptive force of the unconscious with a kind of haunting that reveals the subjective 'I' is already a container for the many. His work is influenced by that of Nicolas Abraham and Maria Torok, who claim that 'inexpressible mourning erects a tomb inside the subject' (1994: 130), or what they refer to as 'psychic crypts', while arguing for a transgenerational haunting produced not strictly by ghosts, 'but the gaps left within us by the secrets of others' (Abraham in ibid.: 171). Frosh accounts for these encryptions and effects as 'things that are so traumatic to lose that the loss itself is denied, even to the extent that knowledge of the existence of the lost object is itself repressed' (2013: 12). Because the object is not recognized and therefore not grieved, its loss acts as a 'present absence', experienced as a kind of psychic haunting (ibid.). For Frosh, reading Freud, identity and haunting go hand-in-hand, insofar as one's identifications are premised on intergenerational losses, repressions and disavowals. 'Haunting is then the *norm*, not the pathological exception,' Frosh observes of Freud's work, 'the present is always filled out by the past, each generation by those that have come before' (ibid.: 120). Fred Moten, taking a similar position, maintains that while subjectivity is defined by the subject's possession of its organizing objects, it is inevitably troubled by the risk and force of their dispossession; 'such that the subject seems to be possessed – infused, deformed – by the object it possesses' (2003: 1). Subjectivity, in this model, is formed by the possession of the psyche's organizing objects and the potential or fact of their dispossession.

Judith Butler proposes that subjectivity is produced through the interplay of psychic dispossession and possession, via the internalization of and projection of others. In order to become a self, Butler suggests, the subject must first 'be dispossessed in sociality in order to take possession of itself' (2004a: 7). This has implications for how we think about sexuality, Butler proffers, for if an *I* can claim to *have* a sexuality, it is a sexuality gained from being previously dispossessed of one, and/or activated through the promise of possession. 'And so when we speak about *my* sexuality or *my* gender, as we do (and as we must)', Butler maintains, 'we mean something complicated by it. Neither of these is precisely a possession, but both are to be understood as *modes of being dispossessed*, ways of being for another or, indeed, by virtue of another' (ibid.: 19).

When we lose people or are dispossessed from a place or a community, Butler argues, we often think we are enduring a temporary condition that will eventually draw to a close. Mourning will be over, we assume, and some semblance of prior order will be restored. But the process can also expose the ties that form the basis of our subjectivity and social relations, whose removal changes us for good. What this experience can reveal, according to Butler, is that there is no independent 'I' that is not composed of 'You'. To lose you is to feel I lose part of myself too. 'On one level, I think I have lost "you"', Butler proposes, 'only to discover that "I" have gone missing as well' (2004b: 22).

To be possessed by something of/or in the past assumes that the past has *dis*possessed itself of something – passed it on as memory, feeling, imprint or relic to be experienced in future by others. While Freud makes a powerful case for the *'return of the repressed'* ([1915] 2001: 154), this book might be described as concerned with the *return of the dispossessed*, and their occupation of and among the people, places and things of theatre and performance. Indeed, I posit that Freud's model of repression already contains within it an idea of dispossession, which is to say, we can only try to exclude that which has already taken hold of us. I supplement this psychical model with a materialist dimension that accounts for how this apparatus operates in concert with places and things. This is particularly apparent in theatre and performance, in which the psychic elements of subjectivity, the social conditions of performance, and the material conditions of production dynamically interact, allowing not only for the staging of that which possesses performance, but its dispossession as thought, image, affect and feeling between performers and audiences, and the stuff of production.

How subjects respond to loss is explored in Freud's writing on 'fort/da' in 'Beyond the Pleasure Principle'. In observing his grandson play with a reel that he repeatedly loses (or throws away) and finds again, Freud maintains that the child was trying to gain mastery over loss. The child learned to cope with his mother's leaving, Freud contends, by 'staging the disappearance and return of the objects within his reach' ([1920] 2001: 15). Lee Edelman posits that we might read in this scene not just the subject's mastery of a lost object, but an open-ended experiment in taking risks and their consequences and the potential for different outcomes to emerge. The theatre and performance examined in this book, in many ways, can be seen to enact its own fort/da scenario, in which the past ritualistically (re)surfaces in the present before fading again. Following Edelman, we might not only see in these practices the theatricalized mastery of loss, but rather experiments in finding form for loss and repossession; what Berlant describes as 'the risks of possessing, ambivalence, being in control, being out of control, being alienated or dissociated, and/or the pleasures of cycling through these' (Berlant in Berlant and Edelman 2014: 79).

Taking a more interventionist and materialist approach in *The Undercommons: Fugitive Planning & Black Study*, written with Fred Moten, Stefano Harney likens the practice of education to a process of possession and dispossession – of being taken over by the ideas of the other and letting go of 'what you might otherwise have been holding onto' (Harney in Harney and Moten 2013: 109).

Harney submits that this happens in an applied way in 'the social space of the text itself' (ibid.), such as in those moments when a group of readers, possessed by an idea, reflect and ask 'how could this become more generalized?' (ibid.). This scene of possession and dispossession is a zone of 'general antagonism', a site of the 'riotous production of difference' (ibid.) that Harney and Moten call 'the undercommons.' 'Being possessed by the dispossessed, and offering up possession through dispossession', Harney tells us, 'is such an experiment and is, among other things, a way to think of love, and this too can arise in study' (ibid.: 110). Harney is writing about text here, but he might also be describing the social space of theatre and performance, which quite explicitly deploy aesthetics and dramaturgies of possession, to transmit knowledge of the past. Certainly, this is a repository of loss, grief and trauma, however, it does not merely repeat and re-enact those hurts in the present. In passing them forward aesthetically and dramaturgically, for the present to learn from, tend to and share, these practices have the capacity to dispossess the past of its heaviest burdens.

The past possessed

The power and effectiveness of queer theatre and performance is often considered to reside in their capacity to explicitly represent identities or to directly intervene in social and political situations. But this book proposes that the terms of visibility by which these markers are assessed are all too easily manipulated by political conservatism and corporate culture that manufacture images of progressiveness to project a vision of inclusiveness. This book traces a different vision of the structure and impact of queer theatre and performance, by maintaining that we must turn to the more tacit means by which the restless preoccupations of history and culture make themselves known. It does so by challenging some prevalent assumptions, by asking: what if the power of theatre and performance resides less *on* the skin than *under* it; less in what is spoken than what remains silent; less on stage than in what is cast off and around it; less on the surface of the present than underneath its protective film? How do theatre and performance unexpectedly reveal the ways in which the minds, bodies, sites, archives, objects and narratives of the present are possessed by a past that cannot be compliantly consigned to history? In what ways do theatre and performance move to the unpredictable rhythms of possessed time?

Mobilizing these questions, discrete chapters focus on how the strategies of channelling and haunting, working through and working out, recollection and replay, reproduction and transformation, occupation and commemoration, intermedial recontextualization and dissemination in theatre and performance evidence the past's possession of the present, and the present's attempts to vie for ownership and control of its ghosts and legacies. If the aesthetic practices and dramaturgical devices of possession reveal the present to be haunted, held, occupied or owned by the past, as I attempt to show, the arc of each chapter also moves to consider how the burdens of history can be *dispossessed* via the discharge of thought and feeling among performers, audiences, sites and generations, and in the encounter with its material remains.

In arguing that theatre and performance can function as powerful forms for hosting the possessions and dispossessions of history, at the interface of psychic experience and material conditions, I propose that this exchange can happen primarily via three mechanisms, of a representational, affective and legal nature. In the first instance, artists and audiences are called on to bear witness to history, in a manner most powerfully described by trauma theorists. For Soshana Felman and Dori Laub, art is a 'precocious mode of witnessing – of accessing reality – when all other modes of knowing are precluded', and it achieves this by inscribing into its representational language, that is, it bears witness to traumatic history, 'what we do not yet know of our lived historical relation to events of our times' (1992: xx). In the second mode, which can operate with and against representation, the emotions and feelings of others can 'enter into another', as part of what Teresa Brennan has elaborated as the 'transmission of affect' (2004: 3). In the third manner, this can happen via material possession or ownership of people, places and things, supported by physical force, economic exchange or legal means. As I track how the past is revealed and shared in this book, it is primarily to the intertwining features of representational effect, affective exchange, and material possession and ownership that I focus my attention.

All three of these mechanisms ask us as artists and audiences to be responsible to the known and not-yet-fully-known past – to deliver the weight of its histories onto the shore of the present and its immanent horizons. This is an ethical injunction that invites us to recognize and share the burdens of the past, and attempt to lighten the load for future generations to carry via emotional, intellectual, artistic and cultural processes of collective witnessing, remembrance and material reconfiguration. Of course, the invitation alone does not preclude its resistance or rejection, as both cultural context and/or individual circumstance need to be capable of supporting this trans-temporal transfer. For this reason, many of the case studies in this book are shadowed by frustrated artistic antecedents, which show us how invitations can both fail and be subsequently reissued with receptive success via creative rearticulation or recontextualization (we can think here of how centuries of queer silence followed *Hamlet*, prior to Dickie Beau's affirmative rearticulation in *Re-Member Me*, as explored in Chapter 1; or how the imprisonment of Wilde and the silencing of his works after his death preceded a century of enthusiastically mining their significance and meaning, as discussed in Chapter 5). In fact, being able to discern how the dynamics of possession and dispossession move through history as well as play out in the present is perhaps the most crucial skill of all in enabling this trans-temporal and intergenerational exchange, and this book strives to help make those structures, languages, emotions and moods legible;

or what we might think of collectively as the grammar of possession and dispossession.

This book is not all about ghostly possession, although every chapter hosts its restless dead. Instead, possession primarily takes the form of the haunting of history – the past's stubborn occupation of the present, and its refusal to recede or rest easy. But possession in theatre and performance is not just a way of holding on to the past, or of being held back by it, but of loosening its grip and releasing it forward. Wilfred R. Bion argued for the container-contained function of psychoanalysis, suggesting that the therapist may hold the thoughts unbearable to the patient, as a parent ought to do for a child, until they might be re-introjected to the analysand in a tolerable form ([1962] 2004: 89–94). In the experience of possession in theatre and performance, we are confronted with what we contain and what contains us, both psychically and materially, and the hope that a recognition of this occupation might not only produce knowledge about the past, but freedom from its most limiting burdens. To be possessed by the past is to know that history has not abandoned us, nor we surpassed it – rather it is inside us, imprinting our minds, contouring our bodies, saturating us at a molecular level. To greet this possession is to wilfully learn this history, to take responsibility for it and to pass it forward, but also to strive to lighten its load via the processing of trauma that comes with rites of remembrance and recognition.

Channelling is a term popularized by nineteenth-century spiritualists to describe the occupation of body by a ghost. One such spirit was Oscar Wilde, who is said to have delivered messages and plays from beyond the grave. Wilde's ghost appears in Chapter 1 of this book, and at various points throughout, as a foundational queer presence that will not let the past be forgotten. It is sometimes chased by the ghost of Hamlet (and his father's ghost that chased him), to ground recent hauntings as part of a long history of Western drama's preoccupation with memory, grief, inheritance and cultural transmission.

In contemporary queer theatre and performance, the term 'channelling' is often used to describe the ventriloquizing of a dead artist's voice. Chapter 1 examines queer performance-as-séance spanning examples from Wilde to Jaamil Olawale Kosoko, but takes as its focus performances by Dickie Beau and Karen Finley that use strategies of channelling to give voice to queer lives lost to AIDS. In Beau's *Re-Member Me* (2017) and Finley's *Written in Sand* (2013), the performers present themselves as *queer conduits* of the dead, to propose that the present is and must always be haunted by those whose lives were lost to AIDS. The chapter explores how channelling, as a technique and dramaturgical device, works not only to mourn the dead, but to insist on their relentless occupation of the present.

The past does not just persist in spectral form, but as memories permeating the bodies, materials, sites, archives and objects of the present. Chapter 2 explores how the history of queer struggle is captured via pugilistic performance, which shows fighting bodies to both store trauma, and the capacity to harness that hurt physically for representation and remembrance in the present. In Cassils's *Becoming an Image* (2012) and Franko B's *Milk & Blood* (2015), we see how queer bodies have been brutalized by the past, and spurred into action for political purpose. This chapter situates queer pugilistic performance within a history of performative combat, examining how it functions as a mode for 'working through' (after Freud) trauma, by 'working out' physically in and for performance. I think of these bodies, haunted and training, as instruments for *exe(o)ricising* history, invoking and releasing its ghosts via physical fitness and transformation.

Chapter 3 is concerned with violence against queer people in public, and the ways via which performers share responsibility for its intervention with audiences. Its central focus is Milo Rau's *La Reprise: Histoire(s) du théâtre (I)* (2018), a production rooted in the brutal killing of the young Muslim gay man, Ihsane Jarfi, in Liège in 2012, and *Burgerz* (2018) by Travis Alabanza, which is concerned with a public attack on the transgender writer and performer of colour. In both productions, the past is made present in performance to testify to its violence against racialized sexual minorities, using theatrical form as an instrument of historical analysis, and as an invitation to fashion alternative outcomes in the present and its burgeoning futures. While the previous chapter prioritized how pugilistic tactics reveal and process trauma, this chapter focuses on the use of collaborative re-enactment to study violence and intervene its reproduction.

How objects absorb and mediate historical violence, and impact queer artists in the present, is a concern of Chapter 4. Focusing on Jeremy O. Harris's play *'Daddy': A Melodrama* and its UK premiere at the Almeida Theatre, London (2022; the US premiere was in 2019), in which people and art are things to be owned, and Rachel Mars's durational installation *Forge* (2022), which centres on the replication of a gate stolen from Dachau concentration camp, this chapter examines how objects contain and transmit racialized violence and trauma, and how material transformation and performative enactment function to divest them of their power. With *'Daddy'* and *Forge*, I explore how the compression of the past into an object functions to represent and contain history, and the ways in which artistic practice endeavours to liberate and distance the past via the reformulation of the object in the event of performance.

Oscar Wilde's status in queer culture waxes and wanes, his style falling in and out of fashion. Recent installations and sited artworks displace some of these narrow tropes and expectations, to position Wilde as the definitive organizing figure of twentieth and twenty-first century queer culture. Chapter 5 prioritizes installation projects that commemorate Wilde via the occupation of specific sites of historical significance, including Artangel's *Inside – Artists and Writers in Reading Prison* (2016), set in Reading Prison and McDermott & McGough's *The Oscar Wilde Temple* (2017), set in an abandoned church, alongside reference to other works. This chapter considers how Wilde is installed in particular sites to trace new paths in queer history and heritage, art and activism, in ways that expand our understanding of the form and remit of Wilde, and reclaim him as a guiding force for contemporary queer performance and performative culture. Moreover, I propose that we might think of the structural dramaturgies shaping these artworks as *rewild(e) ing* practices, that present new curatorial and performative models of commemoration, occupation and engagement.

Chapter 6 examines the programming of theatre and performance as a response to covid-19, exploring how queer history and culture haunted the pandemic and its cultural responses, and how the occasion allowed for the recontextualization and digital dissemination of queer theatre, performance and cultural history in new ways to wider audiences. It addresses a number of productions made for live and mediatized environments, in an apparent effort to mobilize queer theatre and performance history to help reckon with the impact of covid-19, including Belfast Ensemble's 2020 digital production of Mark Ravenhill's *Ten Plagues* (2011), and Split Britches's *Last Gasp* (2020/2021). The chapter explores how this programming worked to recontextualize and recentre queer theatre from being ostensibly a form of historical interest, about and for queer people, to being of urgent and widespread significance and value. It considers how the fresh losses of the present are haunted by losses of the past, which precipitates a kind of emotional ricochet of historical and contemporary feeling, within the context of intermedial performance practice. The chapter explores the effect of transposing queer theatre and performance as a guide to navigate the pandemic, and what this repurposing might mean for the work for queer culture and thought.

Collectively, the artists and artworks represented in this book stage encounters with the past to ask what happens when we meet the dead as ghosts, approach our scars as wounds, feel our grief as love, grasp the things that once held us back as the pliable stuff that might lead us forward? What happens, in other words, if we allow the past to occupy, disturb and inspire the present, instead of sequestering it to an inert or misty hinterland? While individual chapters examine varied evocations of the past through a variety of conceptual lenses, read together they support a singular conviction, which I emphasize in the Epilogue (Chapter 7), that if we do not allow the difficult past to possess the present culturally – that is, to inhabit porous cultural forms via the aesthetics and dramaturgies of possession and dispossession – it will possess us unwittingly, and erupt in unpredictable and violent ways. This, too, is the lesson of Bion's work on containment, in which the container (parent/therapist) and contained (child/analysand) 'conjoined or permeated or both' have the capacity to change one another 'in a manner usually described as growth' ([1962] 2004: 90). The occupation of or by the aesthetic is different to individual possession, or indeed the therapeutic dynamic of containment as outlined by Bion. More accurately, it resembles a dramaturgy of dis/possession, via which the burdens of history are passed on as the present's responsibility to acknowledge, make sense of and own; the weight easing but never quite disappearing with each successive generation.

Conclusion

This book intervenes a social and political climate that largely assumes that the darkest and most troubled days of LGBTQ+ struggle are over. It does so to highlight not only how this is patently untrue of the present, as evidenced by the collision of old and seemingly new struggles and forms of violence, but in particular by tracking how the past routinely returns to reveal its unfinished business – its irreconciled losses, unresolved hurt, ungrieved dead and a passion to expose and share their burden in the present. My hope is that it will not only speak to those queer social and cultural milieus from which it emerges and explicitly references, but help guide our understanding of cultural responses to other difficult histories, including those beyond the expected remit of queer culture.

In confronting our possessions, and the dispossessions scattered around them, we are dealing with the fallout or threat of loss – how to respond to it, how to prepare for it, what to leave behind, what to take forward. Lee Edelman illuminates some of the emotional and material implications of loss drawing on the object-relations school of psychoanalysis. 'Loss is what, in the object-relation, it's impossible to lose; it's what you're left with when an object changes its place or changes its state', Edelman writes (Edelman in Berlant and Edelman 2014: 47). Following Edelman's formulation, we might say that the experience of loss is not defined by an encounter with *absence* but with the *space* shaped by the thing that has vacated – like the palpable presence that fills an empty chair, with which this chapter began. To feel loss it not to feel nothing, but the charge of the still-buzzing outline of the disappeared, and in this, to feel loss is to keep a relation alive. 'Loss, in such a context', Edelman tells us, 'may be a name for what survives' (ibid.). However preoccupied queer theatre and performance are by what has happened, however what is lost still seems to possess us, the surfacing of the past is also a powerful affirmation of what survives – the inevitable turn and return of the dispossessed.

1

Channelling ghosts: The haunted present

Ghosts are summoned in contemporary queer theatre and performance to remember and mourn the dead and to acknowledge their lasting legacy. In Matthew Lopez's *The Inheritance* (2018), the past decade's most commercially ambitious attempt to stage queer history, the lives of gay men in New York City are introduced by resurrecting the figure of E. M. Forster, who serves as a guide. At the end of Part One, numerous gay men appear on stage to welcome Eric into the home of Walter, which was once a refuge for men suffering from AIDS during the height of the crisis. *The Inheritance* also invokes another ghost from queer theatre history, that of Prior from Tony Kushner's two-part play *Angels in America*, whose illness due to AIDS supplies the conditions for his supernatural visions in the play. These hauntings remind us of all those who have died due to AIDS, of the importance of friendship and refuge, but also of the need for queer culture to continue to find forms that might commemorate those histories and house that grief.[1]

The use of ghostly devices on stage is of course not unique to queer theatre and performance but interlaced with the origins and development of theatre. As Marvin Carlson has argued, 'the practice of theatre has been in all periods and cultures particularly obsessed with memory and ghosting' (2001: 7). What concerns me in this chapter, however, is the alignment of queer performance with séance and performer as medium, whose body becomes a conduit for the channelling of memories and voices of the dead. Mary Luckhurst suggests that performers' descriptions of themselves as channels or vessels for entities that they experience as 'other' to be analogous to the discourses of nineteenth- and early twentieth-century mesmerism and spiritualism, as well as early technologies such as electricity and telegraphy (2014: 171). These media produced a material sense of a fourth dimension, which was taken by some to support the possibility of a coexisting spiritual plain.

The history of queerness and channelling in theatre can be traced back to the early twentieth century, in the form of the ghost of Oscar Wilde, whose spirit also appears at various stages of this book. Irish spiritualist Hester Dowden (later Hester Traverse Smith) gives us the most famous accounts, documenting how her body seemingly became host to Wilde's spirit during her séances in London. Wilde's first possession took place on 8 June 1923, and his voice was mediated using a Ouija board and automatic writing. Other visitations followed, during which Wilde's voice is said to have dictated from beyond the grave, resulting in a collection of psychic messages published as *Oscar Wilde from Purgatory*. These transcriptions are presented by Smith as the voice of a 'discarnate personality', who comments on everything from *Hamlet* to the work of W. B. Yeats and James Joyce, while expressing regret about 'the lurid flame of crime' that had been 'attached' to him to tarnish his life (Smith [1924] 2003). In these instances of theatrical mediumship, Wilde's voice was channelled to validate the aesthetic experimentation of those he conjoined, while striving to recuperate him from his emerging status as a wronged queer sacrifice.

Traces of this theatrical mediumship persist in contemporary theatre and performance that use strategies of channelling to give voice to the dead. This chapter is concerned with a selection of such instances, focusing on Dickie Beau's *Re-Member Me* (2017) and Karen Finley's *Written in Sand* (2013), with reference to other examples. In these works, channelling takes the form of the performers using their bodies to seemingly host the voices of the departed, and stage designs that frame the performance space as a site of mediumship. The performer is presented as partially and theatrically possessed by a spirit, who becomes a *queer conduit* for communicating with the living, while also ostensibly grieving the dead. In the context of queer performance responding to the legacy of AIDS, this channelling operates to communicate a sense of the intergenerational impact of catastrophic loss, and the ongoing work of mourning.[2]

Spectral voices

A chorus of overlapping voices announces the opening of Dickie Beau's *Re-Member Me*: 'I remember ... I can't remember ... If he remembers ... I've forgotten ... one of the many things I've forgotten ... probably provoked by memory ... Must I remember?'[3] Resounding like a ghostly incantation at the Almeida Theatre, London, where the production was first staged in 2017, these words evoke a séance in which the voices of deceased or long-standing players in UK theatre are conjured in the present to query the compulsory invocation of the past. These figures' comments have been cut from recorded interviews – some found, some conducted by Beau himself – as they reflect on their careers, in particular the experience of playing Hamlet or watching the eponymous play performed. Relayed over an hour-long performance, these observations circle around the largely forgotten and final performance of Scottish actor Ian Charleson (1949–1990) as Hamlet in Richard Eyre's production at the National Theatre, London, in 1989, a role he played while effectively dying of AIDS. Crucially, in Beau's production, directed by Jan-Willem Van Den Bosch, the ghost's injunction 'remember me' reverberates more as a question than a demand. It queries the same words uttered in Robert Icke's production of *Hamlet*, which it was originally programmed to precede,[4] and ripples across the theatre industry and British culture, including the nation-wide events that surrounded it to mark the fiftieth anniversary of the Sexual Offences Act 1967. Spun as an interrogative, verbally and dramaturgically interwoven, Beau's production asks us to consider how certain forms of cultural remembrance and production operate by wilfully forgetting or inoculating against others, in particular queer histories.

Beau (Richard Boyce) is a UK-based performer and theatre maker whose work has ranged from club drag to theatre and film acting. His individual practice is founded in an unruly archaeological method that responds to found materials – voice recordings, digital cuts, recovered footage, text, images and objects – reorganizing them in surprising, often weird ways to afford them new life in the present. Beau's other main productions to date – *Blackouts: Twilights of the Idols* (2011), *Lost in Trans* (2013), *Camera Lucida* (2014) and *iSHOWMANISM!* (2022) – are all concerned with remembering the dead via their obscure remains by letting their voices speak through the performer's meticulously ventriloquizing lips. Sometimes these are queer icons, including Judy Garland and Marilyn Monroe, classical queer figures such as Tiresias, or mythological entities such as Echo and Narcissus. Beau describes his mode as a type of playback theatre that draws on drag and spiritualist traditions to channel lost or forgotten lives with the aim of serving as 'a live performing archive of the missing' (Beau 2016a).

Beau's *Re-Member Me* finds form in Charleson's illness to elaborate a dramaturgy of contagion, in which the past is given to continuously infect, seep into or occupy the present. On a visual level, we see this impulse play out in Beau's precise lip-synching, as well as via his imitative speech and gestures. Structurally, we can discern it in the swirl of gossip,[5] ephemera, objects and history that contour the project, as well as among the voices, bodies, places, times, feelings and images that crisscross the stage and digital media, creating a sense of psychical and theatrical possession. This model of contagiousness is fundamentally benign, and works to temper some of the deleterious effects of biological and cultural destruction due to AIDS by staging surprise cultural connections and transmissions that carve a place for Charleson within queer culture, and for both Charleson and queer culture within UK and Western theatre traditions. Understood in this context, remembrance emerges as both a mode of thinking and doing – the passing on and piecing together of bodies, relationships and histories in surprising new configurations. Beau's approach offers compelling ways for thinking more broadly about medical and cultural interplay by demonstrating the latter's capacity to translate death, disappearance and amnesia into life-sustaining engagements with history, memory and kinship production.

In the year of *Re-Member Me*'s premiere, the commemoration of queer cultural history was highly topical in the UK, given that 2017 marked the fiftieth anniversary of the Sexual Offences Act 1967, which partially decriminalized sexual acts between men.[6] Programming by numerous institutions reflected an effort to engage with LGBTQ+ history and culture. Across television and radio, for instance, the BBC's Gay Britannia season included a wide range of programmes exploring queer history and culture. Tate Britain hosted a major David Hockney exhibition from February to May, which overlapped with Queer British Art 1861–1967 and which ran from April to October. In July, the National Theatre marked Pride month and the fiftieth anniversary with a Queer Theatre programme strand, which featured an array of rehearsed readings, talks, exhibitions and screenings. *Angels in America* took over the Lyttleton stage from April to August before transferring to Broadway, having had its UK premiere in the same theatre in 1992. Opening in Soho Theatre in November, David Hoyle's *Diamond* reflected on LGBTQ+ life and politics in the UK since the 1950s, refracted through the performer's own biography. Matthew Lopez's *The Inheritance* had its world premiere at the Young Vic in March 2018, whose title in part refers to its meditation on the relationship between a generation of gay men blighted by AIDS and a contemporary one that is not.

The desire to celebrate the partial decriminalization of homosexual acts ran simultaneous to the urge to reflect on some of the more painful and unresolved aspects of queer cultural history. Large cities in the UK, especially London, were devastated by AIDS in the 1980s and 1990s, including the theatre communities in which gay men worked. According to NHS statistics, in 1994 or earlier, there were 26,939 recordings of HIV, 11,516 of AIDS and 8,901 of related deaths, with 88 per cent of HIV diagnoses being among males prior to 1982 (Harker 2010). Across queer communities in the West, incorporating the history of the AIDS crisis into successive generations' sense of the past has been a fraught affair, in part because of a desire to leave the past behind, made possible by changes in societal attitudes and law, and crucially by advancements in antiretroviral treatment. Indeed, the justification for any attachment to this morbid past at all has been thrown into question in more recent years with the development of pre-exposure prophylaxis (PrEP) medication, which has already contributed to the dramatic drop in HIV acquisition (Public Health England 2017: 6).[7] When, from the vantage point of the present, the future of queer culture does not seem so tragically inclined as its past, some question the value of keeping that history alive. Should the dawn of immunity from disease (for some at least) warrant immunity from its remembrance and cultural legacy?

Many are missing in *Re-Member Me*, with none but Beau present on stage. The performer draws on interviews he conducted with actor Ian McKellen and directors Eyre and Sean Mathias, alongside other recordings featuring the actor John Gielgud, Beau's former agent John Wood and John Peter, former chief drama critic at the *Sunday Times*, as they comment on *Hamlet* or those who performed the title role. In addition to McKellen and Gielgud, other famous actors mentioned in the production who played the prince include Simon Russell Beale, Kenneth Branagh, Alan Cummings, Daniel Day-Lewis, Ralph Fiennes, Mel Gibson, Jeremy Northam, Peter O'Toole, Michael Pennington, Jonathan Pryce, Roger Rees, Alan

Rickman, Mark Rylance, Jonathan Slinger and Ben Whishaw. According to Beau, by drawing on all these figures and voices, his aim was to create 'a human Hamlet mix-tape ... Part documentary theatre, part twenty first century séance' (Beau 2016b).

The opening conceit is that Beau feels he will never get to play Hamlet, a role leading actors often pass through and imprint.[8] Expressed against a rendition of the Village People's 'YMCA' (followed by a snippet of Barbara Streisand singing 'Papa can you hear me?'), while wearing rainbow sweatbands, Beau's campness and queerness are given to undermine his capacity to be a leading man. However, the production proceeds to foreground how many of the actors who have played the role were in fact gay men – Beale, Charleson, Cummings, Gielgud, McKellen, Rees, Whishaw and Andrew Scott on the contemporaneous Almeida run – suggesting a persistent if often concealed or tacit connection between queerness and Hamlet. But there is nothing subtle about Beau's sexuality on stage, and in his performance of not being Hamlet, he allows for the queerness of the lineage to be seen while implicitly positioning himself within it.

Charleson's final performance as Hamlet forms the centrepiece of the production. A successful actor in his lifetime, Charleson arrived to play Hamlet fresh from acclaimed performances as Brick in Tennessee Williams's *Cat on a Hot Tin Roof* and Eddie in Sam Shepard's *Fool for Love*. However, Charleson's memory has largely been forgotten within UK national and queer theatrical cultures, partly because he died so young of AIDS-related illness and partly because his performance was over-shadowed by taking on the role from Day-Lewis (following a short stint by Jeremy Northam) who left the production mid-run, to claims he saw his own father on stage (some reports maintained he originally made and later retracted the claim for being misconstrued, and the official reason eventually given was exhaustion).[9] Charleson only played the part from 9 October to 13 November 1989, and seeing as he was visibly sick at the time, his family requested that the National Theatre not make any photographs available to the public following his death.[10] Despite his obvious illness, most audiences did not know that Charleson was so unwell, or that Hamlet would be his final role, dying as he did eight weeks after he left the production. For a small number of people, however, including his friend McKellen, this knowledge made Charleson's feat all the more momentous and Hamlet's meditation on mourning and death particularly powerful. Charleson's Hamlet was, to all intents and purposes, dying in front of the audience's eyes.

McKellen relays Charleson's life and final performance in greatest colour and detail. A gifted young actor, Charleson was also involved in the early years of gay activism in the UK. Immediately prior to playing Hamlet in 1989, he performed Greta in Martin Sherman's *Bent* for one night only at London's Adelphi Theatre to raise money for the founding of Stonewall, his body reported to have been covered with Kaposi's sarcoma at the time (Benedict 1995).[11] McKellen recalls concerns among friends who knew Charleson was sick that he should not take on the part as there would be nowhere to hide in a role like Hamlet. During rehearsals, Charleson underwent chemotherapy and radiation and had an operation for a chronic sinus infection, which many reviews reported, without mention of the underlying cause.[12] Charleson also suffered sight problems, and cast members and friends observed his weight loss and facial disfigurement (see interviews in Davison 1999).[13] According to McKellen, Charleson's sickness sort of infected his performance by infusing Hamlet's mortal preoccupations with Charleson's own. 'It was revelatory', McKellen's voice tells us, via Beau's lips, 'an actor talking from his own experience about the prospect of death'.

In his published diaries, Eyre writes that when Charleson agreed to take on the role in August 1989, they did not discuss his HIV positive status (which he received early in 1986), but that it was 'there as an unspoken subtext' (2003: 82). According to fellow cast member Judith Coke, Charleson performed his dying with intent: 'he made the deliberate choice to play the part of a dying man – or, at least, a man in love with death, because he was in a unique position to do so' (quoted in Davison 1999: 173). Coke even recalls Charleson say of himself: 'I bet I'm the best qualified Hamlet they'll see – I'm not coming back from the bourn, either, and I want to see the truth of it' (ibid.).

Speaking the line 'Oh that this too too solid flesh would melt', the voice of actor Suzanne Bertish tells us in Beau's production, Charleson collapsed on the floor of the Olivier stage, to which the audience responded with a standing ovation. 'Oh. I remember that. At the end, and I have never seen this, in England, for a Shakespeare ... at the end two thirds of the audience just stood. Not a few people. Just stood! They knew they had witnessed something deeply profound', she says. This had the effect of rupturing the integrity of the play's representational mode, as unlike other actors, Charleson was effectively dying himself. According to McKellen, this made Charleson's delivery all the more impactful: 'You know, you play Hamlet, we all know he's going to jump up at the end and take the curtain call and go off to a club. Turn up and give this performance again tomorrow. But with Ian ... He's dying in front of our eyes'. Charleson took the knowledge of this own imminent death, McKellen submits, 'and gave that to Hamlet', making for an extraordinary performance, standing ovations and critical acclaim.

The voices recounting Charleson are either lip-synched by Beau on stage or across digital screens (Figure 1.1). Occasionally, Beau stands out front, other times he mimes in silhouette. He dresses and undresses mannequins standing in for the cast of Hamlet at one point, using costumes retrieved from previous productions, surrounded by medical screens. In this moment, Charleson's illness is added to Hamlet's layered performance history, and Beau's theatre practice framed as both surgical and replete with care. As if representing Charleson's death, and foreshadowing his own with a mute body double, Beau places a mannequin on a medical stretcher. If *Hamlet* is, as Carlson asserts, the 'most haunted of all Western dramas' (2001: 4), Beau's production is explicitly and markedly so,

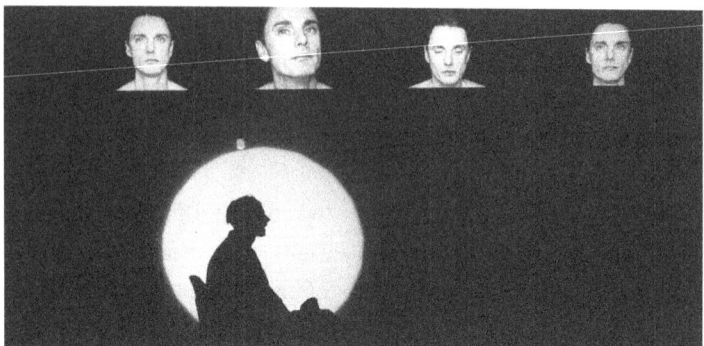

Figure 1.1 Dickie Beau lip-synchs the voices of the absent and dead, on stage and via digital screens, in *Re-Member Me*, Almeida Theatre, London, UK (2017). Photographer: Robin Fisher.

with every performer mentioned, speaking and present, already a spectre or one in the making – including Beau.

Plagues of history

Hamlet evokes the past's occupation of the present by conjuring both ghosts and a sense of lethal contagion. In Act III, Scene II, while preparing for revenge, we see these ideas conjoin when the protagonist's soliloquy likens his time of action to 'when churchyards yawn and hell itself breathes out / Contagion to this world' (2006: 325). This comparison imagines a noxious portal between life and death that no one can escape, and indeed it stirs Hamlet's own desire to 'drink hot blood' (2006: 325). The word 'contagion' appears again in Act IV, Scene VII, when Laertes announces his plans to take Hamlet's life with a poisoned sword. This reference sits alongside many other allusions to corruption and contamination in the play, and it is poison which is largely responsible for the drama's infamous mound of corpses. Here, contagion may also operate as a veiled reference to the bubonic plague that had erupted intermittently across Europe since the fourteenth century with devastating effects, ending with the Great Plague of London in 1665-6. A number of major outbreaks occurred during Shakespeare's own lifetime in London, with those of 1563 and 1603 each eliminating one quarter of the city's population, while often forcing the closure of its theatres for prolonged periods of time, including in 1581-2, 1592-3, 1603-4, 1608-9, 1609-10, 1625, 1630, 1636-7 and 1640 (Gurr 1992: 78). *Hamlet* was written sometime between 1599 and 1601, so it is highly possible that Shakespeare was reckoning with the plague's real impact as well as its metaphoric force. We can say, then, that *Hamlet* has been steeped in plague since its origins – absorbing and emitting it in historical and metaphorical ways. Elsinore, like Thebes before it, is a sick city, and almost everyone is affected while Hamlet strives to locate its source.

Audiences are also implicated in these dramaturgies of contagion. Some spectators of Shakespeare's theatre knew of the plague's very real threat, and the dangers of its acquisition in crowded public spaces, but we can only speculate that for some it was a risk worth taking. However, audiences are unlikely to have paid much heed to the difference between medical and cultural contagion due in part to a less distinct sense of where the body stopped and the world began. We can see this play out in Hamlet's own braided references to contagion, which simultaneously signal the stench of decaying bodies, the open border between death and life and the fuel for vengeance: contagion is real and symbolic, but it is also a theatrical trigger. Similarly, but in a very different context, at the initial outbreak of the AIDS crisis among queer communities in Western urban centres, some audiences and performers believed they were putting themselves at risk by attending or making theatre due to confusion and misinformation surrounding the acquisition of HIV/AIDS. In some theatres, particularly those with openly gay performers, fears circulated that AIDS could be acquired through all bodily fluids, including saliva and sweat, via make-up, costumes, wigs and close bodily contact (Shnayerson 2013). These ideas did not necessarily colour most audiences' experience of watching Charleson's Hamlet, as he did not actively foreground his personal life, although he was degenerating before their eyes. Nonetheless, as his friends have disclosed, Charleson deliberately channelled his experience into his portrayal and even requested that his condition be made known to the public after his death in a bid to raise awareness of HIV and AIDS (McKellen 1990).

Beau's *Re-Member Me* channels this production history by enacting a dramaturgy of contagion constructed around techniques of imitation, cross-fertilization and transmission. In the opening segment, Beau performs a Hamlet mixtape sequence that stutters around a line drawn from Act V, Scene I: 'Have I something in me dangerous / Something in me / something in me / Have I something in me dangerous'. Beau presents himself in this refrain as merging Hamlet's anxieties surrounding inheritance and poisoning, with Charleson's illness, and his own sense of being possessed by a lineage whose provenance and potential he is grappling with to understand. If Hamlet, Charleson and Beau do indeed have something dangerous inside them, it is perhaps the possibility of locating queerness at the centre of the Western dramatic canon, while insisting that those dispossessed through the stigma of sexual shame, illness and grief should be allowed to occupy centre stages.

While the common medical understanding of contagion is a transmissible disease, less sinisterly the word draws on the Latin *con* (with, together) and *tangere* (to touch).[14] In 'Totem and Taboo', Freud describes touching as 'the first step towards obtaining any sort of control over, or attempting to make use of, a person or object' ([1913] 2001: 33-4)'. Embedded within the etymology of contagion, however, is not just the threat of control or use, but the relational and affective possibilities of contagious thought and practice – the touching together as well as the tearing apart it denotes. This layered conceptualization permits us to understand a contagious dramaturgy as one invested in the proliferative cross-contamination and circulation of matter and emotion via structuring techniques, representational media and affective technologies on stage as well as among audiences. In the case of *Re-Member Me*, we witness Charleson's prematurely halted life and career revived via dramaturgical strategies that allow their impact and legacy to ignite the present. If, for Aristotle in the fourth century BCE, tragedy purges the emotions, especially pity and fear ([1895] 1907: 23), *Re-Member Me*'s queer dramaturgy unleashes a flow of voices, images and ghosts that refuse to be stopped by aesthetic or historical closure.

The live production is not only haunted by absent bodies but also by visual scratches and auditory scrambles across digital media. In playing with machinic spectres like this, the production also nods to the Wooster Group's *Hamlet* (2007), which is haunted by intrusions of Richard Burton's lauded film portrayal of the prince. More can be found in Icke's *Hamlet* in which Elsinore is surrounded by CCTV footage and televised news that variously relay mysterious apparitions and short circuits. In one sense, these devices and effects give weight to Simon Critchley and Jamieson Webster's claim that '*Hamlet* is arguably the drama of surveillance in a police state' (2013: 48), but on the other they create a sense of Beau's world trying to break through – especially if you had seen his production before Icke's at the Almeida, as originally scheduled. That which has been untransmissable due to AIDS, and cultural hostility towards homosexuality, becomes transmissible in Beau's production, with histories and bodies passed around and pieced together in new and often extraordinary ways.

This dramaturgy not only derives inspiration from AIDS's viral form, but from regulations enacted by the law. The Sexual Offence Act 1967 did not fully legalize male homosexuality but rather decriminalized it under certain conditions. In fact, some reports claimed that gay people were policed more aggressively in its wake. According to research conducted by Peter Tatchell, 420 men were convicted of gross indecency in 1966, and by 1974 this figure had increased to over 1,700. This continued into the 1980s and 1990s, in no small part owing to the anxiety and paranoia generated by AIDS. Over 15,000 gay men are estimated to have been convicted in the decades that followed the 1967 Act (Tatchell 2017).

The fact that the act did not herald clean progress is evidenced by the introduction of Section 28 in 1988 to the Local Government Act 1986, which affected England, Scotland and Wales. The clause compounded the homophobia of the time, which was heightened due to the anxieties around the transmission of HIV/AIDS, and not unrelatedly, the transmission of homosexuality and queer culture. Enacted on 24 May 1988, the amendment stated that a local authority should not

(a) intentionally promote homosexuality or publish material with the intention of promoting homosexuality;
(b) promote the teaching in any maintained school of the acceptability of homosexuality as a pretended family relationship. (Local Government Act 1988: 27)

While the clause continues to state that these conditions 'shall be taken to prohibit the doing of anything for the purpose of treating or preventing the spread of disease' (Local Government Act 1988: 27), it is itself clearly invested in inoculating against the transmissibility of homosexuality and queer culture.

Discussing the effect of Section 28 on queer theatre of the time, Catherine Silverstone suggests that while it did not have significant direct legal impact, it had a number of implicit consequences. Silverstone maintains that the clause offered a legal basis for homophobia in local authority contexts and encouraged self-censorship, with 'the potential to minimize gay or lesbian visibility as constituted by various groups, particularly in the arts where "fringe" theatre groups are often dependent on local authority funding' (2011: 96). Additionally, Silverstone argues that the wording also 'links homosexuality with the spread of disease and works to reinforce negative perceptions of homosexuality, especially in relation to gay men, compounded by the HIV/AIDS crisis' (2011: 96). Despite these damaging effects, Silverstone claims it had the unexpected effect of galvanizing queer culture against its own containment, spurring on the birth of Stonewall and queer theatre, including path-breaking work by Gay Sweatshop.

If we were to describe the dramaturgy of law, and Section 28 in particular, we might perceive its structure to be hierarchical and divisive, directed at the separation and containment of people, culture and values. But this is not all the law is. For Roy Cohen in Kushner's *Angels in America*, speaking from the inside as an attorney, 'the Law's a pliable, breathing, sweating ... *organ*' (1992: 66). Beau's production shares a sense of the law's porosity and physicality, its capacity to be intercepted by culture as well as to regulate it. As an intervention in commemorating the Sexual Offences Act, *Re-Member Me* endeavours to rewrite the law's punishing effects by becoming a conduit for recording otherwise ignored or vilified subjects and histories. The production does not so much as un-closet queer Hamlets as it allows for now widely known aspects of performers' sexuality and queer cultural history, including AIDS, to filter into our understanding of the role and its legacy, and the impact of queer performers in the UK. While Charleson's final performance is central, we also hear McKellen recall how gay actors were reluctant to come out in the 1980s as the word 'gay was thought to be the worst thing you could say about a young person, or any man'. Gielgud was charged for cottaging in 1953, which gravely affected him personally, as well as damaging his career.[15] While Beau is not directly affected by these laws, he believes he may be perceived as being too gay to play Hamlet for contemporary sensibilities. As the production unfolds, however, homosexuality and Hamlet are recurring bedfellows. Despite the opening conceit, Beau shares a lot in common with Hamlet, as he reckons with the ghosts of his forefathers to reflect on his significance in the scheme of things. But Beau also exceeds Hamlet's dilemma by being the conjurer of the production, who controls the order of bodies and spirits. Around Beau, the stage is scattered with the traces of old productions and frustrated ambitions that are ultimately channelled into a different theatrical purpose.

The single isolated artefact that records Charleson's performance as Hamlet is a review for *The Sunday Times* by John Peter, whom Beau meets to interview in preparation for the show. It is a glowing account, which focuses on Charleson but spins out to make comments on his acting more broadly. The show closes with an audio recording of Peter reading out his original review:

> The way someone like Charleson can transform a production is a reminder that actors are alive and well, that directors can only draw a performance from those who have one in them, and that in the last analysis the voice of drama speaks to us through actors, the abstract chroniclers of the time, and princes not lightly to be dethroned.

The final lines echo Hamlet's own closing words, in which he confirms: 'Fortinbras: he has my dying voice' (2006: 459). That Fortinbras now has Hamlet's voice can be taken to mean he is his ordained surrogate in a way that mirrors Beau's assumed relationship with Charleson and the other queer voices he invokes. If, as in the ACT UP campaigns, silence equals death, for Hamlet death equals silence – 'the rest is silence' being his last utterance (2006: 460). In his lip-synching, Beau is also often silent, but only to choreograph these equations of silence and death into a different relation, so that a chorus of queer voices, living and dead, may enter into dialogue with long-standing existential dilemmas of UK theatre and canonical Western drama more broadly.

Mourning rites

If the rush of voices at the outset of Beau's *Re-Member Me* signals that we are participating in theatre-as-séance, it is the stage design of US-based Karen Finley's *Written in Sand* that initially suggests we are gathered to commune with the dead. The title of Finley's performance evokes the act of spelling out names on a beach, but also of their transience under the rush of tide. In The Pit at Barbican, where I attended the production in 2015 (as part of SPILL Festival), this gesture was translated into small mounds of sand poured across the stage, studded with candles, to frame the show as a sombre ritual of commemoration and mourning. Complementing this tone was the Ribbon Gate installation in the Barbican's foyer, which invited passers-by to tie a ribbon in memory of a loved one who died of AIDS. These presentational tactics countered the tendency Marc Arthur has observed of responses to AIDS in the United States, which is to draw 'a historical line that situates AIDS as history rather than an ongoing crisis' (2021: 19).

Drawing on previous performances and publications, in *Written in Sand* Finley weaves together fragments of memory, text, letters and poetry from between 1983 and 1994, a time when her friends were suddenly succumbing to AIDS. In 1994, for instance, US health departments reported a peak of 34,974 cases of AIDS among men who had sex with other men to the Centre for Disease Control (Centre for Disease Control 1995), while Ronald Regan's administration framed it as a retributive plague from God to kill gay men, while refusing to fund research. *Written in Sand* began its life intervening in this tumultuous context, with the installation *Momentro Mori*, first produced in 1992, which featured a sand-filled chest, in which visitors were invited to write and erase the name of a loved one lost to AIDS. In a 1993 iteration in a gallery in Buffalo, New York, sand spilled across the studio floor, which visitors were also invited to trace names on, without wiping them clear. In 1997, an empty chair was included, to allow visitors to sit and reflect on the installation. The iteration about which I write here emerged in response to an invitation to participate in an exhibition looking back at the prior twenty-five years of the AIDS epidemic – *NOT OVER: 25 Years of Visual AIDS*—at La MaMa La Galleria in New York in 2013.

Set on a stage of ground undulating and light flickering, in *Written in Sand* Finley is accompanied by multi-instrumentalist jazz musician Paul Nebenzahl. Over the course of the performance, Finley recites a series of spoken word verses that jostle over and against Nebenzahl's wrenching score – more like incantations than songs – swiftly dipping in and out of trance-like states. Occasionally she speaks to the audience off-script, or consults notes on a lectern, swapping her reading glasses between her head and hands. Finley recounts the numerous friends she lost to AIDS, citing all the names crossed out of her address book and the litany of funerals she attended. Such was the frequency of her attendance that a family member suggested it 'must get easier to mourn with the more that die', between small talk of cosmetics and diets.[16] 'Sometimes', Finley blasts, 'I pretend those are my problems'. The sense of queer disposability that this exchange evokes resonates with Judith Butler's claim that the lives of gay men lost due to AIDS were often considered to be ungrieveable, because of the sheer scale of death, and the assumption that heterosexual love is more important than homosexual love (1997: 138–9).

Ignorance surrounding the virus is echoed in Finley's recollection of a woman who removed all the toothbrushes and shavers from her bathroom when her HIV-positive brother came to visit, replacing a glass with paper cups. In the weeks after one man's death, his lover, still unable to cry, is encircled by the traces of his former presence: a vacant rocking chair, an unworn shirt, thumbprints, writing. 'I can't take your positive attitude', Finley tells one dying friend, 'when your body is covered with speckled spots of disease'. Bodies ravaged by illness and Kaposi sarcoma are recalled with a tenderness that affords them dignity in the present, while Finley's body becomes a vehicle for all the unaccommodated anger and repressed sadness of the time. Like the 'mother spirits' referred to in the 'I See You Child' section, who are called upon to direct the trapped soul of a recently deceased child, Finley's performance endeavours to guide both the dead and the living through the impasse of enduring grief (Figure 1.2).

Figure 1.2 Karen Finley performing in *Written in Sand*, The Pit, Barbican, London, UK (2015). Screengrab of the production's promotional video.

Elin Diamond has suggested that Finley's performance work in the late 1980s and 1990s offered the spectacle of her shuddering body as an image of 'permanent catharsis' (1995: 166), via which the world's hurt might be recycled and rebalanced. In *Written in Sand*, however, physical and vocal vibrations appear not just to process pain but to invoke the dead. While this sense is true of the overall experience, Finley appears to explicitly conjure the departed when she re-enacts a conversation with experimental performer and drag artist Ethyl Eichelberger, who committed suicide in 1990 while sick from AIDS. Finley interweaves her recollections with Eichelberger's voice, as if she is playing host to his incarnate form. 'Karen, if I have my way, I'm going to be coming back in a more evolved state', he tells us, via Finley. In this sequence, Eichelberger crosses over from the past to the present, the dead to the living, via the conduit of Finley's body.

In her rendering of theatre-as-séance, Finley's performance resonates with Jaamil Olawale Kosoko's *Séancers* (2017). Performed by Kosoko to an eery electronic score, and surrounded by a storm of mannequin parts, iridescent paper shreds and foil fabric, the performance explores the histories of violence and mortality that shadow the performer's personal life and cultural heritage as a queer Black person in the United States. While Finley, and indeed Beau, primarily summon those who have died of AIDS, Kosoko conjures their Black ancestors, intellectuals and close relatives who have passed. If Finley and Beau suggest that the dead exist in or come to occupy the bodies of the living, Kosoko grapples with the suspicion that to be Black is to always live as 'the walking dead',[17] and their performance asks whether anyone existing in this way really lives at all.

Perhaps the most distinctive element of *Written in Sand* is the way Finley uses her voice in performance. She speaks her laments into a mic, sometimes checking notes on a stand, occasionally skimming lines before finding her footing again. When delivering the performance's core scripted passages, the cadence of Finley's voice rises and falls, sometimes hypnotic in its circular rhythms. Occasionally it sounds high pitched and strained, like a radio signal searching to land on the right frequency. At other points, it crackles under the weight of sadness and rage. Her hand, at certain moments, waves back and forth from her chest towards the audience, as if she is guiding the passage of sound. Finley delivers most of her performance standing up, occasionally sitting down to rest, her body often appearing to wrestle with the words to coax them out. Her personal elegies are interlaced with songs by famous figures who have also died from AIDS, including Freddie Mercury and B-52's Ricky Wilson. The intensity of Finley's recollections is modulated by laughing with the audience, or checking in with Nebenzahl. The overall effect is a sense that Finley is not experiencing these emotions in any kind of naturalistic way, nor seemingly trying to claim that she is living them out before us in real time. Rather, the grief she communicates shuttles somewhere between her remembering it and experiencing it, on behalf of herself, the audience and those whose lives she represents.

Finley's fragmented, layered, multi-vocal presentation can barely be described as a solo performance. In many ways, it resembles a medium trying to accommodate and release the memories and voices of others. As Ben Brantley recalls of a New York production, Finley opens by suggesting the show could be called 'Karen and Her Dead Friends': 'Could we make sure, she asks, that we've left some seats for those we love who have departed this life?' (Brantley 2014). This is not Beau's kind of mediumship, in which the performer ventriloquizes the voices of the absent and dead, but the kind in which Finley channels her own memories of the dying and dead, demonstrating the unfinished work of mourning decades later. No matter how hard she tries to conjure the departed, however, *Written in Sand*, like *Shock Treatment*, invariably concludes with the dead's silence:

> I wish I could relieve you of your illness.
> I wish I could relieve you of your life.
> I wish I could relieve you of your death.
> But it's always
> Silence at the end of the phone.
> Silence at the end of the phone.
> Silence at the end of the phone. ([1990] 2015: 144)

Double trouble

Stephen Frosh suggests that 'every generation has something that haunts it' (2013: 1). While this book catalogues numerous hauntings affecting queer culture, the AIDS crisis is certainly a defining phenomenon. In my discussion of performances by Dickie Beau and Karen Finley, I have endeavoured to track and understand the ways in which they invoke memories and voices of the dead, to both remember and mourn those who died of AIDS-related illness. Using strategies of ventriloquism and heightened speech, supported by the stitching together of images, objects and testimony, the works conspire to create a sense that the performers are themselves possessed by the voices and memories of the dead, and that performance is a communal experience that allows us to come together to remember lives at risk of being forgotten. In this configuration, performance offers itself as a means to host the possessions of the past – not to fix and imprison them, but to take ownership of their processing and assimilation. As Jacques Derrida claims, 'to conjure means *also* to exorcise' ([1993] 2006: 59).

One way we might try to understand the scenes of bodily occupation that both performers stage is via Freud's notion of the *unheimlich*, sometimes directly translated as the unhomely or the uncanny. 'Many people experience the feeling in the highest degree in relation to death and dead bodies, to the return of the dead, and to spirits and ghosts', Freud tells us, and some languages can only translate the *unheimlich* as 'a *haunted* house' (Freud [1919] 2001: 241). Encounters with the double, the reanimated dead or the familiar made strange can produce an uncanny feeling of not only navigating a haunted house, but of being one ourselves. In performances by Beau and Finley, we witness the dead revived as the performers' bodies become such houses for the hauntings of history. But the performers' bodies as hosts can never fully accommodate these ghosts; they must remain unhomely, open, porous, to allow the spectres to keep moving, and clear space for other hauntings still. As these ghosts must never be contained by one body, so history can never find a single home, nor become a single story.

It should be clear that these performances function as rituals of mourning as well as remembrance, which invoke the dead so that the artists and contemporary audiences might reckon with their passing. In 'Mourning and Melancholia', Freud famously distinguishes between mourning and melancholia as differently inflected responses to loss. The mourner eventually accepts the loss of the lost loved object, or 'command to reality' ([1917] 2001: 245) as Freud puts it, while the melancholic remains attached, refusing to accept its loss. The psychic attachment to that which is already lost becomes a constituent part of the melancholic's subjectivity. According to David L. Eng and David Kazanjian, in mourning 'the past is declared resolved, finished, and dead', while in melancholia 'the past remains steadfastly alive in the present' (2003: 3–4). Understood in this light, melancholia might be described as 'an ongoing and open relationship with the past – bringing its ghosts and specters, its flaring and fleeting images, into the present' (ibid.: 4). While mourning makes peace with the past and puts it to rest, melancholia seeks 'new perspectives on and new understandings of lost objects' (ibid.).

Freud may have believed that mourning was a finite process, and melancholia its failed foil, but the performances examined in this chapter make claim for a kind of grief that cannot and should not finish; a relationship to the past that is neither pure mourning nor melancholia. In foregrounding an idea of the past as possessing the present, in particular the subjectivity of the performer and space of performance, Beau and Finley propose that remembrance and mourning should be tempered with an understanding that the past flows into the present, as the dead walk among the living.

Trauma theorist Cathy Caruth has argued that traumatic events that are not processed and assimilated will continue to 'possess' the person who has experienced it. The traumatic event 'is not assimilated or experienced fully at one time,' Caruth posits, 'but only belatedly, in its repeated *possession* of the one who experiences it' (1995: 4). Or, as Lauren Berlant whispers it in parentheses: '(we know that we cannot possess a trauma, but are possessed by it)' (2011: 80). The suggestion by Caruth and Berlant that trauma is a *thing* that occupies us, and thus turn *us* into an occupied *thing*, echo Saidiya Hartman's concern that a perpetual attachment to the past, to the dead, can devoid us of agency, desire and life in the present, when she asks: 'Can we mourn the dead without becoming them?' (2002: 771).

This vision of trauma as possessive goes some way to explain how it takes hold of subjectivity. However, Caruth's more individualist model might be complemented by theories that claim trauma can also possess individuals and cultures intergenerationally. Nicolas Abraham deploys the figure of the phantom to account for intergenerational haunting, an image and metaphor that incorporates 'the dead who were shamed during their lifetime, or those who took unspeakable secrets to the grave' (Abraham in Abraham and Torok 1994: 171). As it transmits trauma across generations, Abraham suggests that the 'phantom effect' may fade (ibid.: 176), although its deliberate staging 'constitutes an attempt at exorcism, an attempt, that is, to relieve the unconscious by placing the effects of the phantom in the social realm' (ibid.). 'Haunting' is the term Frosh uses to refer to how individuals or generations communicate with one another 'at a spatial or temporal distance' (2013: 5).

A concern not just with the trauma of mass illness and death but with cultural transmission haunts both *Re-Member Me* and *Written in Sand*. This plays out in *Re-Member Me* in its meditation on the relationship between queer death and the transmission of queer culture, which finds itself amplified by Hamlet's own preoccupations with lineage. If Beau is our not-Hamlet, Charleson is the ghost summoned to alert us of the obscuration of queer culture within theatre history. Soon into the performance, a voice asks: 'Do you feel there is an acting tradition that is passed on from one generation to another?' We hear Gielgud respond: 'I think it's a great advantage for one's survival in people's memories if you've played the great classics'. Gielgud's comment acknowledges the status of *Hamlet* in the building of artistic reputation and legacy, but in Beau's production it also alerts us to the impact of AIDS on the death of generations of gay men. While Finley's work is less preoccupied with canonicity and the transmission of art, as such, her performance is similarly invested in an attempt to keep alive memories of her friends and collaborators. In a 1993 issue of *Newsweek*, devoted to discussing the effects of AIDS after the initial outbreak, this point was made forcefully by Gordon Davidson, artistic director of the Mark Taper Forum in Los Angeles, which originally produced Kushner's *Angels in America*. According to Davidson: 'The problem, aside from the horror of the deaths, is that the system by which we encounter art is a system of passing things down, and when you break the circuit the way it is being broken by AIDS, the damage may be irreparable' (Ansen 1993).

In his work on barebacking subcultures, Tim Dean has discussed how the wilful acquisition of HIV via unprotected sex should not so much be understood as an antisocial gesture but as one invested in the creation of kinship across bodily and generational divides. This is a form of kinship in which relationships are forged around those who have acquired and transmitted the virus, from one person to another, from one generation to another, such that the 'human immunodeficiency virus may be used to create blood ties, ostensibly permanent forms of bodily and communal affiliation' (2008: 82). Exchanging viral load instead of wedding rings, Dean proposes, invites us 'to think about barebacking as the basis for not only one's sexual identity but also one's place in a kinship network' (Dean 2008: 82). Dean's reading of barebacking takes seriously how biological or medical contagion breeds social formation in the form of kinship construction. His research dwells on a time in the United States just before the advent of PrEP and marriage equality, which have already broadened the way queers might think about sexuality and health, social participation and recognition. While it may be difficult for some to imagine so-called bug-chasing as affirmative intimacy and not traumatic repetition, particularly given legal and medical changes since Dean's study was published, the project's sense of the need, within some communities, to stay close to the history of HIV and AIDS in its identity construction is convincing and something that also runs through *Re-Member Me* and *Written in Sand*. However, in both of these works, performing across boundaries of time, place, form and embodiment becomes a strategy for forging and preserving queer attachments; supplementing, if not supplanting, conventions of legal partnership and structures of theatrical authority and cultural hierarchy.[18]

The enmeshment of kinship in historical attachments more closely resembles what Elizabeth Freeman describes as erotohistoriography. For Freeman, erotohistoriography denotes a mode of historical inquiry that accedes to the persistence of the past in the present and our desirous attachments to this unfinished business, using the body to effect, figure or perform that temporal encounter. 'Erotohistoriography admits that contact with historical materials can be precipitated by particular bodily dispositions', Freeman posits, 'and that these connections may elicit bodily responses, even pleasurable ones, that are themselves a form of understanding. It sees the body as a method, and historical consciousness as something intimately involved with corporeal sensations' (2010: 95–6). Central to Freeman's model is the notion that the body is both a material and historical contact zone, an interface of biological, affective, conscious and unconscious transmissions.

Beau and Finley stage an encounter with the past by positioning their bodies as radically open meeting points for other bodies, voices and feelings in history and the present to enjoin. Their performances of channelling and haunting figure memorialization and mourning as central to the sustenance and reproduction of queer culture. These attachments are not just consciously willed, but the means by which we are already possessed by history, for to be a subject *of* history is always to be a subject possessed *by* history. As sites and scenes of possession, theatre and performance illuminate the ways in which bodies, subjectivities, feelings and histories intermingle across time, reminding us of our ancestral heritage, present responsibilities and inescapable destiny within the commune of queer ghosts.

Conclusion

According to Carlson, theatre is a 'repository of cultural memory', but it is also open to modification and readjustment in new circumstances. 'The present experience is always ghosted by previous experiences and associations', Carlson tells us, 'while these ghosts are simultaneously shifted and modified by the processes of recycling and recollection' (2001: 2). *Re-Member Me* and *Written in Sand* may channel the dead in very deliberate ways, but part of the modification they produce is to keep those ghosts alive, so that we might remember them and not let others suffer similar fates in future. What is lost and what remains are inseparable in their work, for as Eng and Kazanjian put it, 'what is lost is known only by what remains of it, by how these remains are produced, read, and sustained' (2003: 2). Emerging from both of these examples is not an image of the past as quarantined, distant and distinct to contemporary life, but rather as always necessarily occupying our memories, bodies and culture, however below the surface of recognition. The task of remembrance, these works suggest, is to tune into the past's strange frequency, to channel it and give it expression; to know how to amplify, mourn and celebrate the voices of the dead, and to know when to let them fall silent.

2

Muscle memories: Exe(o)rcising history

In Franko B's *Milk & Blood* (2015) and Cassils's *Becoming an Image* (2012), the artists fight their way through the event of live performance.[1] They hurl their bodies into action, respectively against a boxing bag and a mound of clay, under the glare of lights, cameras, spectators and the mounting pressures of time. Pugilism, which I take to include both fist fighting and manual grappling, is the primary object and means of artistic production, which physically and figuratively takes to task unresolved queer battles – personal and cultural. Understood in light of the artists' wider bodies of work and the subtler details of production context – both were originally created as site-responsive works – this fighting additionally lands with the explosive force of a punch through time, unleashing the pent-up strains of violence and survival throughout history. By the end of each vigorous performance, the artists are visibly exhausted, their bodies and the surrounding materials streaming and glimmering with sweat. The borders between flesh and matter, art and life, past and present are exposed as always already porous, and we are left with a landscape of shimmering surfaces and material remnants that will, in time, dry out and disappear.

Franko and Cassils are celebrated queer performance artists, whose work navigates the leaky intersections of desire, sexuality and embodiment, often by exploring their bodies' capacity for material resistance and transformation. For Franko, this has predominantly included bloodletting practices and visual artwork throughout the course of his career, which began in the 1990s; and for Cassils, whose career began in the 2000s, this has involved bodybuilding and feats of physical strength and endurance. In *Milk & Blood* and *Becoming an Image*, however, the thrust of each performance is less to invasively rupture bodily parameters than to show what bodies already hold, can release and do. Each performance stimulates and forensically tracks the progressive effects of fighting over time, both for the solo performers themselves and for those whose struggle they strive to bear witness to.

This chapter situates these examples of pugilistic performance within a lineage of performative combat in theatre and performance, examining how they strive to *exe(o)rcise* histories of violence and abuse, via strategies of working through and working out. In doing so, I develop an argument around working out a performative complement or even reverse-orientation to Sigmund Freud's psychologically centred idea of 'working-through', a term he uses to describe the psychoanalytic process and one that has prevailed in understandings of the processing of pain and trauma ([1914] 2011). Reading these pugilistic performances in the context of the slide between working through and working out allows us to perceive the body as both the object of loss and trauma, and in practised form, the key instrument for releasing memory and activating change.[2] To *exe(o)rcise* the past, the performances profiled in this chapter suggest, is to centralize bodily training and material transformation in confronting and remodelling history.

I begin by situating pugilistic performance within a longer tradition of theatre and performance that utilizes fighting imagery and tactics, including queer practices. Turning to Freud's model of working through, I consider how it might be challenged or energized by a more performance-centred conception of working out, as represented by the practices of Franko B and Cassils. In their performances of training and combat, absented people, places, passions and practices are forced into presence. Pugilistic performance labour functions as a vehicle for directing memory, desire and struggle – individual and cultural, contemporary and historical – and as an engine that produces it in the present. These examples of queer pugilism, the chapter argues, expose unresolved queer battles and the necessity of embodied action to their negotiation in the present.

Performing combat

Franko and Cassils belong to a broader tradition of theatrical performance and performance art that has harnessed fighting imagery and tactics within its practices, drawing on boxing's inherently performative behavioural codes and visual shocks. Since the early twentieth century in particular, theatre has demonstrated interest in mining disciplinary parallels, whether by explicitly staging boxing, drawing on its aesthetics or aligning the practices conceptually. Initially, this was consistent with an expanded interest in boxing in the late nineteenth century among writers and artists. In 1878 Eadweard Muybridge produced the first sequential photographs featuring moving horses, and his ground-breaking experiments with Thomas Eakins in the 1880s generated over one hundred thousand images of humans and animals in motion, including men boxing and shadowboxing. The public interest in boxing's presentation of the body in motion was also seized on by the emerging film industry, becoming a staple of nickelodeons. Early filmmakers, including the Latham brothers and Enoch J. Rector, were also interested in boxing because it appealed to working-class male audiences and had the potential to be commercially profitable. But boxing also held technical and practical appeal: cinema was initially fascinated with tracking movement above all else, and given that large cameras were difficult to move around, placing them by a boxing ring permitted the capturing of intricate action without much physical exertion on the crew's part (Boddy 2008: 154).

Bertolt Brecht admired the physicality and aggression of boxing and believed that its fans represented ideal theatre spectators.[3] His *In the Jungle of Cities*, first produced in 1923, is composed of a drawn-out, semi-pugilistic encounter between George Garga, a poor immigrant from the prairies, and Shlink, a prosperous Malay lumber dealer. In the 1927 prologue to the play, Brecht describes the text as 'an inexplicable wrestling match' ([1927] 1994: 436), while the programme note for the 1928 Heidelberg production frames the fight more specifically as a microcosm of 'class struggle' (ibid.: 436). Brecht's interest in boxing partly emerged from his fascination with America, as he perceived the practice as a quintessential form of national mass culture, intimately connected to urban life and modernity. In a distilled, more verbal form, the sorts of aggressions found in Brecht's drama pattern David Mamet's plays, in which characters are always on the brink of fighting, such as in *Speed-the-Plow* (1988). Mamet, like Brecht, admired boxing as a particularly national sport and also for its capacity to simplify more complex and entrenched social, cultural and economic power games (Nadel 2011). As Mamet puts it: 'Boxing, a reduction of capitalism, is about whacking the other guy in the head until he passes out, or whacking him sufficiently in the body to cause him to lower his arms so that one may whack him in the head' (2007).

While Brecht and Mamet represent important instances of boxing's permeation of theatre performance in the twentieth century, more recently still a number of productions have explicitly put the practice on stage as a tool to negotiate experiences of marginal identity and sexuality. For instance, Marco Ramirez's *The Royale* (2015) focuses on the life of the famous Black boxer Jack Johnson, as does Howard Sackler's 1967 play *The Great White Hope*. Roy Williams's *Sucker Punch* (2010), set in a London boxing club in the 1980s, illuminates racial tensions in the context of labouring Black masculinity, while Mojisola Adebayo's *Muhammad Ali and Me* (2008) explores the influence of Ali on a young Black girl growing up in foster care in the UK in the 1970s and eventually grappling with her gender, sexual and racial identity. In Peggy Shaw's *You're Just Like My Father* (1993), the performer reflects on her butch lesbian identity and her relationship with her working-class Irish father, who was a boxer, by shadowboxing on stage. This work is clearly influenced by the artfulness of boxing, informed by its deft but brutal choreography, a continuum occasionally glimpsed in Ali's own self-aware dance interludes. It is also inspired by boxing's capacity to work out aggression by formally and aesthetically containing it, rerouting it toward social or professional mobility, not least among the queer, working class and communities of colour that dominate those represented in this list.[4]

Performance that portrays fighting, even with stage training, differs somewhat from that which enacts it in real time, making alternative physical demands on bodies and possibly soliciting different reactions from audiences. Suffice it to say, alongside this tradition of staged fighting there is an equally rich history of performance artists incorporating boxing practices and aesthetics within their work. Johnson, the subject of Ramirez's *The Royale*, is widely known as a famous champion boxer, although he is less remembered for fighting the nephew of Oscar Wilde, poet-pugilist and early Dadaist innovator Arthur Craven, aka Fabian Lloyd. In an attempt to avoid the First World War, Craven travelled from Paris to New York in 1916, stopping off in the Canary Islands with the hope of raising some money to support his travels by agreeing to fight Johnson. There was no hope of Craven's winning, but he acted in the experimental spirit of Dadaists of the time, who saw themselves as men of action and art. In this, Craven's boxing can be seen to prefigure aspects of conceptual and performance art.

These early stirrings of pugilistic performance art find fuller expression in the work of Joseph Beuys, who remains an important touchstone for queer performance art. Beuys founded the Organization for Direct Democracy through Referendum in 1971 and staged actions, gave talks and created exhibitions to communicate the radical ideas concerning direct action democracy emerging from the group. As part of the Documenta 5 exhibition in Kassel in 1972, Beuys installed an office for the organization, in which he debated with gallery visitors for one hundred days. On the final day, Beuys competed in a staged fight against local art student Abraham David Christian – *Boxing Match for Direct Democracy* (1972) – resulting in a sculpture of the same title. The pugilistic aesthetic has since appeared in various iterations, including boxing sequences by the Kipper Kids in the 1970s and 1980s, and in more recent work by E. J. Hill (*O Captor, My Captor,* 2014) and Li Liao (*Attacking the Boxer from Behind Is Forbidden,* 2015).

While the relationship between performance and pugilism in this range of examples shifts between subtle and direct, represented and enacted, the collective practices are united in the sense that the fight takes place in relationship to an obvious opponent against whom an individual ostensibly fights. Franko's and Cassils's fighting more obviously belongs to a tradition of solo queer performance, where the object is not only some sort of personal expression and transformation – a reckoning with an internalized opponent or an urge to testify – but also a confrontation with the violent or violated ghosts of the past via the materials and circumstances of the present. The work out of the present, we might say, strives to work through the aggressions of the past.

Puncturing the past

Franko B is an Italian-born, UK-based performance and visual artist whose work has long mined the relationship among trauma, sexuality, vulnerability and endurance. In *Milk & Blood*, the performer confronts personal and cultural history through the medium of a solo boxing session. In this approximately forty-minute performance, the artist engages in ten to thirteen rounds of boxing (roughly two minutes each) with a bag filled with milk. Over the course of the performance, Franko spurts words that echo previous preoccupations: 'tortured, betrayals'; 'destabilised, fired up, abandoned, mental'; 'overdose, wars, pain'; and 'rejected, naked'. This vocabulary is drawn from his staccato text "Insignificant" (2015), in which the titular term appears 127 times out of 843 words. In the text, the repetition of "insignificant" appears to undermine every intermittent grave concern, while spoken in performance it threatens to undercut Franko's physical achievement.

Originally set inside Toynbee Hall, London, where I saw it in 2015 and 2018, the performance summons the histories of marginality and violence, power and privilege with which the building has been concerned.[5] Established in 1884, Toynbee Hall was founded to bridge the gap between Londoners of different economic and cultural backgrounds, via hosting a citizens advice bureau, classes and clubs. Some of Franko's earlier explorations of childhood abandonment and institutionalization (the performer tells us he grew up in a Catholic orphanage in Italy) can be seen to persist in the original production context of *Milk & Blood*, with the Hall having once been home to the East London Juvenile Court, where trials took place between 1929 and 1953. In this ghosting of historical function and cultural context, Franko's performance also invokes histories of child welfare and justice, especially with regard to disciplining poor and socially disadvantaged boys and young men.

The efforts of Franko's strenuous live action become apparent as he starts to breathe heavily, while sweat flows over his body. There is no live human opponent in this performance, even if there is antagonism and resistance: the boxing bag opposes and mirrors Franko as, we will see, the clay opposes and mirrors Cassils. In enduring these rounds of boxing, it is clear that Franko has trained for the occasion – and in many ways this is also a scene of training – but his is not the kind of hard, domineering, normative male physique we might expect from a boxer. Franko's body looks both forceful and soft, resilient and vulnerable, as it indeed it has been throughout his performance career.

Franko's body bears the scars of previous bloodletting performances and the marks of faded tattoos, and it invites us to reflect on his long performance art career and what battles he may still be fighting. While some of the artist's more recent work includes stitch art, sculpture and installation, Franko is best known for using his own blood in live art, often letting it against his typically whitened naked body in works such as *Mama I Can't Sing* (1995), *I'm Not Your Babe* (1995), *Oh Lover Boy* (2001). In these works, Franko presents himself as a ghostly child – a figure seemingly trapped in time – whose sense of loss and yearning drip in scarlet rivulets across his blanched skin-canvass. Unlike in his previous work, however, it is no longer Franko who is bleeding but the boxing bag, dripping milk down itself and over Franko's padded, gilded body and the performance space (Figure 2.1).

In an interview in 2016, Franko suggested that the boxing bag can be playfully seen as a gold dildo or penis that he beats until it ejaculates. If it evokes a penis, in releasing milk it also evokes a breast, such that Franko's actions stage a fight between ideas not only of masculinity and femininity but of sexuality and nourishment. *Milk & Blood* also references a much earlier work by Franko, the 2001 short video of the same title, in which a young man (Josef Kleeb) drinks milk from a glass jar, dressed in blood-stained vest and briefs. The video seems to toy with our expectations of what is innocent and nurturing, what is sinister and acceptable, by asserting a visual link between two different bodily fluids – milk and blood – as the artist Andres Serrano did before him (e.g. *Milk, Blood*, 1986). The title *Milk & Blood* also echoes both the biblical reference to milk and honey, which appears in the Book of Exodus (33:3) when God tells Moses he will lead the Israelites to a land 'flowing with milk and honey', and the life of thirteenth-century Saint Katherine of Alexandria, whose veins released milk rather than blood when she was martyred. But if a visual and conceptual link is insinuated between blood and milk, it is also successive in terms of Franko's career: now milk, rather than blood, freely flows.

Figure 2.1 Franko B fights with a milk-filled golden boxing bag, which leaks across the floor, in *Milk & Blood*, Toynbee Studios, London, UK (2015). Photographer: James Bullimore.

Writing about boxing photography, Lynda Nead suggests that the sport civilizes a fundamental human aggression by mediating it through codes, rituals and rules. Boxing may be violent, Nead maintains, but it is distinct from real-world violence insofar as it is 'regulated, held back; it is set limits rather than being excessive and beyond control' (2011: 310). Approaching boxing as a theatrical and spectacular phenomenon, Nead proposes, allows us to examine the 'affects and aesthetics of violence and representation' (ibid.). Nead may well be correct on this, but part of the complicated allure of boxing is that violent combat also has the capacity to undo this theatricality and spectacularity through excessive force, bodily breakdown or the strain of corporeal impact and its remains, as we witness in Franko's performance. As Joyce Carol Oates has claimed, boxing strains to be a metaphor for anything else: 'Life is like boxing in many unsettling respects. But boxing is only like boxing' ([1987] 1997: 4).

In his writing on Franko's earlier bloodletting work, Stephen Di Benedetto has suggested that it is chiefly organized around a 'fluid dramaturgy' (Di Benedetto 2002). Fluidity may at least be one aspect of this performance too; however, neither blood nor milk are the most distinctive referents anymore, but sweat. As it pours from and over Franko's body, across the glistening surfaces of his costume, the bag and the surrounding space, the performer's copious perspiration mingles with milk, becomes almost extinguishable from it. Both are elevated beyond the abject by shimmering in concert with the gold material surfaces. Indeed, in an interview Franko describes being drawn to gold for its radiance, wishing to harness its energy and optimism 'to get out of the ghetto and to make something of your life' (2016). If bloodletting in previous performances seemed to speak to Franko's vulnerability, and even to emit a call to care, here sweat seems to testify to the struggle involved in working through personal and cultural traumas, in making art and sustaining an artistic career. Sweat takes on a luminescent quality, which authenticates not only Franko's labour in performance but also his resilience over time and that of those whose lives he evokes.

It celebrates performance's capacity to alchemize these experiences and matters into something altogether more precious.

Fighting matters

Cassils is a US-based and Canadian-born transgender visual and performance artist, bodybuilder and trainer whose work explores violence enacted on queer bodies and the labours of bodily fashioning and preservation. Frequently exposed in performance and the subject of Cassils's work, their muscled body reveals corporeal transformation as an artistic and athletic enterprise, an ongoing experiment in form with the materials of the flesh. Despite the obvious strength of Cassils's body in action, their performances are equally invested in exploring its fragility by testing the limits of its capacity for self-definition and endurance.

One of Cassils's earlier works, *Cuts: A Traditional Sculpture* (2011), is a multimedia durational artwork in which the artist uses bodybuilding and nutrition to develop a hypermasculine frame, or approximately twenty-three pounds of muscle in twenty-three weeks. Reinterpreting Eleanor Antin's 1972 *Carving: A Traditional Sculpture*, in which Antin recorded the effect of crash dieting on her body, Cassils's project generated video, photography and painting. In *Tiresias* (2010) the artist presses against an ice sculpture of their body until the object slowly melts via convective heat. In *Inextinguishable Fire* (2007), Cassils is set aflame; the action at the National Theatre, London, in 2015 performed live with a previously created film of the action screened on an outside wall. All of these performed artworks involve elements of endurance and display, the artist's body working with and against the material and aesthetic effects of ice and water, oil and sweat.

Similar concerns feature in *Becoming an Image*, although in a much more obviously pugilistic form. While I largely draw on the 2013 performance at the National Theatre Studio, London, as part of SPILL Festival, the artwork was originally created in response to the ONE National Gay & Lesbian Archives in Los Angeles – the oldest active LGBTQ organization in the United States, founded in 1952 – and performed in the building. The archive contains more than two million items, including books, periodicals and articles; art, film, video, photography and audio recordings; and ephemera such as costumes, records and personal papers, including those of Laud Humphreys, Michael Kearns, Bob Flanagan and Sheree Rose. Cassils's response to the archive invites us to consider the fights of LGBTQ+ culture contained within it but also Cassils's own struggle as a transgender individual and artist. It also asks us to see the queer past not as a distant repository of the dead but as coexisting with the present, demanding our attention and intervention.

Becoming an Image accommodates an audience, a photographer and the performer, with live performance, photographs, an audio track and up to 2,000 lb of clay. In the course of the performed artwork, Cassils wrestles and sculpts the mound, as if they are striving to unearth, fight and create something all at once. In this, the most obvious predecessor to Cassils's piece is Kazuo Shiraga's *Challenging Mud* (1955), in which the performer both wrestles with and effectively paints across a clay-covered floor. But Cassils's work ostensibly takes place in the dark, broken only by the flash of the photographer's camera – in a manner previously effected by David Parson's dance performance *Caught* (1982), in which a photographic flash creates the impression that the dancer is flying. In *Becoming an Image*, this photographic action has the effect of dicing the live movement into frames, which in their shocking brightness and unpredictability are almost uncomfortable to register. Light pierces our eyes to communicate a sense of the out-of-sight, often proximate violence enacted on queer bodies. It also conveys the sense that these bodies are being 'worked out' of darkness by light. Performance produces the action, *is* the action, but photography and video recording make performance visible and documentable. According to Cassils, the performance aimed to point 'to the ts and qs often missing from historical records', and to call 'into question the roles of the witness, aggressor and documenter' (Cassils 2013), which can be variously mapped onto the live artwork's three participating parties.

Cassils ultimately engages the block of clay like an opponent, mercilessly punching it, kneading it, dragging it around. Clay, dust, breath and sweat swirl into the air and around the poised viewers, illuminated by shards of light. Cassils may be the human agent, but the material does not give in easily, resisting at every move. With Cassils's body displayed, on one hand this looks like a scene of retribution, not of queers being violated but of fighting back. But the block of clay, which measures roughly the same height and width as Cassils's own body, is also a double, so that everything done to it seems like a form of self-infliction or remodeling. What Jack Halberstam has described as the transgender 'project of dismantling and remaking' gender binaries is forcefully enacted in Cassils's work, 'a sculpting of flesh and molecular form' (Halberstam 2018). We are asked to view transformation laterally, as an interrelated corporeal and artistic enterprise. This struggle is productive insofar as we witness Cassils's self-made body make and unmake their mirror-material, recasting the line dividing art, fighting and life. The atmosphere also feels charged and erotic, with the effect of Cassils's intense work and feeling showing on and showing off their gleaming, athletic physique (Figure 2.2).

Writing about the performance at Edgy Women Festival, Montreal (2013) – in particular her subsequent encounter with the kneaded block of clay in museum presentation at Ronald Feldman Fine Arts, New York – Amelia Jones claims that the clay captures a sense of the performer's intense labour, through its marks, smells and the phenomenological quality of 'having been made' (Jones 2015: 20).[6] The clay works phenomenologically for Jones, and she recounts its 'affecting my physicality, my sense of scale and (through identification) my desire to act or react in return' (ibid.). It has absorbed human qualities, Jones maintains, has become a 'hunk

Figure 2.2 Cassils is captured mounting clay in *Becoming an Image*, Perth Institute of Contemporary Arts, Australia (2019). Courtesy of the artist and Ronald Feldman Gallery, New York. Photographer: Manuel Vason.

of clay-flesh' (ibid.). Jones ponders: 'Surely it smells of sweat? It has the texture of skin. It is a body to me. It reanimates Cassils's actions' (ibid.). The quality of 'having been made' pertains to the art object for Jones, but in its mirroring of Cassils and the artistic histories that surround them, it also communicates a sense of other lives and artworks having also been actively manufactured. In its pummeled state, however, we cannot claim that the object has simply been made, but partly made and partly destroyed; formed, deformed and reformed. For Jones, this visible labour shows the ways in which subject and object can become one, and how, following Bruno Latour, humans and nonhumans are networked and enmeshed in one another (ibid.: 34). Cassils's clay may be understood as networked matter, as Jones argues, but it even more powerfully bears the marks of unleashed rage and longing, not just to create art but to pound out its hidden histories. Indeed, here labour is very much the effect of activated desire – Cassils's passions and those of the archival figures and artworks invoked, and even the queer bodies the performer can more broadly be taken to stand in for. This labour is arduous but also sensual and erotic, inviting viewers to encounter it through the grammar of desire.

This artwork seems quite obviously about the hunger for bodily (self-) fashioning and representation and the labours of enduring violence, transformation and survival. But central to its impact are the aesthetics and affective qualities of sweat. At the outset of the performance, Cassils's white flesh looks like the surface of a classical marble statue, which is gradually softened into life by perspiration, produced under the heat of lights and physical duress. Eventually, Cassils's body, the clay and the space in which they do combat are glossed with the performer's perspiration. In the interaction between Cassils's already-exercised body and the mound of clay, it is as if we are witnessing marble become flesh become clay become artwork with objects, bodies and histories moistened as well as lit back to life.

Richard Dyer discusses the effects of glowing or shining in photography and film for different gendered and racialized groups. Sweat tends to confirm the natural aggression and desirability of men, Dyer proposes, and the dirtiness of non-white skin and women. When idealized white women appear on photographs or on screen, Dyer proffers, they tend to glow with a light that suffuses the body, while working-class or non-white women shine as if sweating. Dyer writes: 'Idealised white women are bathed in and permeated by light … Shine, on the other hand, is light bouncing back off the surface of the skin. It is the mirror effect of sweat, itself connoting physicality, the emissions of the body and unladylike labour, in the sense of both work and parturition' (Dyer 1997: 122).[7]

Cassils's performed labour, accentuated via photography and film, seems to play around with the relations between gender, shine and glow. Sweat on skin, against clay, reflecting and refracting light in the saturated performance space is a byproduct of work that becomes an aesthetic effect that dissolves ideas of normative embodiment. The body leaks, shines and glows, becomes pliable and in turn makes malleable its clay body double. Dyer submits that built bodies, especially white male bodies, are 'hard and contoured, often resembling armour', defining resistance to 'being merged into other bodies' (Dyer 1997: 152). But Cassils's sweaty performance disturbs binarized distinctions around the conventions of male-female embodiment. Cassils's body is hard in its musculature but also soft in its porosity and pliability, when read next to its clay body double. It is shining but also glowing, seeping but evaporating, fixed but also transforming, in a way that materially foregrounds the varied historical bodily labours of queer cultural production.

Exe(o)rcising history

Displays of working out, and perhaps boxing in particular, have historically been important tactics in male self-fashioning. Broderick D. V. Chow traces their origins to the late nineteenth century, to the 'physical culture' displays of weightlifting and strongman shows in popular musical hall entertainments. These theatrical shows, Chow suggests, sought to 'spread their message of ideal health, fitness and manliness' (Chow 2017). But any body or identity dependent on repetitive action and display for its sense of integrity and authority might well be accused of being grounded in anxiety and uncertainty. In one sense, Franko and Cassils locate themselves within this tradition of male bodily and cultural production in their presentations of fitness, skill and aggression. But they are not strictly projecting male bodily ideals: Franko's body strains under the pressure, and Cassils both conceals and reveals their transgender identity in the use of breast bandaging, for instance. Indeed, if anything, we might say that masculinity is itself being worked through by being worked out – not produced but experimented with; built and unbuilt, as Halberstam might put it. Fighting in these performance works does not affirm heroic masculine prowess; rather, masculinity is presented as something to be formed and deformed, split and spilt.

As I have already indicated, however, masculinity or gendered embodiment are not the only referents here. Both performances, in light of the artists' wider bodies of work and production contexts, ask us to see the fights enacted as personal and cultural, of the present and the past. These artworks are *about* work and *of* work – art work in verb rather than noun form. In using boxing forms to physically engage with specific queer personal and cultural histories, Franko and Cassils do so at the intersection of the psychic and material. That is to say, both are invested in the psychic and material effects of queer struggle and trauma, the manner in which they impact the body through channelled rage and exhaustion, and as I indicated at the outset, the ways in which these may be 'worked through' by being 'worked out'.

In the American Psychiatric Association's *DSM-5* (*Diagnostic and Statistical Manual of Mental Disorders*), Posttraumatic Stress Disorder (PTSD) was removed from the category of anxiety disorders and placed under 'Trauma and Stressor-related Disorders'. The shift marked an emphasis in understanding trauma as arising from exposure to specific events. While not all stressful events provoke trauma, the *DSM-5* definition of trauma requires 'actual or threatened death, serious injury, or sexual violence' (2013: 271). And it must be as a result of three qualifying types of exposure, the manual states: direct personal exposure, witnessing of trauma to others and indirect exposure through trauma experience of a family member or other close associate. Without needing to claim that Franko or Cassils actually experience PTSD, in their work they enact an idea of trauma at the intersection of the personal and the cultural, and they invite us to step closer to witness it in their artworks and to confront it among ourselves.

The most seminal writing on trauma and its treatment comes from Freud. In 'Remembering, Repeating, and Working-Through' ([1914] 2001), Freud claims that if a patient cannot fully remember the past, they repeat it in various ways, via acting out and in transference. Freud uses the term '*work through*' (155) to describe the process by which patients of psychoanalysis come to process their symptoms and adjust to new realities. While Freud does not offer a precise definition of the term himself, he recounts that 'the patient repeats instead of remembering, and repeats under the conditions of resistance' (151). This resistance takes the form of grasping from 'the armory of the past the weapons with which he defends himself against the progress of the treatment', Freud suggests, while the therapist's task is to 'wrest [those weapons] from him one by one' (ibid.). It is this movement from resistance to yielding arms that is a critical feature of Freud's idea of working through. Charles Rycroft describes working through as 'the process by which a patient in analysis discovers piecemeal over an extended period of time the full implications of some INTERPRETATION or INSIGHT', as well as 'the process of getting used to a new state of affairs or of getting over a loss or painful experience', using the example of extended mourning ([1968] 1972: 179). Psychoanalysis invites the patient to remember, through free association or acting out, and to work through, as Adam Phillips describes it, 'the paralyzing past to reopen the future, the potentially more satisfying future' (Phillips 2016: 376).

What we find in Freud's account and among its interpreters is the idea that remembrance is a type of repetition, which can also be a form of working through, largely taking place via free association and transference in the context of the analytic encounter, but of course manifest in daily and sleeping life too. That is to say, psychoanalysis does not exactly assert a binarized distinction between mind and body, although it does posit narrative and verbal expression as its core targets and tools. As M. Guy Thompson contends, working out should be thought of as work, as labouring through 'our resistance *to be* candid' (Thompson 1994: 200).

Milija Gluhovic has argued that along with theories of testimony and witnessing, 'trauma theory has become one of the key modes within which performance and other scholars analyse the transmission of experiences of extreme suffering and violence (and is central to the field of transnational memory studies)' (2020: 31). The point is reflected in the earlier work of Deirdre Heddon, which explored the centrality of traumatic testimony to autobiographical performance in the late twentieth and early twenty-first centuries. But Heddon submits that one of the main differences between performed testimony and psychoanalysis is that the former takes place in public and the latter in private: 'Live performance is explored as a response to trauma that not only shares some of the effects of psychoanalysis, but which might also be usefully differentiated from this strategy given that performance is public rather than private' (2008: 14). Additionally, in performance art, and in queer performance art in particular, the body, rather than the mind or narrative, often figures as the leading force of testimony and action, and in this regard, it has much to offer our understanding of processing pain and trauma.

In the performances by Franko B and Cassils, remembrance is not so much about creating a coherent historical narrative for the self, as it is in psychoanalysis, but the material re-membering or putting back together of bodies and experiences in time and place. Physical training, rehearsal and the combative gestures we witness in performance are the repetitions by which the past is given a future in the present, to paraphrase Phillips, and working through follows the form of working out – a reckoning that the whole body must undertake. It requires not only vulnerability but a practised and enduring resilience.

Recent studies maintain that trauma does not only belong to or originate in the individual but rather can be inherited, either through psychic connections with family or even gene expression, as posited by epigenetic studies. As Mark Wolynn puts it: 'Even if the person who suffered the original trauma has died, even if his or her story lies submerged in years of silence, fragments of life experience, memory, and body sensation can live on, as if reaching out from the past to find resolution in the minds and bodies of those living in the present' (2016: 1–2). Franko's and Cassils's works also convey a sense of unresolved inherited pain – not just familial (which Franko's previous work has explicitly addressed) or even genetic but cultural – passed down from the LGBTQ+ community, other marginalized figures with whom they identify, and those who would cause this injury.

The importance of the physical body to the experience and repair of trauma is increasingly confirmed by research. In his hugely popular and influential book *The Body Keeps the Score: Brain, Mind, and Body in the Healing of Trauma*, psychiatrist and PTSD researcher Bessel van der Kolk, for example, argues for centralizing the body in discussions of and the treatment of trauma, suggesting that while talking therapies and even medication may be important to traumatic expression and recovery, so too is bodily engagement and empowerment, or what he describes as permitting the body to 'have experiences that deeply and viscerally contradict the helplessness, rage, or collapse that result from trauma' ([2014] 2015: 3). This perspective is affirmed by scientific studies that examine the role of exercise in processing trauma and regulating mental health (e.g. Hegberg, Hayes and Hayes 2019), as well as by somatic practices that are increasingly of interest to performance studies. Van der Kolk's model chimes with what many queer performance artists have long understood: that the body cannot be excised from the mind in any processing of the past, and that any kind of working through must also be a form of working out – a re-membering and a retraining the body in the present. The pugilism of Franko and Cassils, in this regard, offers us two visions of bodily resilience and transformation, which cut across lines of age, embodiment and cultural context. It allows us to see the processing of pain and trauma as both a psychic and a physical, an emotional and a material enterprise, with the emphasis on the physical and material in particular filling a blind spot in well-trodden psychoanalytic interpretations of what working through might entail. This process requires not only vulnerability in life and art, Franko B's and Cassils's work suggests, but practiced and enduring resilience.

What remains

Working out describes an approach to physical activity, but the phrase also evokes the freeing of a stuck object or problem; here, personal and cultural injuries. In the case of Franko B's and Cassils's performances, when their bodies step out of frame following their actions, what we are left with materially are shimmering surfaces of pulp. To 'beat to a pulp', of course, is the expression used to capture a fundamental aim of boxing: to reduce the opponent to soft, amorphous matter. Pulp was an important category in the first volume of Klaus Theweleit's *Male Fantasies: Women, Floods, Bodies, History*, a psychoanalytic interpretation of the violence of the German Freikorps as they fought the revolutionary German working class, based on the language and imagery contained in the troops' diary entries and writings. The Freikorpsman's body is imagined as solid and sealed, while enemies are figured as wet and formless. One of the recurring substances that encapsulated this was pulp, which Theweleit claimed would emerge 'whenever the will to fight collapses' ([1977] 1987: 394). Pulp is matter made soft by being broken down with force and moisture. For Theweleit, it is psychically associated with the fluidity of female bodies and represents the dissolution of the male ego into pure matter (ibid.: 394–5). Something of the quality of pulp pertains to the products of both Franko's and Cassils's pugilistic art, most obviously discernible in the mess that remains spread across the surfaces and spaces of their actions. The production of pulp – this beating to a pulp – is not just the effect of milk and clay but also the production of sweat: it both precipitates and conjoins it.

Sweat is not only produced by the body in action in performance, but it also becomes an evolving feature of performance's aesthetics and affects – the seepage that lubricates and the sheen that lights its material effects and mutations. Sweat's emission authenticates the effect of intense bodily work in the production of performance, taking on the qualities of a temporary skin that makes labour momentarily visible and palpable. This is work that Franko and Cassils do for us, the viewers, and also for those they labour to bring to our attention. It also impresses a sense of queer culture's dutiful investment in the abandoned people and contexts referenced in the works. Oozing from the pressured seam where the physiological and the psychic intertwine, the perspiration on these queer bodies reveals them to be productively at work but also erotically contoured and porous. Sweat is central to the aesthetic expression and affective experience of labour and desire in overdrive, invested in marking presence. In these performances, sweat emerges as a queer sort of bodily residue that signals the labours of embodiment and cultural production, ushering the past into the present while *exe(o)rcising* its hurts.

While I have already signalled some fighting bodies in performance history, we do not have to look too far down similar histories to encounter explicitly leaky bodies: Vito Acconci's semen (*Seedbed*, 1972); Carolee Schneemann's mucus (*Interior Scroll*, 1975); Ron Athey's blood (*Four Scenes in a Harsh Life*, 1993); Andres Serrano's urine (*Piss Christ*, 1987); Marina Abramović's (and Ulay's) viral tears (*The Artist is Present*, 2010)[8] and Ragnar Kjartansson's mother's spit (*Me and My Mother*, 2000), to name a brief selection. In these works, body fluids often have a queer resonance, transgressing corporeal or relational norms. Abramović and Ulay's *Breathing in, Breathing Out* (1977) is perhaps a seminal instance of artists testing the body in relationship to breath and sweat. In the work, the performers inhale and exhale each other's breaths, until they sweat profusely and pass out. Theatrical performance shares an interest in sweat as an effect of bodily pressure and work. It is a central idea in Lynne Nottage's play *Sweat* (2015), for example, which examines the impact of deindustrialization among residents in Pennsylvania.

Sweating bodies recur throughout Tennessee Williams's oeuvre too, often as symptoms and signals of sexual secrets and distress; or, as Shonni Enelow has issued, sweat works to draw attention to the labour of theatrical production for actors (2019). By and large, however, we either do not notice sweat in live performance or assume its invisible or covert release as an incidental byproduct of human activity. When sweat does explicitly feature in performance, as it does in Franko's and Cassils's work outs, it captures a striking sense of the body's real-time physical and psychological pressure.

Sara Ahmed has described feminist concepts as 'sweaty concepts', insofar as they 'show the bodily work or effort of their making' (2013). She does so with reference to Audre Lorde's *Sister Outsider* in which the author recounts her experience as a Black lesbian in a white straight male world, claiming that 'in order to withstand the weather, we had to become stone' ([1984] 2019: 156). Lorde's statement appeals to Ahmed insofar as it captures the cycle by which we become hard: we build defences to survive the relentless pounding on the surface of the body. Ahmed presents this as a danger of 'making ourselves into harder matter, matter that will less easily shatter', and therefore less able to receive each other's impression' (2014). We must, Ahmed cautions, 'struggle not to let ourselves become too hard; we have to struggle to stay open enough to receive the warmth of an impression' (ibid.). For Ahmed this is the challenge of living a queer-feminist life.

Ahmed's approach to sweat is primarily conceptual here: she embraces it as a metaphor for exploring the labour of producing social relations. In Franko's and Cassils's work, we can see its implications phenomenologically and materially at play: the hardness of fighting bodies is countered by the softness of the sweating forms and by the marks left on their respective materials. Following Ahmed's line of thinking, we might think of sweat as forming a crucial feature of pugilistic performance's queer dramaturgy; one that not only captures the labour of individual struggle and cultural production, but also cautions against being relationally too hard and too closed, or indeed too soft and too porous. Exhausted bodies are vulnerable and resilient, and their seepage and sheen invites us toward a more sensual awareness of the impact of violence and occlusion on our bodies and those of others. Performance transmits the impressions of others in history while leaving its own distinctive mark.

I began this chapter by arguing that Franko and Cassils are invested in tackling residual individual and cultural battles in their pugilistic performances. Pugilism is the main means by which the traumas of the past enter the present, but the performers' perspiration authenticates the labour of this work on an individual and a cultural level. Sweat serves as a temporary aesthetic skin that reminds us that while the pain of the present will quickly recede from view, it will not necessarily disappear. Performance labour, in all its vigour and messiness, is what allows these experiences to enter into the sphere of representation while also resisting the capacity of a single mode of representation to neatly capture and contain them. If we agree that violence has been at the heart of queer struggle, then these performances can be taken to indicate that this aggression needs to be routed physically as well as psychically to give it expression and meaning. Working through and working out are necessarily intertwined – a question of minds and bodies conspiring together in the ring of life and cultural production.

Conclusion

The history of queer culture is punctuated with fights – for rights, recognition and representation – and pugilistic queer performance emerges as both a practice and a metaphor to remember old battles that have receded from view or that persist in some form in the present. This represents a passionate, physicalized reckoning with personal and cultural pasts to assert the unfinished work of queer bodies, activism and art. In Franko's and Cassils's live artworks, we witness the effort to *exe(o)rcise* queer bodies and histories back into life by making the performers' own labour phenomenologically felt and materially apparent across their saturated bodies, artistic materials and performance surfaces. Old wounds and sidelined people, places and practices enter representation through the work of the performers' bodies. In different ways, these queer bodies are soft and vulnerable but also resilient and transformative. They testify to the often unseen work involved in queer life – its pressures and achievements in the present and across history – and the need for ongoing artistic and activist resilience and intervention.

While dominant theories of trauma, which have also been popular within queer studies, have privileged working through as a primarily psychic function, the processing enacted in the examples discussed here is a strenuously psychological as well as physical exercise. The queer pugilism of Franko B and Cassils not only emphasize the ongoing importance of 'the fight' and its associated traumas to performance art and queer culture, but also calls for a recalibration of how we think about the relationship between the mind and the body in relation to histories of violence, on the edge of paralyzing trauma and the horizon of dynamic change.

3

Re-enacting violence: Sharing responsibility

Shortly after Milo Rau's *La Reprise: Histoire(s) du théâtre (I)* (2018) opens, the ghost of Hamlet's father appears on stage. In this recollection of the events surrounding the murder of Ihsane Jarfi in the Belgian city of Liège, in 2012, performed by professional and non-professional or first-time actors, Johan Leysen, an experienced and celebrated performer, muses on the nature of dramatic character and the function of tragedy. 'Once, I played the ghost of Hamlet's father', he announces to the audience, followed by lurching a request to the crew: 'Mist, please' (Rau and Ensemble 2021: 41). Johan proceeds to recite the ghost's speech from *Hamlet*, as diaphanous fog encircles him:

> I am thy father's spirit,
> Doom'd for a certain term to walk the night,
> And for the day confin'd to fast in fires,
> Till the foul crimes done in my days of nature
> Are burnt and purg'd away. (Rau and Ensemble 2021: 42)

'That's theatre!', Johan concludes, abruptly side-stepping the role of Hamlet's father; 'A dead person speaking, a ghost' (ibid.).

Theatre might well be a place where ghosts speak, or as Johan has heard claimed, at least listen. But as he conveys to us in his own performance, and as Dickie Beau reminded us in *Re-Member Me*, as discussed in Chapter 1, theatre is also a place where actors become those ghosts, and where those actors playing ghosts are remembered.

While this might be the opinion of Johan, a performer ostensibly playing himself, director Rau's vision is somewhat different than theatre-as-séance. Rather, in Rau's view, theatre is a site where the dead can speak and listen, not so that they can be individually missed and mourned, but so that the past might be collaboratively recollected, forensically studied and socially understood by those gathered to make and witness the action.

This chapter is less concerned with channelling the dead as ghosts, as we saw in Chapter 1, or *exe(o)rcising* traumatic history, as discussed in Chapter 2, than with collaborative theatrical responses to violence against queer people, in particular racialized sexual minorities. It takes as its focus *La Reprise*, which is rooted in the brutal killing of a young Muslim gay man, and *Burgerz* (2018) by Travis Alabanza, which is concerned with a public attack on the transgender writer and performer of colour.[1] The dead and those at risk of death are close to the surface of these productions, although in each work the performers function less as conduits for the deceased, than as vital agents who endeavour to recollect and replay the past with the help of the audience, in order to take shared ownership of the burden of its hurt and relief. The past is made present in performance to testify to its violence against racialized sexuality minorities, using theatrical form as an instrument of historical analysis and socio-political intervention.

Recollecting history

Milo Rau is a Swiss theatre director and artistic director of Belgium's NTGent since 2018. In 2007, Rau founded the touring production company the International Institute of Political Murder (IIPM), based in Switzerland and Germany, which is dedicated to exploring 'the multimedia treatment of historical and sociopolitical conflicts' (IIPM website).[2] *La Reprise* is emblematic of IIPM's mission, and it belongs to a series of productions that explore histories of the theatre through situated sociopolitical case studies. These histories also nod to Jean-Luc Godard's *Histoire(s) du Cinema* (1988–98), a four-chapter, eight-part project that examines the development of cinema throughout the twentieth century. Within Rau's oeuvre, *La Reprise* follows in the wake of *The Congo Tribunal* (2015), which featured victims, perpetrators, witnesses and commentators on the Second Congo War; *Five Easy Pieces* (2016), in which child actors played out the crimes of the child molester and serial murderer Marc Dutroux; and *120 Days of Sodom* (2017), an exploration of the limits of representation in response to Pier Paolo Pasolini's controversial last film *120 Days of Sodom* and the work of the Marquis de Sade. While Rau's body of work is not exclusively focused on queer objects of inquiry, it is singularly invested in exploring how violence and conflict are mediated through different representational forms, including the reach and limit of theatrical performance.

La Reprise shares some ground with *The Laramie Project* (2000). Created by Moisés Kaufman and members of the Tectonic Theater Project, *The Laramie Project* is a landmark example of verbatim theatre, which drew on a large number of community responses to the 1998 murder of young Wyoming gay man Matthew Shepard.[3] While *The Laramie Project* absents Shepard from the stage, to focus on Laramie and its remaining residents, *La Reprise* keeps its victim centre stage. Rau channels the investigative force of Kaufman's production, but directs it at understanding both Jarfi's murder and what theatre can do to mediate historical violence, or even to intervene it. What Jill Dolan claims of *The Laramie Project* might also be said of *La Reprise*: 'It uses performance to attempt to create a "we" – from the odd collection of people who comprise the play's community to the performers and spectators who come to participate in its dialogue' (2005: 114).

In the 2018 production at Théâtre National, Wallonie-Bruxelles, Belgium, which I refer to here, the action unfurls as a staging of the original casting process at Théâtre de Liège. This presentation takes on the quality of a courtroom interrogation, which is live-streamed and projected on the back wall of the stage. Speaking in French and Flemish, the performers (including storeman Fabian Leenders and the dog sitter Suzy Cocco, accompanied by her dog) share their responses to Jarfi's murder and the trial of his killers, and their experience and understanding of theatre. These scenes are intercut with more charged re-enactments, in which the cast of six replay the beating and murder of Jarfi, the attack played on stage and mediated up close on a screen. In this, *La Reprise* is not verbatim theatre in the style of *The Laramie Project,* which seems to take its intervention as an essential good, but rather it queries the ethics of a theatrical mode that would raise the dead to find meaning for the living.

Although Jarfi is represented on stage by performer Tom Adjibi (Figure 3.1), we are not provided with a full biography, nor an intricately narrated account of his killing. We are told that Jarfi was Muslim and gay, and that he was picked up by a car full of men while leaving a gay bar, and beaten to death, and this is shown in one of the production's scenes. Sébastien (Foucault) indicates that the city was struggling economically, with the closing of steelworks in 2012 contributing to the loss of thousands of jobs, implying that this economic pressure had bearing on the psychology of its residents. When Jarfi was murdered the same year, Sébastien tells us, 'it was like a symbol for the final decline of the city' (Rau and Ensemble 2021: 42).

While Rau's production is concerned with tragic subject matter, his production does not absorb and replay Jarfi's murder in tragic form, via which, in the Aristotelian sense at least, resolution might yield catharsis. Rather, it replays the murder in episodic spurts, interspersed with staged interviews, as something the community of performers and spectators needs to make sense of and take responsibility for in the present. We might read in this supple shape a Brechtian impulse to stage historical violence, with plenty of formal room to critique and assess it. Carol Martin argues that while *La Reprise* indexes real-world tragedy, it unravels the conventions of

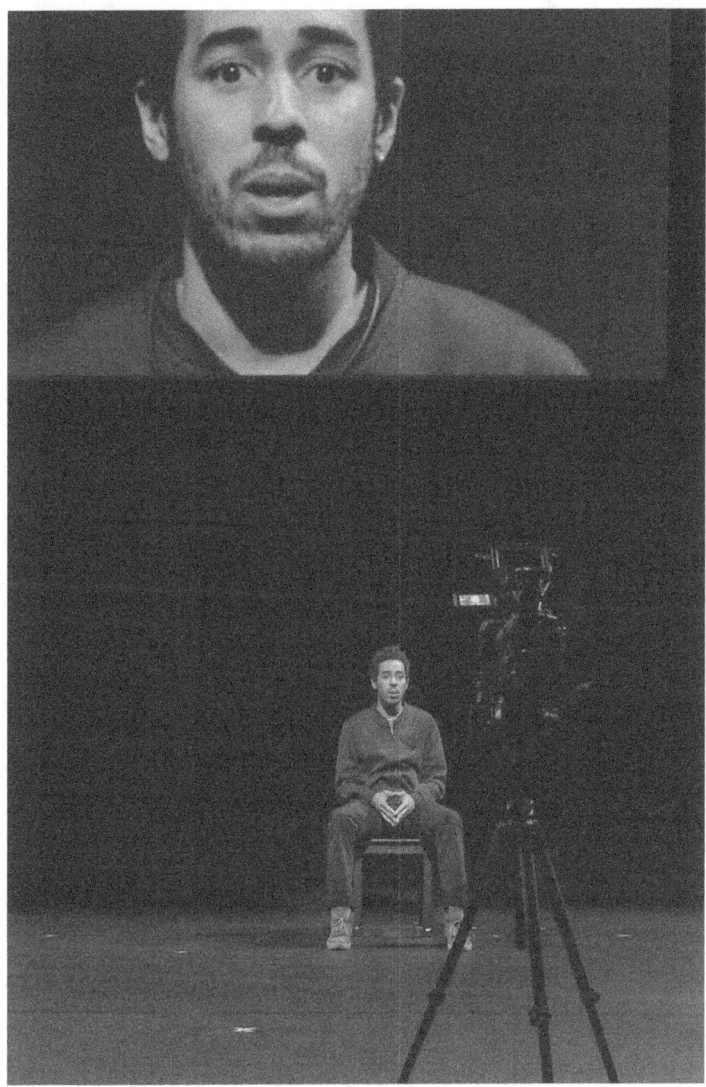

Figure 3.1 Tom Adjibi, who plays Ihsane Jarfi, is interviewed as part of the staged casting process in *La Reprise*: *Histoire(s) du théâtre (I)*, Théâtre National, Wallonie-Bruxelles, Belgium (2018). Photographer: Hubert Amiel.

dramatic tragedy, by abandoning rising tensions, climax, catharsis, resolution, offstage violence and heroes of noble social status. Unlike Aristotle's estimation of the tragic hero as having a noble character, Martin suggests that Rau's protagonists are 'common men and women enmeshed without redemption in a tragic mythos' (2021: 55). These 'common men and women' resemble those identified by Terry Eagleton as the tragic figures 'found loitering on every street corner' (2003: 94) following the democratization of tragedy in the wake of the Enlightenment. Jarfi's murder may be tragic by all accounts, but Rau's form does not allow us to get lost in its emotion, nor grant us the comfort of assuming that this tragedy belongs to a sequestered past.

The production's cool reporting of Jarfi's killing finds resonance in its concern with 'the banality of evil', a phrase projected on screen to signpost the production's Chapter 3. Plucked from Hannah Arendt's reporting of the 1961 televised trial of Nazi SS officer Adolf Eichmann, the phrase aligns Jarfi's murder with the killing of other minorities in history, which in the twentieth century finds it most horrific realization in the Holocaust.[4] Eichmann's trial took place at Beit Ha'am, a theatre turned into a courtroom for the proceedings, and in Rau's courtroom turned theatre, we are reminded of the long history of theatre's role in the pursuit and critique of justice.

Sébastien (Foucault), in his recollection of the trial of Jarfi's murderers, is preoccupied with the constellation of birthdays that surrounded the killing – a murderer's girlfriend and Jarfi's colleague on the night of the attack, Jarfi's mother the following day – which seemed otherwise at odds with the darkness of the episode that unfolded around them. 'An unbelievable coincidence', Sébastien tells us, 'or maybe just something very ordinary' (Rau and Ensemble 2021: 43). But if the production is struck by the banality of evil, it is also persuaded by the clarity of goodness. For Sébastien, this was manifest during the trial when he recalls Jarfi's ex-boyfriend speaking directly to the murderers: 'I'm going to try to describe the man you killed. He was a good person' (ibid.: 48). Sébastien recounts how he tried to explain to the court killers 'what it means when a human life disappears, how it hurts, how it is irreparable' (ibid.: 48). The pain of death may be irreparable, but Rau's production lays claim to theatre's capacity to anatomize injury and its causes, and in so doing, to help us process and respond to it differently.

In *La Reprise*, the performers are as concerned with the nature and function of theatre as they are with remembering Jarfi. In one exchange, Johan asks Suzy, the ostensible amateur performer, if she has ever made theatre before, and when she responds affirmatively, he asks her if she can cry on command. 'You have to think of something sad', he advises (ibid.: 43). Even though Suzy tries to think about a friend who has died to stir tears, she cannot bring herself to cry. The Stanislavskian idea that emotional memory might be activated to fuel a performance is evoked in this scene, although the pressure to emote on command is given as no convincing measure of emotional authenticity, nor the capacity to be an effective agent of reflection in the theatrical present.[5] Indeed, expectations of emotional authenticity in theatre belie the extent to which what appears as spontaneous and sincere often relies on repeated practice. Even Suzie, whose non-professional presence seems intended to embed a hypernatural authenticity, cannot avoid acting in the repetition of her performance over time, while skewing some of its expected skillset. For Rau, theatre is both truth and fiction, the product of action repeated in life and in the rehearsal room. 'The question of how you come to a total, true fictionalisation, is the basic question at the heart of theatre', Rau claims (Rau in Fisher 2019).

La Reprise also incorporates performance history within its structures. Towards the end of the performance, the character playing Jarfi, who has been ostensibly murdered on stage, steps centre stage to face the audience, to sing 'The Cold Song' from Henry Purcell's semi-opera *King Arthur* (1691), with a libretto by John Dryden. With this song, the Cold Genius wakes from his slumber, and begs to be frozen again:

> What power art thou, who from below / Hast made me rise unwillingly and slow / From beds of everlasting snow? / See'est thou not how stiff and wondrous old, / Far unfit to bear the bitter cold, / I can scarcely move or draw my breath? / Let me, let me freeze again to death.

In one sense, this rendition within *La Reprise* speaks to how the production has awoken Jarfi, and how his spirit asks to be let rest again. But the song's most famous rendition was arguably by Klaus Nomi, the gay German singer who came of age in New York in the 1970s, by combining operatic and the New Wave styles of the time. Nomi was known for his falsetto voice, sharply stylized looks and highly theatrical stage shows. 'The Cold Song' was one of Nomi's final releases and public performances, mere months before he died of AIDS-related illness in 1983. When Tom sings 'The Cold Song' in *La Reprise*, his hands outstretched from sides emulating Nomi, he is also situating Rau's production, and Jarfi's murder, in a longer history of queer death.

Asked by Sébastien what the most radical act on stage would be, Tom recalls a scene in a book by the theatre maker Wajdi Mouawad, in which he imagines an empty stage with a chair in the centre, with a noose hanging overhead: A character tells the audience that he is going to stand on the chair, put the noose around his neck, kick the chair away and hold onto the rope to stop himself from being strangled. 'The character climbs on the chair, puts the noose around his neck and he kicks the chair away', Tom reports; 'Either someone will save him and he survives. Or, the audience doesn't move and the character dies. The actor dies' (Rau and Ensemble 2021: 46).

The image Tom shares returns to haunt his own production in its closing moments. He ponders on how theatre should end, before recalling and performing his easier instructions calmly and impassively:

> There is an actor.
> There is a chair in the center of the stage.

There is a noose hanging over the chair.
The actor climbs on the chair.
He puts the noose around his neck.
He says that he is going to kick the chair away.
It's the final scene.
Either someone will save him and he survives.
Or the audience doesn't move, and he dies. (ibid.: 53)

According to Hans-Thies Lehmann, '"the spectacle of death" becomes "bearable or different" when it "only" seems to be staged. Representation as such puts us at ease and deceives us about terror' ([2014] 2016: 29). In this constructed spectacle of both the death of Jarfi and Adjibi, the performer stares down the audience with a gentle smile, the rope never quite gripping his neck. Following Lehmann, we might decide that this scene renders death bearable by making its constructedness or theatricality obvious. In the performer's searching look across the sea of spectators, however, it also passes on the responsibility for action from the stage into the auditorium, from the performers to the public. These ghosts, dangers and duties are now ours to manage.

Writing about this closing moment, Martin claims that Rau 'holds a mirror up to theatre in ways that reveal how the world we live in is created' (2021: 55). In so doing, Martin proposes, Rau 'asks spectators to avoid confusing the fictional with the real and ending up with their neck in a noose' (2021: 60). Certainly, this final moment enacts a Brechtian distinction between showing and doing, replacing a cathartic resolution with a question for the audience on how to act. This amounts to no sincere challenge to the audience to intervene in the staged action, and in the very end, it is the actor who releases himself from the noose. With the final image, both cast and audience are liberated from the historical ties that bind, and from any delusion that theatre is reality, but left with an injunction to intervene violence wherever it may occur.

In interview with Mark Fisher, Rau cites Heiner Müller as claiming that theatre is a dialogue with the dead. 'The dead', Müller submits, 'have to be exhumed, over and over again, because it is only from them that the future can be obtained. Necrophilia is love of the future. It is necessary to accept the presence of the dead either as interlocutors or as destroyers of dialogue – the future comes only from dialogue with the dead' (1991: 31). The idea of a future at all, of course, is predicated on a working sense of what belongs to history, that is, to an order of the past whose ghosts do not continuously return to haunt the present. As Müller put it to Sylvère Lotringer in 1981: 'To banish the ghoul of history, one must first concede the very existence of history. One must know history. Otherwise it can always return in the old established ways, as a recurring nightmare or Hamlet's ghost. One must first analyze history to be in a position to denounce it, to banish it' (1986–94: 78).[6] For Rau, theatre's dialogue with the dead has typically moved in in one direction, in which the living try to communicate with the deceased. It is theatre's repetitive impulse, according to Rau, which holds hope that the dead might eventually speak back. 'What we can do by delivering, by doing this ritual again and again', Rau says, is 'talk to the dead and perhaps they will hear you' (Rau in Fisher 2019).

The published performance text of *La Reprise*, which can be translated as *The Repetition*, opens with an epigraph from Søren Kierkegaard: 'Repetition and recollection are the same movement, except in opposite directions; for what is recollected has been, is repeated backward. Whereas the real repetition is recollected forward' (Kierkegaard in Rau 2022).[7] For Kierkegaard, recollection is characterized by a backwards relation to past events, tinged with sadness and anxiety for that which has been, whereas repetition brings the past into the present, finding pleasure in its security: 'Repetition's love is in truth the only happy love. Like recollection, it is not disturbed by hope nor by the marvellous anxiety of discovery, neither, however, doesn't have the sorry of recollection. It has instead the blissful security of the moment' ([1843] 2009: 3).

According to Kierkegaard's distinction between recollection and repetition, the former characterizes an orientation towards the past, and the latter the present. In the Kierkegaardian sense, recollection can be seen to constitute the interviews that form part of the performers' staged questioning, in which they recall what they knew about the Jarfi case and their experience of theatre. Repetition, on the other hand, takes the form of scenes in which the performers re-enact Jarfi's murder. Recollection recalls the tragic event at the heart of Rau's production, but repetition allows for it to be studied by the community of performers and spectators in the present as part of claiming group ownership. *La Reprise* is a form of investigative theatre, but not quite in the style of tribunal theatre that claims to stage the facts of an event that has already been. Rather, it is a genre that examines how history is produced by narratives and representations, which need to be reworked in the present in order to be delivered into the future. That which possesses us, we might say, can only be put to rest by taking ownership of its meaning and form in the present.

Rebecca Schneider discusses re-enactment as a specific kind of repetitious replay, which she sees as being a key feature of 'twentieth-century academic "memory industry"' (2011: 2). Focusing on war re-enactments specifically, Schneider suggests that they 'try to bring that time – that prior moment – to the very fingertips of the present' (2011: 2). Extending this metaphor of tactile time, Schneider writes: 'Touching time against itself, by bringing time *again and again* out of joint into theatrical, even anamorphic, relief presents the real, the actual, the raw and the true as, precisely, the zigzagging, diagonal, and crookedly imprecise returns of time' (2011: 16).

Schneider invokes Elizabeth Freeman's writing on queer temporality, to propose time's tendency to both pass on and resist passing on; its capacity to unsettle an idea of the present and for the present to unsettle an idea of the past. What Freeman describes as time's 'mutually disruptive energy' (2010: 84) is taken up by Schneider to claim that 'the bygone is not entirely gone by and the dead not completely disappeared nor lost, but also, and perhaps more complexly, the living are not entirely (or not only) live' (2011: 15).

Via *La Reprise*'s recollections and repetitions, filtered through the performers' experiences of auditions, and memories of the trial and murder of Jarfi, the historical incident is revived, and its victim resurrected in the temporary time of performance. The past is given as both deeply personal and particular, but also of universal urgency. As Rau tells Fisher: 'This is not a historical or journalistic work, it's a play. Somehow the case of your son will be changed so it can become a metaphor for what can happen to everybody' (Rau in Fisher 2019). In sharpening a distinction between recollection and repetition – that is, turning backwards and forwards as in Kierkegaard's thinking – Rau opens dialogue with a ghost, allowing it to rest, by releasing its story as one for us to take responsibility for in the future. According to Martin's positive reading, the interaction of the time frames of past and present 'position the ritualized public space of theatre to expose and transform political realities' (2021: 59). However, I think the production is ultimately much more ambiguous about the appropriateness of the form of its intervention. In the juxtaposition of documentary theatre and Shakespearian tragedy, in particular *Hamlet*, the production seems certain that theatre has a role to play in reviving and questioning the dead, although it is less sure of the most ethical genre or mode with which to do so, and leaves this too as a question for the audience to consider.

Street harassment

Travis Alabanza is a UK-based writer and performer, whose work explores transgender experience as it intersects class, violence and constructions of race. Alabanza's early performance work includes the solo biographical show *Stories of a Queer Brown*

Muddy Kid (2015), and they have also worked to animate trans of colour histories in the UK. As part of Duckie's 'Gay Shame' club performance night in 2019, for instance, Alabanza re-staged the Black trans performer Zsarday performing 'I am Telling You' (from *Dreamgirls*) at the Black Cap, Camden, London, in the 1980s, the footage spliced together as part *of Out and About! Archiving LGBTQ+ history at Bishopsgate Institute* at the Barbican's The Curve in 2022.[8] Alabanza's first major performance credit was a lead role in an adaptation of Derek Jarman's punk film *Jubilee* for the Lyric Theatre (Hammersmith) in 2018. *Overflow*, written by Alabanza, was first produced by Bush Theatre London in 2020, and explores trans and cis female friendship in the confines of a club toilet.

As with *La Reprise*, Alabanza's *Burgerz* involves the recollection of violence against queer people, although in this case it is writer and performer Alabanza who is its victim. Alabanza's experience concerns being assaulted in public, when a burger was thrown at them by a passersby. First produced at Hackney Showroom, London, in 2018, and directed by Sam Curtis Lindsay, the performance is structured as an inquiry into the risks faced by trans people in public, not least trans women of colour, often deemed to be objects of debate and attack. For Alabanza, this violence takes many shapes, and they posit that even ignoring it is also a form of enacting it. As with Rau, Alabanza's approach is to collaboratively replay the scene of violence, in order to dissect it and understand it better, and to stall the repetition of similar violence in future, taking us through the cooking of a burger in the theatre to its throwing. As Alabanza describes their rationale in performance: 'If I become obsessed with how the burger works, how it flies, how it smells and how it lands then maybe I will have some agency over it' (Alabanza [2018] 2021: 7).

Alabanza is focused on the particularity of their own attack, but also finds in the burger a metaphor for trans embodiment insofar as its preparation appears to be surrounded by choice – for the box, the bun, the toppings, and for the burger over a hotdog: 'This is

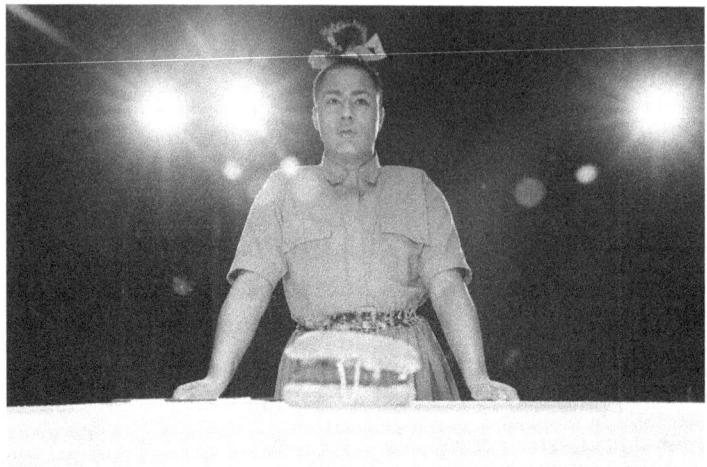

Figure 3.2 Travis Alabanza performing in *Burgerz*, Hackney Showroom, London, UK (2018). Photographer: Dorothea Tuch.

where people believe the burger has some freedom. We've got the bun, the bed, the patty – and now, we finally feel we have a choice. That the bun becomes your liberal playground, toppings are where you can make you … You!' (ibid.: 10). They also liken the box in which the burger comes to the identities we use to categorize and contain bodies: 'What came first? The Burger or the Box for the Burger? Man or woman. Or the cages made for man and woman' (ibid.: 23–4; Figure 3.2).

In *Burgerz*, Alabanza's portrayal of the scale of violence against trans people is supported by numerous official reports. For instance, a 2017 Stonewall report claimed that two in five trans people (41 per cent) and three in ten non-binary people (31 per cent) in the UK have experienced a hate crime or incident because of their gender identity in the last twelve months, and that one in eight trans employees (12 per cent) had been physically attacked by colleagues or customers. More than a third of trans university students (36 per cent) in higher education, the report uncovered, experienced negative comments or behaviour from staff in the last year (Stonewall 2017: 7).

The close relationship between discursive and physical violence is deftly exposed in Alabanza's narrative. In particular, they relay the toxic nature of UK media coverage of trans issues, suggesting it lay fertile foundations for harassment. In illuminating how the media essayed to locate trans people at the centre of a strategically choreographed culture war, Alabanza highlights the complicity of journalists in their violent scapegoating. Alabanza references a 2017 article by Janice Turner in *The Times*, running under the incendiary headline 'Children sacrificed to appease trans lobby', which sought to attack Alabanza and their publicized efforts to use the female changing rooms in a clothes store. 'There were photos of me in every major newspaper, misgendering me, pulling apart my appearance, telling me I was an imposter', Alabanza recounts; 'people were tweeting at me saying they wanted me to die thousands of times a day; in the street people would come up to me and call me a freak; a group of mums told that theatre I was working in at the time that I should lose my job' (Alabanza [2018] 2021: 42). Alabanza yearns for a world in which trans bodies are neither seen as objects of attack nor as in need of fixing: 'Why when I say I'm trans does someone ask, "What will you have done?" "What is next?" As if trans can never be a destination, as if trans is a synonym for broken body' (ibid.: 35).

Shon Faye argues that trans people have been dehumanized and reduced to a talking point to be debated. 'It turns out that when the media want to talk about trans issues', Faye posits, 'it means they want to talk about *their* issues with *us*, not the challenges facing *us*' ([2021] 2022: 9). In this, Faye exposes how trans people are frequently targets in the right-wing media, alongside 'Muslims, immigrants generally, Gypsy, Roma and Traveller communities, Black Lives Matter, the fat acceptance movement, and feminists challenging state violence against women' (ibid.: 14). Representational equality alone will not solve this problem, Faye maintains. What is needed, she argues, is a materialist trans politics, rooted in retributive justice that would 'reallocate resources to the most vulnerable trans communities in their struggle to resist state violence (like police harassment, imprisonment or deportation), poverty and dispossession, and achieve better labour conditions' (ibid.: 12).

One way we might think of this struggle for justice is as a fight for freedom, and this is a sentiment that pulses through both Alabanza's and Rau's work. Both productions speak to how racialized sexual monitories are held hostage to everyday violence in public, and performance's capacity to mediate these experiences. Joshua Chambers-Letson contends that we live facing 'historical and social conditions that produce an unjust distribution of death toward, and exploitation of, black and brown life and queer and trans bodies, actively shortening black, brown, Asian, indigenous, queer, and trans of color life with alarming and mundane regularity' (2018: 4). Performance, Chambers-Letson proposes, is a 'vital means through which the minoritarian subject demands and produces freedom and More Life at the point of the body' (ibid.: 4). But this freedom, or More Life, as Chambers-Letson phrases it, has already been colonized by white liberal politics. 'Freedom, within white supremacist liberal capitalist modernity', Chambers-Letson tells us, 'is largely understood to be a possession or right: the freedom to own, to enter the market, or to buy and sell one's labor' (ibid.: 6). This mundane habitualization of violence is akin to what Saidiya Hartman describes as racism's 'diffuse violence', that is 'the everyday routines of domination, which continue to characterize black life but are obscured by their everydayness' (2002: 772). The terror of racism, as Hartman contends, is often concealed by seemingly rational reports of crime, poverty and pathology.

As a trans performer of colour, Alabanza is aware of being vulnerable to violence in public, but also to how the temperature of the room changes when issues of race are introduced; how it heats up, becomes airless and smaller (Alabanza [2018] 2021: 31–2). They may have once been arrested for stealing, Alabanza confesses, but theft, in the form of colonialism, is very British tradition (ibid.: 32).

Colonization and its racial politics continue to shape how we think about gender, Alabanza submits, as one of its tools was the violation of gender: 'Black bodies have known what it means to be de-gendered, hyper-gendered, misgendered since the beginning of your slavery' (ibid.: 33). Alabanza has experienced this too, not just in street harassment, but in expectations to be 'more masculine because you're Black' (ibid.: 32).

Writing about queer and trans feminist performance, Sandra D'Urso, Tiina Rosenberg and Anna Renée Winget emphasize that survival is one of the most urgent concerns for many trans people, and particularly trans people of colour, and that 'this struggle for trans survival is grounded in colonialism' (Rosenberg, D'Urso, and Winget, 2021: 9). They invoke the work of María Lugones, who maintains that coloniality is the organizing force of all social classification. 'With the expansion of European colonialism', Lugones argues, 'this classification was imposed on the population of the planet' (2008: 3). Since then, Lugones maintains, 'it has permeated every area of social existence and it constitutes the most effective form of material and inter-subjective social domination' (ibid.). Accordingly, 'coloniality' is not identical to racial classification. Rather, Lugones proposes, coloniality 'is an encompassing phenomenon, since it is one of the axes of the system of power and as such it permeates all control of sexual access, collective authority, labor, subjectivity/inter-subjectivity and the production of knowledge from within these inter-subjective relations' (ibid.). While colonization's most brutal and public gestures are geopolitical, the term also describes the processes by which we psychically cannibalize otherness in identity formation. As Diana Fuss writes: 'a certain element of colonization is structurally indispensable to every act of interiorization' (Fuss 1995: 9).

In an interview with Bridget Minamore, Alabanza bemoans the separation of racial and trans politics, claiming that 'talking about transness and gender is the blackest thing I know' (Alabanza in Minamore 2019). 'When I look at my mum or my aunties who are dark-skinned black women,' Alabanza continues, 'they're being misgendered, degendered, too. When we look at what happened to black women throughout slavery, and how their sexuality was perceived and treated, it's all linked. It's who's failing at being a woman' (ibid.). Racism contributes to Alabanza's victimization, but it is to their Philippine ancestors that they turn to in dreams for comfort. Alabanza conjures an image of the bakla (or baklâ), a term used to describe male to female transgender, third gender individuals or effeminate gay men in Philippine culture, who were assimilated in the pre-colonial order, but subject to violence following Spanish invasion. 'We are both floating in a time before we were punished. Floating in and out of genders', Alabanza recalls of their vision (Alabanza [2018] 2021: 48). The bakla hold Alabanza in their arms and lift them onto the finger tip of the Femminiello (typically a third gender figure in Neapolitan culture), just above the atmosphere, who says: 'Darling, we have held so much more for centuries. We were not always treated like dirt, we were once seen as blessed. Of course I can hold you on my fingers, that power never leaves you' (ibid.: 49). In this dream, Alabanza reminds us how the history of Western invasion and colonization is deeply implicated in the violation and pathologization of indigenous gender categories.

Whereas a mixture of professional and non-professional actors form part of Rau's effort to revisit the murder of Jarfi, in *Burgerz* Alabanza enlists the audience for assistance. First, they invite a man on stage to help cook the burger and re-enact the experience. He stays on stage for most of the performance, and serves as a surrogate for the man who attacked Alabanza, now compelled to listen, support and serve. Finally, in the closing moments, a woman from the audience is invited to take the man's place, to represent the woman who ignored Alabanza's assault. Although Alabanza begins by hoping that replaying their attack will help develop some agency over it, they ultimately feel that this approach is insufficient:

> But truth is – there isn't really a way to do that with this. Whenever I get down to it, whenever I really say it out loud, whenever I utter

the words to someone else, or myself or even as I do it now, they still don't feel like my words to tell. It still feels exactly as violent and as horrible as when it happened. I can't lie and say I have any control. (Alabanza [2018] 2021: 53–4)

Alabanza therefore supplements their repetitions with a vow, read by a female audience member, from a recipe book:

I vow to protect you, more than others have before. I vow to protect you, as in the plural, as in more than just you. I vow to realize that in my safety, in my comfort, in my silence, comes your danger, hurry, and entrapment. I vow to know that I can't possibly be free, whilst you the plural, are still hurt. I vow to know that I cannot remain silent when others are hurting, to recognise that silence is part of the hurting, I cannot, on my own, make them stop. (Alabanza [2018] 2021: 59)

This moment shifts the focus from the person who physically assaulted Alabanza, to the woman and all the others walked by and did nothing. As in Rau's production, the audience is responsibilized to intervene in the violence should it be repeated again, and the conditions that enable it.

Group work

A Council of Europe Parliamentary Assembly report, published in 2022, recognized that 'significant progress has been achieved towards making equal rights a reality for LGBTI people throughout Europe', while warning of the rising number of hate crimes experienced by LGBTI people (Council of Europe Parliamentary Assembly 2022).[9] In 'Combating rising hate against LGBTI people in Europe', the authors warn of 'a marked increase in hate speech, violence, and hate crime against LGBTI people, communities, and organisations across many member States of the Council of Europe', noting that a significant proportion of hate speech, vilification and scapegoating of LGBTI people, as well as broad attacks on the exercise of their civil rights, have come from political figures and leaders, including government representatives, as well as from religious leaders' (ibid.). The report goes on to condemn 'highly prejudicial anti-gender, gender-critical and anti-trans narrative', and the ways they 'deny the very existence of LGBTI people, dehumanise them, and often falsely portray their rights as being in conflict with women's and children's rights, or societal and family values in general', identifying that some of the most virulent attacks have come from Hungary, Poland, the Russian Federation, Turkey and the UK. Most alarmingly, the report argues that 'legislative processes aimed at improving the protection of the rights of LGBTI people have stalled, and in some, progress previously achieved has been undone' (ibid.).

Rau and Alabanza are attuned to the fact that violence against LGBTQ+ people is not of the past, and to the ways in which they can still be scapegoated for the anxieties of other social groups. In their work, we see how this is often most sharply felt by queer or trans people of colour, when racism, homophobia or transphobia collide. Rau and Alabanza re-perform recent historical violence against racialized sexual minorities, not to explicitly critique the kind of leaders identified by the Parliamentary Assembly report, but to charge the audience with the role of co-conspirators, witnesses and agents of change. In Rau, this opening up of theatrical form is evidenced in the use of non-professional as well as professional actors to bring Jarfi's death to stage, as well as via the closing moment that invest the audience with the power to let someone live or die. In Alabanza's case, the involvement of a cis white man and woman in the replaying of their attack functions as an effort to compel the audience and public to confront their own complicity with violence, and to rehearse for a different response in future.

Claims to the radical nature of audience participation in theatre belie the extent to which all audiences are participatory. As Gareth White insists: 'Of course all audiences are participatory. Without participation performance would be nothing but action happening in the presence of other people' (2013: 3). But in theatre as testimony – that is, in theatre that testifies to ostensibly real world events, as in the examples considered in this chapter – the audience is deliberately and strategically implicated in bearing witness to the stories recollected and re-enacted. That this act of witnessing frustrates easily turning away is echoed by Derek Goldman's argument that 'witnessing runs directly counter to the idea of the artistic event as merely a form of escapism – implying that as witnesses the performance has exposed us to something that shifts us in some way and that will make us continue to engage and grapple with its contents, perhaps both privately and in our dialogues and interactions with others' (2017).

In these re-enactments, the past is not merely imitated or reproduced as it was, in a manner that might suggest seamless temporal continuity and linear progression. Instead, the past is replayed in order to be interrupted, paused and accelerated so that we both experience ourselves inside and outside time, immersively reliving it and adjacently critiquing it at once; part of the violence enacted, but potentially also part of its remedying or stalling in future. In a kind of Brechtian fashion, the performers dip in and out of the past's re-enactment and its narration, showing and telling, to emphasize that what is repeated is being done differently, with the audience's own participation as central to history's disrupted resolution in the present. The collaborative replaying of the past might ultimately be seen as a kind of possessing of the past on behalf of those who are dispossessed by it, sharing among theatre makers and audiences the responsibility of transmitting it into the future, while committing to an alternative course of collective action.

Conclusion

Scenes of historical violence form the backdrop of this chapter, in which racialized sexual minorities are attacked in public by passers-by, leading to death as well as to physical and psychological injury. Rau and Alabanza ask the audience to bear witness to these experiences, and for Alabanza urgency is supplied by the fact that their own life story is being shared. The past is given to be alive in both productions – not as an intangible and affective haunting, as in previous chapters – but as an unresolved relationship with the audience or public. The naturalistic retelling of the past is disrupted by extending an invitation to the audience to actively participate in replaying it, and doing it differently, by reckoning with their status as implicit conspirators and agents of future change, and by querying the ethical and political potential of theatre to rise to such a challenge.

Eirini Kartsaki lays claim to repetition's generative power in performance, by suggesting repetition's force 'is the force of desire for more' (2017: 7). In Rau and Alabanza, this 'desire for more' is not a longing for more violence, but a wish to enact it only to understand it better; to dispossess its aggressors of power by taking back control of the tools and terms of queer social participation and representation. Re-enactment is less a tool of repetition, than a tactic of historical analysis, used to charge the audience with the responsibility to act differently in future. History is repeated only to be reoriented via the intervention of shared understanding and collaborative action.

4

Arresting objects: Transforming matters

While violence against LGBTQ+ people is often enacted directly on the body, as explored in the last chapter, it is also concentrated in objects deemed capable of holding, representing or reproducing its shocks. When those objects circulate as artefacts to be displayed or sold in the present, they are charged with an over-determined responsibility to both evidence their brutal former deployment, as well as their ability to commemorate and neutralize that danger in the present, by assuring us that history can be contained within material borders. This chapter considers how certain kinds of objects become embroiled in the mediation and negotiation of the past, when fashioned by the will to possess subjects of violence as objects, and a counter-desire to dispossess those objects of their power. Focusing on Jeremy O. Harris's play *'Daddy': A Melodrama* (published in 2022 alongside its UK premiere, following a 2019 US premiere), in which people and art circulate as commodities, and Rachel Mars's durational installation *Forge* (2022), which opened at Testbed, Leeds and centres on the replication of a gate stolen from Dachau concentration camp, the chapter examines how objects absorb and transmit racialized violence and trauma to queer artists in the present, and how performance functions to divest them of their power via the distancing and distorting effects of material reproduction and transformation. While neither work is about an exclusively queer historical event, they both nonetheless expose the ways in which history occupies the present, demanding retrospective inquiry and future orientation via artistic intervention.

I approach the idea of possession in this chapter from the perspective of commodity fetishism, by exploring how objects become charged by an idea of history that promises privileged access, status or understanding to those who can own them. In particular, I think of these forms as *arresting objects*, which fix an idea of the past in the place of the present, and in so doing, risk turning those subjects who encounter them into *things* hollowed of agency. Such objects have the capacity to still the past in the present, including those lives they represent and those whom they appear to enrapture. With '*Daddy*' and *Forge*, I explore how the compression of the past into an object functions to represent and hold history, and the ways in which artistic practice endeavours to loosen the grip of the past via the destruction and reformulation of the object.

Projecting props

Harris's play '*Daddy*' is preoccupied with things – how they represent us, how they control us, how they might liberate us. It is also concerned with what happens when objects circulate as commodities, and how those involved in these transactions risk become objects themselves. This was one of the strands of the US-based playwright's breakthrough drama *Slave Play* (2018), which uses role-play to explore how racial identity and sexual practices interact. Similar issues play out in '*Daddy*' in the context of a new relationship between a young Black artist named Franklin (Terique Jarrett) and an older white art collector named Andre (Claes Bang), and the fraught intersections of queer sexuality and racial identity that define their interpersonal dynamic.

The action takes place by the pool of Andre's Los Angeles home, shortly after he and Franklin meet for the first time. They are occasionally joined by Franklin's two friends, Max (John McCrea) and Bellamy (Ioanna Kimbook), art dealer Alessia (Jenny Rainsford) and Franklin's mother Zora (Sharlene Whyte) at various points in the play. Under Danya Taymor's direction, in the London premiere the pool jutted into the audience, so that those in the front row were frequently doused with water. In Harris's introductory 'Notes on Style', which accompany the dramatic text, the playwright identifies his inspiration for this setting as David Hockney's iconic 1972 *Portrait of an Artist (Pool with Two Figures)*. But in the production, the pool is not just an artistic reference point, but a site of leisure, baptism and rebirth shared by the performers and audience.

Andre becomes 'Daddy' in the play via his capacity to possess, by turning art in commodities and people into things. As soon as the play opens, we learn of this ability via the impressive collection of queer art he keeps at home, including pieces by Diane Arbus, Alexander Calder, Georgia O'Keeffe, Roy Lichtenstein, Cindy Sherman and a room full of Jean-Michel Basquiat artworks. Andre not only appreciates Franklin's art, but also quickly starts to perceive him as an object of visual pleasure to be enjoyed, initially by calling him Naomi (Campbell), and latterly by referring to him as his son, whose sexuality and career he seeks to control. Andre's relationship to art is not just one of neutral owner, but as his fascination with Franklin comes to suggest, one of neocolonial collector.

These obsessions with objecthood are chiefly explored in the play's preoccupation with dolls. The new exhibition Franklin has been preparing features soft dolls of Black boys, designed for the production by Tschabalala Self, reminiscent of Cabbage Patch Kids or Original Doll Babies. The dolls, Franklin initially says, remind him of himself, and are intended to evoke 'a sense of nostalgia' while 'recontextualizing what it means to be a black man' (Harris 2022: 35). As preparations for his show progress, Franklin's dolls become more expressive, on account of his developing relationship with Andre, whom he has come to habitually call 'Daddy'. Franklin wants each of the dolls in the exhibition to look smart and stand to attention for all the daddies who observe them in the gallery, as he does for Andre. 'I want each of the daddies in the room to see me', Franklin muses, 'Dressed smart. Standing at attention. Just like daddies always like' (ibid.: 50).

'*Daddy*' carries the subtitle 'a melodrama', which helps us understand the play's expressive register. The melodramatic form is rooted in the eighteenth and nineteenth centuries, distinctive for its sentimental style and sensational tone. The term 'melodrama' emerges from the French word *mélodrame*, which includes the Greek 'mélos' meaning song and 'drame' meaning drama, reflecting the tendency for song and music to be threaded throughout the form, in order to amplify its emotional range. '*Daddy*' features songs performed by a trio of gospel singers, which also draws on the chorus convention from Greek tragedy, who come in and out of the action to respond to it through song and music, often disapprovingly trolling the main characters. Its core musical refrain, however, is George Michael's 1987 track 'Father Figure', in which the voice promises to be a father figure to his would-be lover. In the melodramatic form, studded with tragic conventions, Harris finds a shape to accommodate the amplified characterizations and expressive breadth of his play world.

Franklin initially decides to call his show 'Daddy' to reflect the impact of his relationship with Andre on its development – the dolls are at once inspired by Andre's capacity to demand controlled self-presentation, and Franklin's ability to solicit investment by captivating his imagination. Andre recognizes that Franklin also has power over him towards the end of the play, by claiming: 'You knew the minute we met that if you could get me, have me, if I would have you, that I would become worthless in your arms, didn't you?' (ibid.: 140). In the dolls, Harris identifies two different vectors of possessiveness – they are at once artistic artefacts which can be owned for money, and representations of an artist skilled at owning father figures by captivating them with his appeal.

While Franklin relates the dolls' expressivity to Andre, the latter senses they have a longer history. When he meets Franklin's mother Zora, Andre suggests that it is she who belittled and paralyzed him, 'like the dolls you played with in your room all those hours all those nights' (ibid.: 127). Franklin discloses that he started making the dolls when he discovered his mother forcing his father to leave. But Zora sees her son as acting out a racist white fantasy, in which Black people are turned into objects to be owned, like slaves or the trophies of white saviours. 'You make a room full of white folk walk around with little coon babies on their arms like they were Madonna or something', Zora exhorts, 'Ha! Angelina Jolie' (ibid.: 68).

Dolls, and Black dolls in particular, as Bill Brown has insisted, contribute to 'the riddle of person or thing' (2006: 199) which characterized debates surrounding the legal and ontological status of Black people as slaves or property in the United States. This is reflected in Jasmine Sanders's essay on the 2022 *Black Dolls* exhibition at the New York Historical Society, in which she proposes that the doll is 'freighted with the signifiers of race and skin color' (2022). 'This object is "not-I" but *is* a human likeness', Sanders writes, 'muddling and redrawing distinctions between person and thing' (ibid.). Sanders's claims that dolls have long troubled ideas of 'personhood and autonomy', insofar as they are 'analogous both to children (disempowered, diminutive) and to slaves (purchased, traded, maltreated)' (ibid.). She cites Julia Charlotte Maitland's *The Doll and Her Friends; or, Memoirs of the Lady Seraphina*, in which a doll describes herself and her friends as 'a race of mere dependents; some might even call us slaves' ([1852] 1893: 2).

Zora is keen to inform Andre that Franklin's ancestors were workers, not slaves – subjects, not things – connecting his artistry to his family's history of manual labour and craft, and not the commercial art market: 'Furniture folk. Lots of work with our hands. Before that we were tobacco folk ... Franklin still found a way to keep working with those hands' (ibid.: 77). She suspects that Franklin has been taken over by an evil spirit, and prays to God, *her* Father, for a solution. Andre repeats this image of interiorized possessiveness, by describing 'burrowing' his way inside Franklin when they met. But Zora also claims that she owns her son: 'That's my baby. His whole life I felt what he feels' (ibid.: 104).

The play text of '*Daddy*' includes an epigraph from Hilton Als's *White Girls*: 'there's the bizarre fact that queerness reads, even to some black men themselves, as a kind of whiteness. In a black, Christian-informed culture, where relatively few men head households any more, whiteness is equated with perversity, a pollutant further eroding the already decimated black family' ([2014] 2018: 183). The point is underscored by Mojisola Adebayo and Lynette Goddard, writing about Black British queer theatre, who posit that 'homosexuality is associated with white people and is therefore also seen by some as a betrayal of blackness' (Adebayo and Goddard 2023: 17). In Zora's eyes in particular, Andre's queerness and whiteness are intertwined, and manifest in a will to possess, dominate and therefore destroy all that he desires. Ultimately, Franklin seems caught in an ownership battle that involves his mother, Andre and his art, which is given to be at least partly rooted in the effects of his own absent father.

Stage directions in the play tell us: 'Franklin propulsively regresses from Young Man, to Boy, to Baby from act to act until he emerges as himself again' (ibid.: 11). The arc of the play, therefore, takes the form of a kind of regression, in which Franklin must repeat his trauma of abandonment, which manifests as a will to ownership, before he can be self-determining. When Franklin stands alone in the pool, in Act Three, the stage directions liken it to amniotic fluid, from which he is emerging. The process peaks during Andre and Franklin's wedding ceremony in the third act, which takes place in the former's property. By the pool slump three new large dolls representing Franklin, Andre and his mother (Figure 4.1). Franklin sucks his thumb throughout, and appears to have a breakdown, during which he hears his mother and Andre speak in tongues, tormenting each other and him, while the water around him seems

Figure 4.1 Franklin (Terique Jarrett), surrounded by the dolls he has made representing his mother Zora (left) and partner Andre (right) in *'Daddy': A Melodrama*, Almeida Theatre, London, UK (2022). Photographer: Marc Brenner.

to boil. The wedding ceremony becomes a Southern gothic rite of purification, via which Franklin seems to release the spirits which occupy him.

If *'Daddy'* functions as a ritual of cleansing and exorcism, what are we to make of the objects so central to its operation? Andrew Sofer suggests that objects on stage hover 'between actor and prop, sign and substance, mimesis and kinesis, liveness and deadness', and in this operate as a 'synecdoche for performance itself' (2016: 684). Sofer's description chimes with Freud's assertion that a feature of a brush with the uncanny is 'uncertainty whether an object is living or inanimate' ([1919] 2001: 230). Franklin's dolls similarly straddle the line between living and inanimate, in both representing characters in the play and functioning as art objects. Via their uncanny rendering, Harris's play explores what happens when a subject becomes an object, via forms of psychological or economic control, and how we might recognize and reverse the transformation.

In trying to understand this movement between subjectivity and objecthood, the object-relations psychoanalysis of Donald W. Winnicott proves useful. Winnicott uses the term 'transitional objects' to describe those things that facilitate the child's separation from the mother and introduction into the life of the external world. Transitional objects and phenomena, Winnicott tells us, belong to an 'intermediate area of experience, between the thumb and the teddy bear' ([1971] 2005: 2–3). The thumb and the teddy bear are often the child's first possessions, Winnicott suggests, which substitute the mother's breast and the form of its introjection (ibid.: 19). Despite the term, Winnicott tells us that the objects themselves are not transitional, but the child who develops around and with them: 'It is not the object, of course, that is transitional. The object represents the infant's transition from a state of being merged with the mother to a state of being in relation to the mother as something outside and separate' (ibid.: 19–20). Transitional objects help the child develop 'a sense of "me" and "not-me", or inside and outside me', Winnicott submits, and come to 'associate meaning as a "function of intake and output"' ([1965] 2018: 45).

For Winnicott, the infant develops a sense of subjective security and independence by being supported through the 'holding phase' and delivered into the 'living phase' by his caregiver. During this stage, the infant learns to navigate the world of objects that surrounds and separates his self from his caregiver. The term 'holding', for Winnicott, denotes 'not only the actual physical holding of the infant, but also the total environmental provision' (ibid.: 43). As Jan Abram summarizes, 'the parents must provide their infant with an environment that is suited to his needs' ([1996] 2018): 196). In the therapeutic relationship, Abram adds, 'it is the setting in analysis that provides the necessary holding environment for the patient' (ibid.: 196). By extension, we might see the performance-audience relationship mirror something of this therapeutic structure, in which we are aesthetically or dramaturgically held to share an encounter with troubled history.

Winnicott's theory of holding resonates with Wilfred R. Bion's claims about the container-contained function of psychoanalysis. According to Bion, the therapist may hold the patient's intolerable thoughts, until such a time as they might be re-introjected in a more bearable form ([1962] 2004: 90). However, whereas holding is a necessarily positive feature of care-giving, the container-contained relationship can be mutually destructive. In its damaging form, patients may feel a 'sense of imprisonment' or of being tormented by 'expelled particles of ego' (Bion 1967: 39), which take the form of 'bizarre objects'. These bizarre objects are the outcome of excessive productive identification, 'compounded partly of real objects and partly of fragments of the personality' (ibid.: 81).

Franklin's dolls and thumb-sucking, which so heavily feature in '*Daddy*', make the play look like an experiment in enacting the transition Winnicott describes. The young artist endeavours to surpass his parental attachments, and his status as a racialized object in a white art world, by fashioning dolls that might hold his projected sense of self. In this, we might say that Franklin is battling with what W. Ronald D. Fairbairn describes as 'bad objects', which are those figures in the external world that once sought to control the child, and which must in turn be controlled *by* the child via the interiorizing mechanisms of individuation, thus setting up a dynamic of fighting to possess the self. 'However much he may want to reject them, he cannot get away from them', Fairbairn tells us; 'In a word, he is "possessed" by them, as if by evil spirits' ([1952] 1994: 67). 'This is not all', Fairbairn continues, for 'the child not only internalizes his bad objects because they force themselves upon him and he seeks to control them, but also, and above all, because he *needs* them' (ibid.). During his breakdown in the last act, Franklin's dolls also take on the quality of 'bizarre objects', as defined by Bion – part real, part fragments of expelled personality. In the economy of the art of the world, however, Franklin struggles to escape his status as object, insofar as he becomes doubly fetishized as an artist and for his object doubles.[1]

Structures of containment

If the father is both objectifying and fetishized in Harris's play, in Sylvia Plath's poem 'Daddy', patriarchy itself is squarely fascistic in the way it reproduces violent men in successive generations, and enables abuse via the eroticization of pain. The poet compares her father to a Nazi in the poem, who terrorized and brutalized her like a Jewish prisoner: 'I have always been scared of *you*,/With your Luftwaffe, your gobbledygoo./ And your neat mustache/ And your Aryan eye, bright blue./Panzer-man, panzer-man, O You — /Not God but a swastika' ([1962] 2008 : 223). Plath also implies that the dynamic prevailed in her marriage to Ted Hughes, suggesting a brutality at the heart of the father figures who surrounded her: 'I made a model of you,/A man in black with a Meinkampf look/And a love of the rack and the screw. /And I said I do, I do' (ibid.: 224).

Striking a less confrontational tone, but equally interested in the shadow of Nazism, Rachael Mars's durational installation *Forge* invites us to reflect on the intergenerational effects of the Holocaust via gender and sexual politics, and material remains. While Mars's work, as a performer and maker, often explores queerness in humorous terms, the starting point for *Forge* is the sombre stealing of an entrance gate at Dachau concentration camp in 2014, bearing the slogan 'Arbeit Macht Frei' (Work Sets You Free), which was subsequently replaced with a replica.[2] The original gate at Dachau was made by Hermann Peter, who was imprisoned in the camp because of his oppositional writings against the Nazis. Even though the stolen gate was eventually found in Norway, the reproduction has remained *in situ*, while the original has been kept in the former camp's museum. Mars's project is interested in the effects of this substitution, for its ambiguous capacity to both reproduce violence and distance it. The project asks: What happens to the gate's power and meaning when it is recycled in this way? Is it possible to dispossess history of its dark potency in the reproduction and transformation of its objects? How can the present honour the power of one of the most powerful symbols, such as the gate, while also experimenting with its material displacement and disintegration?

Located northwest of Munich, Dachau was the first concentration camp established by the Nazi government in March 1933. The number of prisoners incarcerated between 1933 and 1945 approximated 200,000 with the number of deaths across the camp and subcamps exceeding 31,000, although the precise figure will never be known. The inmates were composed of Jews, political prisoners, Roma, Jehovah's Witnesses and homosexuals. All were subjected to a programme of forced labour, medical experimentation and starvation, many of whom were killed in mass shootings or at the gas chambers in Hartheim.[3]

In Weimar Germany, between the 1920s and 1930s, there was a vibrant social scene for queer people, which centred around bars and cafes. While in German criminal code, paragraph 175 criminalized male homosexuality, during these years LGBTQ+ people tended to be observed and monitored rather than persecuted. Many doctors did not perceive LGBTQ+ people as deviant, which was supported by the work of Magnus Hirschfeld's Institut für Sexualwissenschaft (the Institute for Sexual Science) based in Berlin.[4] In May 1933, four months after Hitler came to power, Hirschfeld's institute was attacked with its books burned in the streets. From the mid-1930s, under Heinrich Himmler, the anti-gay laws enshrined in paragraph 175 of the German Criminal Code, including new revisions, were enforced more ruthlessly.[5] Male homosexuality was considered to be contagious and at risk of spreading throughout the population and undermining the state, and therefore particularly dangerous. As Kathrin Braun describes it, 'male homosexuality was a contagious force that caused mental illness, weakness, venereal diseases, prostitution, and crime and that threatened to undermine the strength and fitness of state and society' (2021: 86).

Between 1935 and 1945, there were nearly 100,000 indictments according to paragraph 175 of the German Criminal Code, and about half of the men charged were convicted (Zur Nieden in Braun 2021: 80). In 1940, Himmler decreed that the criminal police were to place all homosexual men who had seduced more than one partner in preventive detention, after they had served their prison sentences (Bastian in Braun 2021: 80). Thousands were deported to concentration camps and only a minority survived. While the exact death toll is unknown, it is estimated that the death rate of homosexual men in camps was around 60 per cent (Zinn in Braun 2021: 80).

Some reports conjecture that among approximately 200,000 inmates, Dachau imprisoned approximately 800 male homosexuals.[6] Less is known about what we would consider now to be transgender individuals, or the experience of lesbians, who were not outlawed by paragraph 175, although it is assumed that those in the camps were there for other reasons. From 1938, detained homosexuals were assigned a pink triangle to identify them clearly. The power of this coding is dramatized in Martin Sherman's 1979 play *Bent*, which although written at a time when less was known about the treatment of gay people in Nazi Germany, is concerned with the sending of two gay men to Dachau. In the camp, Max meets Horst and asks about the pink triangle he wears, to be told: 'If you're queer, that's what you wear. If you're a Jew, a yellow star. Political – a red triangle. Criminal – green. Pink's the lowest' (Sherman [1979] 2004: 88).

The Nazis enjoyed spectacle as a mask for suffering, and central to the implementation of their ideology of racial purification was the circulation of images of cleanliness, strength and solidity. The gates at Dachau are among the most iconic artefacts of Nazi architecture, with the slogan 'Arbeit Macht Frei' appearing on a number of them, including at other camps. The slogan reflected the arduous physical labour endured by detainees, for whom freedom would never be the outcome. This had particular resonance for gay people, who laboured for long hours in challenging conditions under the expectation that hard work could straighten them, even though it would often result in death from injury. Some detainees were even castrated or experimented on as a 'cure' for homosexuality. Nazi architecture, according to Hitler, was 'ideology become stone', or 'the Word in stone' (Taylor 1974: 81–3), and the gates reflected this commitment to enduring resilience.

While Mars's queerness implicitly evokes this history, the more contemporary and personal impetus for her project was David Cameron's announcement in 2015 of his intention to create a Holocaust Memorial in the UK, the very same year he described the Mediterranean refugee crisis on ITV News as a 'swarm of people coming across the Mediterranean', evoking Nazi era propaganda of migrants, and especially Jews, as pests, as subsequent Conversative administrations have echoed.[7] As in Cameron's case, we can see how the drive to commemorate the past can also be used as a strategy to obscure or repeat violence in the present in more insidious ways. Mars's grandparents were refugees from Nazi Europe, who were welcomed to England because they were deemed to be not fiscally at risk, having secured jobs in advance of arrival. But a number of their relatives, and Mars's ancestors, perished in camps.

Mars believes that it is her responsibility to remember her forbears and carry their memories forward. In this, Mars is inspired by the work of Dina Wardi, who argues that in most families of survivors, one child serves as a 'memorial candle' for all the relatives who died during the Holocaust. This child, according to Wardi, serves as a generational link between the past, present and future, who 'heals the trauma' of the generational breach, by endeavouring to fulfil the expectations of their parents, 'but also, to some extent, those of the entire Jewish people' (1992: 6).

When *Forge* was first presented at Testbed, Leeds, in 2022, the entrance to the installation was painted with the hot pink of Nazi-era pink triangles, later taken up by ACT UP as its primary logo graphic. Over three days, for seven hours a day, Mars forges a replica of the stolen Dachau gate, accompanied by a soundscape created by Dinah Mullen. During this time, visitors come and go, watching Mars engage in the labour of manufacturing the reproduction, utilizing the welding skills she acquired during the pandemic. While the Jewish female body is often perceived as pale and intellectual, Mars tells me in conversation, she wilfully positions herself as a manually labouring queer presence at the centre of *Forge*. Wearing double denim and a protective visor, Mars works to realize the gates, bending and blasting the metal into her desired shape. Attendees also wear visors for protection against the sparks of fire produced by welding, which have the effect of framing the action as if it is happening on a widescreen. Every twenty to forty minutes, Mars takes a break to avoid the fumes produced by the welding (Figure 4.2).

Although Mars's project is, on the one hand, invested in replicating the gate, it is foremost concerned with the impossibility of perfecting this gesture, and arguably the ethical impropriety of such an act. In the exhibition accompanying the show, Mars is keen to record the disparate and heterogeneous origins of her materials, tools and collaborators. For instance, although she assembles the gate during the installation, its material base is substantively impure, made out

Figure 4.2 Rachel Mars welding in *Forge*, Testbed, Leeds, UK (2022). Photograph: JMA Photography.

of lengths of steel supplied by UK companies A1 Steel and F. H. Brundle, imported from Turkey or maybe Germany; no one is sure. The steel has been cut and forged by metal worker Jeni Cairns at her workshop and home in Coates, Peterborough, UK. Mars uses a Kemppi welder to cast approximately sixty-seven pieces of metal, and the tool was manufactured in Finland. Her Plymovent PHV Portable Fume Extractor was manufactured in the Netherlands. She uses a different font to recreate the distinct 'Arbeit Macht Frei' banner, as if to reproduce the style precisely would be an act of violence. For the same reason, Mars does not spell out the phrase, but uses the letters to create surprisingly witty anagrams, that refuse to let the text's meaning fully occupy the present – 'arithmetic', 'afterbirth', 'aftermath', 'aftercare'. Additionally, Mars draws focus less on the gate as a fetish object, than on her labour as a performer, invested not only in the making of a gate but in the commemoration of history, and the transformation of meaning through the material transmutations of welding.

While most of the project involves the making of the gate, the closing forty minutes shift in focus. Attendees are brought outside to a courtyard, washing their hands as they exit as part of a cleansing ritual. Here a prayer is spoken, and a brass band plays the theme music from the camp film *Flashdance* (1983), which follows the story of a female welder and aspiring dancer in Pittsburgh. In centring a brass band that plays a song about a welder who wants to be a dancer, the final scene seems to celebrate some of the other uses of metal – its capacity not just to contain and possess us, but to release us via kinetic vibration and musical form. In the same spirit, at the end of each installation, Mars recycles the steel for reuse, so that with each iteration the metal finish deliberately deteriorates. Her ultimate plan is to melt it into spoons at the end of the project, transmuting the violent form and function of the metal into something that supports generosity and hospitality. Mars explains her intention to melt the gates into spoons as a will to extend our dining tables in grief: 'Let's really live. Let's live and let's feed each other and animate that nourishment' (Mars 2022: 29).

Mars's attempt to reproduce a historical object is matched by her efforts to spoil this intention. For instance, the sober forging of the gate indoors is eventually interrupted by jubilant music outside. The gate is not a precise reproduction, but a deliberate distortion of the original. So on the one hand, Mars brings the past into the present, but she deprives it of some of its historical power via reproduction. In the act of transforming metal into a gate and then transmuting it into spoons, Mars implicitly asks if these new objects remain inherently contaminated by virtue of their origin, or if material and symbolic reconfiguration have the capacity to break a dark historical chain.

According to Jewish law, and the concept of *tumah*, the dead body is considered impure and capable of contaminating other things around it. Therefore, it must be ritualistically washed to purify it and to contain this threat. In a conversation with artist and educator Jacqueline Nicholls, printed in a programme note that accompanies the show, Mars wonders if her installation contaminates the present with the past, or has the capacity to contain and ritualistically purify it. In the text, Mars reasons:

> The closest that the metal of that gate has got to the Holocaust is my body. Over these three days. But the metal is being wilfully transformed into this problematic shape, which has absolutely to do with death … And we're inviting people to witness that act, or to be around it. So are they are actually around a dead body? (Mars 2022: 26)

Even though Mars concludes that the installation experience does not equal direct contact with a dead body, its proximate and representational nature prompts her to allow for ritual washing to take place.

Nicholls suggests that Jews in Europe had a very rich life, and that over-dwelling on how they died in the Holocaust casts too much focus on the last minutes of their lives. 'Knowing that they were just rounded up and shot is not remembering them', Nicholls writes, 'That's remembering how they were murdered' (Nicholls in Mars 2022: 28). Instead, Nicholls suggests we must reproduce the joy and generosity that defined their lives by extending tables in hospitality.

Holocaust memorials are charged with the task of commemorating the dead without a marked grave and sometimes with no record of death at all. Memorials are typically static constructions around which visitors move. Often this is done with due reverence, but sometimes also curiosity, and a less noble hope to be photographed at the memorial in question, in order to assert sympathy by photographic association. Such has been the case with the *Memorial to the Murdered Jews of Europe* in Berlin, which became a surprisingly popular backdrop for gay men's profile pictures on the social networking application Grindr in the 2010s, some of which were gathered for the 'Grindr Remembers' blog, with one such image featured in Mars's accompanying programme note. Even commemorative monuments, Mars's inclusion of this photograph suggests, cannot be easily policed and protected from the apparently contaminating effects of whimsy or narcissism. The subject of Holocaust memorials as sites of leisure is raised in Alan Bennett's *The History Boys*, first staged in 2004, in which the central teacher Hector, eventually accused of molesting the boys, says: 'They go on school trips nowadays, don't they? Auschwitz. Dachau. What has always concerned me is where do they eat their sandwiches? Drink their coke? ... Do they take pictures of each other there? Are they smiling?' (Bennett [2004] 2008: 71). In Mars's project, the historical memory and traumatic legacy of the Holocaust is recast via the remoulding of its architecture, such that she describes it as 'an attempt at containment' (Mars 2022: 26).

Mars's artwork is interested in the ways in which a commemorative monument can be deemed to be both morally good and bad. Alongside this, she is also suspicious of memorialization via static objects, which are vulnerable to over-determined signification, human intrusion and decontextualization. Instead,

Mars's durational performance not only desecrates the object, but also purposefully uses it as the basis for reflecting on the labour and violence of the camps and their memorialization, and the possibilities of finding shared pleasure amongst the ruins of history. If the Nazis enjoyed careful and codified image-making, Mars's project is committed to exploring what happens to the desecration of those images via their reproduction as a form of destruction, and the transformation of objects into implements and symbols of sharing and hospitality.

Reproduction and destruction

Tim Dant describes fetishism as 'the worship of objects' (1999: 40). He suggests that both Karl Marx's and Sigmund Freud's ideas of fetishism owe much to a 'pre-humanistic scheme in which spirits, sometimes residing with material objects, were treated as a significant part of the ontological order of the world' (ibid.: 41). In one of his more rigid texts, Freud describes fetishism as a male order of desire, in which the fetish object serves as a 'substitute for the woman's (the mother's) penis that the little boy once believed in and – for reasons familiar to us – does not want to give up' ([1927] 2001: 152–3). For Marx, fetishism accounts for how commodities are imagined to contain inherent value, rather than to represent 'the peculiar social character of the labour which produces them' ([1867] 1982: 165). Whether the object is imagined to be possessed by a spirit or value, its fetishization produces a sense of over-determined presence, via a fantasy of interior abundance, aimed at concealing its essential hollowness and the social relations particular to its production. Owing to this structure, David Marriot suggests that fetishism is always about 'repudiation and loss' (2010: 215). The fetish object is libidinally charged to conceal loss, Marriot maintains, distinguishing fetishism as the commemoration of loss through its denial.

In her collection of essays on 'evocative objects', Sherry Turkle writes that '*When objects are lost, subjects are found*' (2007: 10). By this Turkle seems to mean that subjectivity is premised on the internalization of psychic object-others, but also that we develop a sense of who we are in the pursuit of lost objects – whether people or things – in our everyday lives. We come to know who we are via the losses we pursue. If fetishism both commemorates and conceals loss, as Marriot proposes, it does so by assuming that the fetish can somehow be possessed or controlled. However, as Lauren Berlant has pointed out, even though we may think we control our fetishes, it is they that 'control or possess the person who thinks she possesses it' (2012: 34).

Bill Brown has argued that if 'the history *of* things can be understood as their circulation', that is their social life, 'then the history *in* things might be understood as the crystallization of the anxieties and aspirations that linger there in the material object' (1998: 935). In '*Daddy*' and *Forge*, objects take on the quality of fetishized commodities, circulated for their assumed capacity to distribute value in the form of proximity to a person or an event. But in each work, the object's ability to mediate history without obscuring subjectivity is questioned, until the objects themselves are discarded or dissolved.

The wilful destruction of the art object has precedent in the twentieth and twenty-first centuries, via practices that function to question the object's material resistance and enduring presence as sources of value. Banksy's *Girl with a Balloon*, which self-shredded moments after it was sold for £1,042,000 at Sotheby's in 2018, represents a recent version of this style of work, taking on the form of a prank destined to go viral on social media. If Banksy's auto-destroying art can be seen as an inquiry into the value of absence and presence, however, it ultimately demonstrates that capturing these experiments is itself highly lucrative, when the half destroyed object sold for £18.5 million in 2021 under the title *Love is in the Bin*. According to Jarad Pappas-Kelley, the destruction of the object in art changes our understanding of art as 'as a timeless and fixed entity', to one 'that both burns and is burning – putting forth and pulling down; an art that is perpetually shipwrecked, undone, and given form through this moment inhabited' (2019: 4). Pappas-Kelley invokes Paul Virilio here, who posits that all technologies incorporate the tools of their ruination: 'When you invent the ship, you also invent the shipwreck ... Every technology carries its own negativity' (1999: 89). As the shipwreck carries the tools of its undoing, according to Pappas-Kelley, so art carries the germ of its own future destruction. 'Art has a capacity to forestall through a ship's wreckage, to catch our breath', Pappas-Kelley tells us, 'revealing this interplay between what is lost yet still there – shipwrecked, yet still docked' (ibid.: 11). If art loses monetary value in its destruction, it gains in a different order of immaterial power. As Johnathan Jones puts it: 'art does not die so much as multiply its power when it disappears' (2013).

The history of self-destroying art takes us to the work of Gustav Metzger, who developed ideas of auto-destructive art in a series of manifestos written between 1959 and 1965, typically delivered as lecture-demonstrations. Metzger's vision for auto-destructive art imagined a scenario in which public monuments self-destruct, producing objects from their effacement. When the object is destroyed, in Metzger's vision, its remains are removed and scrapped, clearing space for the presence of absence. In 1961, along London's South Bank (not far from where Cassils would perform their indestructability in *Inextinguishable Fire* in 2015, as referenced in Chapter 2), wearing a protective mask and clothing, Metzger painted hydrochloric acid onto nylon canvasses, producing beautiful flares of rapidly disintegrating material. In performing on and against the object, the artwork was simultaneously created and destroyed.

A Polish Jew, born in Nuremberg in 1926, Metzger's ideas were formulated in the wake of his family being arrested by the Gestapo in 1939, after which he was sent to England under the Kindertransport scheme.[8] In Leeds, Metzger studied carpentry at the O. R. T. Technical Engineering School from 1941 to 1942, which had relocated from Berlin where it was established to train Jewish boys fleeing Nazism, followed by working as a joiner at the Harewood Estate. His parents and other family members died in Poland during the Second World War, while his two sisters escaped. While auto-destructive art's immediate target was the threat of nuclear war following the dropping of atomic bombs on Hiroshima and Nagasaki in 1945, the Holocaust powerfully shadows and fuels the work. The impact of both is felt in Metzger's belief that auto-destructive art enacts social destruction so that we might critically confront 'the pummelling to which individuals and masses are subjected', as he writes in the second publication, 'Manifesto Auto-Destructive Art' ([1960] 2019: 66). In its ruination, the object draws heighted awareness to the risks, causes and processes of destruction in the social sphere, as well as to the durability and survivability of the human body.

In '*Daddy*' and *Forge*, historical violence takes the form of turning subjects into objects, commodifying and discarding them through structures of containment and control. Certainly, objects commemorate this violence, but not in a way that suggests the historical narrative is complete. Instead, they seek to reroute and recycle violence via the distorting and distancing effects of reproduction and the alchemy of material transformation. It is not so much the case that an exclusively queer past is evoked, than that the past is projected, compressed and stalled in the queer subject's objects – in this chapter dolls and a gate – in the hope of storing violence within material borders. But this kind of containment, as both examples expose, risks leading to a localized fetishization of the past via the object, making it too-present and too-distant all at once. As '*Daddy*' and *Forge* seem to ultimately suggest, to avoid its arresting effect on time, the object, like the past, must be continuously remade through reproduction, recontextualization and reformulation; forms of destruction which are also, inevitably, radical forms of creation.

In his famous essay 'The Work of Art in the Age of Mechanical Reproduction', Walter Benjamin contends that technologically reproduced art loses its aura of authenticity, which challenges the 'authority of the object' ([1935] 2007: 221). While reproduction strives to close the distance between viewers and art, by increasing access for the masses, it also has the effect of destroying the aura of the original, which is the powerful, intangible quality of its singular emergence in place and time. In *'Daddy'* and *Forge* too, reproduction-as-destruction becomes a strategy to commemorate and represent history in a safe, containable way and to distance the present from the heat of its aura. In reproducing objects of violence, the past is not just summoned as fetish, but distorted of its original approximation, and diffused of its power.

Conclusion

This chapter has examined how objects commemorate and stand in for historical violence, absorbing its force and rendering it apparent, although veiled and contained, in the present. It has also demonstrated how the object's capacity to both hold and distance the present from the past runs the risk of reproducing suffering as a fetish, prone to being capitalized on by those who collect pain for pleasure. In *'Daddy'* and *Forge*, racialized violence overshadows the present of queer artists, who confront their cultural histories in the objects they make, unmake and trade to survive. It is only in the reproduction-as-destruction of the object that the violence it indexes and gathers can be discharged and remoulded, to re-present the past and protect the present from the burn of its unmediated glare. If the reproduction of the object refuses to let history settle in an over-determined thing, so too does it allow those who have been objectified by its production or arrested in fascination to return or ascend to the world of subjects. In this realm, the past cannot reside solely in objects, but it must be produced and reproduced in the fleshier interface of bodies and things, so that queer people and their material cultures are not just objects of curiosity to be controlled, but subjects of history-making.

5

Wilde spirits: Occupation and commemoration

On 28 February 2021, the graffiti artist Banksy painted a mural on the wall of Reading Prison, showing a man escaping the building using tied sheets flowing from a typewriter. The artwork was immediately taken to allude to Oscar Wilde, the prison's most famous detainee, while bolstering a campaign for Reading Borough Council to purchase the disused building in order to transform it into an arts and cultural hub. 'Oscar Wilde is the patron saint of smashing two contrasting ideas together to create magic', Banksy claimed in a statement published by the BBC; 'Converting the place that destroyed him into a refuge for art feels so perfect we have to do it' (Khomami 2021). In May of the same year, the Council's bid for the jail was rejected by the Ministry of Justice because the offer of £2.6 million was deemed too low. Reading Prison will be always be remembered as a site of detainment, a place created for the holding of the 'outcasts' referred to in the inscription on Wilde's tomb.[1] But it is not just a structure for the possession of the dispossessed, nor indeed their ghosts, but a place that has inspired free thinking and artistic production, against the odds. As Banksy's image suggests, Wilde may have been incarcerated in the prison, but his art, ideas and inspiration live on, forever scaling the walls of his time and place in history.

I use the occasion of Banksy's intervention in the sale of Reading Prison to explore how contemporary culture endeavours to possess and contain Wilde – as an idea, object or site – and the ways in which Wilde resists this commodification by possessing contemporary culture as a restless ghost or disruptive spirit, overspilling his assigned boundaries. The attempt to sell the prison is tied to the question of how the building's history will be remembered and given meaning, and begs considering how that which possesses *us* might be transformed by the histories that occupy *it*. Karl Marx wrote that we believe 'an object is only *ours* when we have it – when it exists for us as capital, or when it is directly possessed, eaten, drunk, worn, inhabited, etc., – in short, when it is *used* by us' (1844: 101). This singular focus on *having*, Marx tells us, estranges us from all the other 'physical and mental senses' (ibid.) with which we might encounter and experience the world.

In the installation-based practices examined in this chapter, properties and objects are presented as if possessed by Wilde's spirit, in a manner that resists their easy commodification and ownership, by tracking his diffuse and enduring influence. I focus on two multi-modal installation projects produced in the UK, in which Wilde was invoked as the foundational sacrifice of queer culture, and its key artistic reference point. Via Wilde, in Artangel's *Inside: Artists and Writers in Reading Prison* (2016) and McDermott & McGough's *The Oscar Wilde Temple* (2017), audiences were invited to reckon with some of the forgotten histories of violence and inspiration, activism and art shaping LGBTQ+ culture, and the means by which we come to know, process and preserve them. Moreover, Wilde was presented as the figure capable of bridging other urgent contemporary social and political issues not exclusively about sexuality, but injustice, exclusion and dispossession, and championing the case for ongoing queer cultural production in this spirit.

These works were produced during a time of significant queer commemoration and legal revision. Same-sex marriage became legalized in large parts of the West in the 2010s, including England, Scotland and Wales in 2014, and Northern Ireland in 2020. As discussed in Chapter 1, 2017 also marked the fiftieth anniversary of the decriminalization of homosexuality in England and Wales, which was responded to by numerous artists, cultural institutions and media outlets. It was also the year when the so-called Turing Law was passed, which pardoned all men charged with gross indecency under Section 11 of the Criminal Law Amendment Act 1885, including Alan Turing after whom it was named, and Wilde.

How might we understand this turn to Wilde during this period of commemoration, legalization and pardoning? In this chapter, I initially consider some of the ways in which Wilde's power has been tamed, primarily via cultural commodification and objectification. Countering this tendency, I explore how the siting of Wilde in a former prison and a (re)constructed temple participate in histories of performing and sculpturally siting Wilde, of theatre attendance and pilgrimage. In this way, they faithfully keep Wilde's work and legacy alive, but also reorient him from his more familiar place in mainstream theatrical and literary culture where he has largely become sanitized. I argue that through a combination of historical realignment and recontextualization that traces new paths of Wildean influence and inspiration; and architectural and scenographic innovation that encourage immersive and participatory encounters, we are drawn into a new appreciation of Wilde's time and place in queer culture, and their shared capacity to engage contemporary social and political concerns.

In developing these ideas, I think of these artworks, and some others like them, as *rewild(e)ing* practices, which reseed Wilde across different contexts for new times, while stimulating the renewal and diversification of queer arts. The *Merriam-Webster Dictionary* defines rewilding as 'the planned reintroduction of a plant or animal species and especially a keystone species or apex predator (such as the gray wolf or lynx) into a habitat from which it has disappeared (as from hunting or habitat destruction) in an effort to increase biodiversity and restore the health of an ecosystem'.[2] I like the idea of Wilde as an apex predator, who episodically returns to stalk, devour and generate new queer ideas and practices. On the one hand, I am succumbing to easy word play, of course, as many other commentators have done before me who associated Wilde with wildness. But as I attempt to demonstrate over the course of the chapter, at various points throughout history this alignment also represented utterly serious efforts to bolster Wilde's perceived otherness, whether artistic, sexual or racial. Here I try to honour tones both mischievous and grave, by examining artworks that purposefully harness Wilde's disruptive force, in order to generate new ways of accessing, experiencing and shaping relations of history, artistic form and political alliance. So this chapter is not so much interested in Wilde's dramatic corpus, which many others have written about, than in what Wilde's spirit is invoked and put to work for now, and how this might expand and enliven the substance and shape of contemporary queer performance and culture.

The shadow of sacrifice

While Wilde's status in theatrical, literary and queer culture seems now relatively secured, this was not always the case. During his trial, imprisonment and in the immediate years after his death Wilde was widely shunned and shamed by the society that had once elevated him. One of the most influential voices in the recuperation of Wilde was the German sexologist Magnus Hirschfeld, a leading figure in the destigmatization of homosexuality at the turn of the twentieth century. Hirschfeld was greatly affected by Wilde's prosecution, and its negative impact on homosexuals at the time. In 1905 Hirschfeld visited Cambridge University to meet with Wilde's son, Vyvyan Holland, whose surname was changed to avoid being associated with his disgraced father. While at Cambridge Hirschfeld came across a 'a group of beautiful young male students' who had gathered to read *The Ballad of Reading Gaol* – Wilde's last major work – with his prisoner number attached to their shirts (Bauer 2017: 55).[3] Heike Bauer suggests that this incident reveals that queer communities were already congregating around Wilde shortly after his death (ibid.), but it may also be one of the earliest recordings we have of what we would now think of as a queer public performance of Wilde's work.

Bauer also argues that the alignment of homosexuality with suffering, which Hirschfeld discerns, would reappear at various points throughout the twentieth century, including during the height of AIDS. 'In some ways', Bauer writes, 'Hirschfeld's account of the impact of Wilde's death on homosexual subcultures anticipates some of the responses to the early AIDS crisis when political resolve and vitality was formed out of suffering' (ibid.: 55–6). Bauer points to Neil Bartlett's imaginative biography *Who Was That Man?* (1988), which links Wilde's pain to Bartlett's own experience as a gay man in London in the 1980s, suggesting that it bridged the two foundational events of modern English and American male same-sex history: the trial of Wilde and AIDS (ibid.: 133). The point worth underscoring here, however, is that part of Wilde's enduring appeal since his death has less been his sexuality – which has continued to pose a problem at various stages – than his capacity to stand in as a victim of suffering and defiance with whom many might identify.

Any attempt to understand Wilde's legacy requires considering how he was received and responded to differently within the two cultures that defined him – the Ireland he was born in and the Britain where he lived and worked most of his adult life. Graham Price contends that Wilde's presence can be felt across Irish theatre in the twentieth and twenty-first centuries, in which 'Irish playwrights … have used the Wildean aesthetic in very productive ways in an attempt to create compelling and innovative plays for present-day Ireland' (2018: 1). However, in Ireland, Wilde's explicit recuperation in the mid twentieth century was largely dependent on his capacity to be framed as an eloquent, clever and martyred anti-colonial patriot at the heart of British culture, largely beginning with Micheál Mac Liammóir's production of *The Importance of Being Oscar* (1960), which he wrote, directed and starred in. Traces of this patterning can be found among other works, including Thomas Kilroy's *The Secret Fall of Constance Wilde* (1997), Terry Eagleton's *Saint Oscar* (1989) and David Norris's *Oscar* (1994). While these productions created public space for Wilde's life and work to be discussed, in the lead up to the decriminalization of homosexuality in 1993, Wilde's sexuality was often obscured. For Eibhear Walshe, this largely sapped the subversiveness of Wilde, which was only compounded by his reappearance in the latter part of the twentieth century 'to suggest or even invent a more inclusive sense of Irishness', in light of radical economic, social and legal change (2011: 69). Most strikingly, perhaps, Wilde appeared as a branding insignia across everything from festivals, boats and souvenirs, to epigrammatic quotes on café walls.

Bartlett is an important figure in bridging Wilde's contested Irishness and Englishness. In addition to his aforementioned novel, and the play *In Extremis* (which was written to be performed alongside *De Profundis* as part of the National Theatre in London's programming to mark Wilde's death in 2000), Bartlett's production of *An Ideal Husband* was performed in the Abbey Theatre, Dublin, in 2008, and his adaptation of Wilde's *The Picture of Dorian Gray* appeared in the Abbey in 2012. Other important UK theatrical productions include Eagleton's play and David Hare's *The Judas Kiss* (1998). An Oscar Wilde season at the Vaudeville Theatre in 2018 featured Frank McGuinness's adaptation of *De Profundis* as an interlude between Dominic Dromgoole's direction of *A Woman of No Importance* and Kathy Burke's *Lady Windermere's Fan*. Perhaps the most pivotal moment in invigorating and bridging Irish and UK stagings of Wilde was Steven Berkoff's production of *Salomé* (1988). This was not just because Berkoff's piece opened at the Gate Theatre, Dublin, and continued to tour the UK, but because it found a dark and eerie queerness in Wilde's play, neither possible for nor typical of the rest of Wilde's oeuvre. The silent executioner was played by the openly gay street mime artist Thom McGinty, who would learn of his HIV diagnosis in 1990, and die in 1995 – the first person to make public his HIV-positive status on Irish television. Berkoff's production, in this regard, perhaps unwittingly found a way for Wilde's play to be haunted by the past, present and future of queer cultural concerns.

While Wilde has served as a valuable figure to variously negotiate Irish-UK national politics, reflect on the suffering brought by AIDS and promote tourism, with the rise of the Marriage Equality agenda in the 2000s, approaches to Wilde strained under this normativizing lurch. Conall Morrison's all male version of *The Importance of Being Earnest* at the Abbey Theatre in 2005, a decade before Marriage Equality legislation was passed in the Republic, exemplifies this awkward transition. Morrison's pantomimic production seemed to try and locate homosexuality at the heart of Wilde's best known play, but aligned it with comic female impersonation, which ultimately seemed rather homophobic.

In the last decade, however, Wilde's art and life have again been invoked across diverse forms, to insist on his seminal place within the history of queer culture. What interests me here about some of these works, however, is how they distance – even rescue – Wilde from his own theatrical idiom, approaching him instead via performative interventions that offer innovative ways for understanding his work and legacy. These sited projects firmly insert Wilde's art, sexual criminalization and death into the history of LGBTQ+ rights, lest it be forgotten, while also engaging other urgent contemporary social and political issues. These practices, I argue, not only deepen our sense of queer history, activism, artistic practices and networks, but also signpost new forms and targets for queer performance culture.

Installing internment

Founded in 1844 and formally closed in 2014, Reading Prison (formerly Reading Gaol) was opened to the public in 2016 as part of Artangel's immersive installation *Inside: Artists and Writers in Reading Prison*. Artangel is a UK-based collective with a mission to take 'extraordinary art' to 'unexpected places'.[4] With this project the company curated a range of artists, artworks, performances, readings, talks, tours and events to shine a light on the prison, whose most famous inmate included Wilde, who occupied cell C.3.3.

Following trials at the Old Bailey in London in 1885, Wilde was eventually found guilty of gross indecency for homosexual acts, and forced to spend two years in prison with hard labour, which likely hastened his early death in 1900. Wilde spent the first year at Wandsworth Prison, and the second at Reading, where he endured its Separate System, a harsh regime of solitary confinement, designed to prevent contact between prisoners. These conditions inform the design of the installation, especially the placement of artistic materials and the possibilities for interaction among visitors, artworks and the site. So while Wilde's sexuality and suffering are certainly reflected in the installation, the work of influenced artists also dwell on issues of injustice, loss, isolation and longing, and the threads that connect them all.

Artangel's project broadly functions as an installation that takes over large parts of the old Victorian prison's cells and corridors, filling them with visual art, performances, recordings, lectures and display cases. In some instances, the artwork has the quality of immersive performance, insofar as viewers are embedded in a series of performative and theatrical encounters. But none of these draw on the frequently melodramatic or camp interpretations of Wilde's own commercially popular plays, which have come to define and sometimes impede how he has been understood. Adam Alston describes immersive theatre as that which produces 'thrilling, enchanting or challenging experiences' (2016: 3) as a result of audiences effectively co-producing a show through participation or the prospect of such involvement. Artangel's project does not assign attendees such purposeful tasks, but our movement, viewing and listening experiences are nonetheless guided by the installation's curation, in particular its temporal and spatial design.

The fine curation of time and space to lead us around the site and immerse us in its discrete artworks has a number of effects. First, it reveals to us the prison in which Wilde was detained, while reminding us, via more recent signs of wear and tear, of the thousands of others were held here too. Second, it showcases Wilde's work, and charts how he made way for future artists and activists. Jack Halberstam has suggested that 'queer uses of time and space develop, at least in part, in opposition to the institution of the family, heterosexuality, and reproduction. They also develop according to other logics of location, movement, and reproduction' (2005: 1). The turns of time and space that contour Artangel's installation offer equally resistant and surprising views of queer history and culture. In remapping the prison site and queer cultural lineage, Artangel's project evokes a sense of queer time and space as being very much of the present as much as of the past, available not only to sexual outlaws, but all those otherwise detained, dejected and dispossessed.

Among the more obviously performative gestures presented in the prison, the theatre company Reading Between the Lines performed transcripts of Wilde's trial (*Oscar Wilde on Trial* by Beth Flintoff, directed by Jonathan Humphreys). However, the centerpiece of the project was undoubtedly staged readings of *De Profundis*, Wilde's letter to Bosie (Lord Alfred Douglas), written from his prison cell. Readings were delivered from a table on a raised platform at the top of the old chapel by distinguished performers from across a range of disciplines, including Neil Bartlett, Ralph Fiennes, Kathryn Hunter, Ragnar Kjartansson, Maxine Peake, Lemn Sissay, Patti Smith, Colm Tóibín and Ben Whishaw; with Bartlett's unabridged version taking over six hours. These particular artists represent different ideas of outsider and insider; their fame and success bristling against a range of sexual, national, classed and disciplinary identities. The readings in full had the quality of what Jonathan Kalb has theorized as 'marathon theater' (2011), in which prolonged performance endeavoured to simulate a sense of Wilde's own pained endurance.

Arguably the exhibition's most powerful object, at the top of the raised platform is Wilde's cell door, incorporated into an installation by the French artist Jean-Michel Pancin, titled *In Memoriam* (Figure 5.1). The door forms part of the Galleries of Justice Museum collection in Nottingham, its key being sold to a private buyer in 2016. The same door (along with other artworks, including portraits of Wilde and Bosie by Marlene Dumas) was later displayed at Tate Britain's Queer British Art 1861–1967 exhibition (2017). Positioned at the top of the chapel, the door looks like an iconic statue in a church, or the crucified Christ, which places visitors as praying to or for Wilde. But its shape also resembles a headstone, as if locating us by Wilde's grave. Closer inspection reveals that the door's inside faces us, the viewers, so that we are also implicitly inside Wilde's cell, contained by the same structure that once detained him.

While performance undoubtedly features in this project, as indicated earlier, the artwork predominantly takes the form of a sited installation. Claire Bishop reminds us that installation art 'loosely refers to the type of art into which the viewer physically enters, and which is often described as "theatrical," "immersive" or "experiential"' (2005: 6). What differentiates installation from other media, Bishop proffers, is that 'it addresses the viewer directly as a literal presence in the space. Rather than imagining the viewer as a pair of disembodied eyes that survey the work from a distance, installation art presupposes an embodied viewer whose sense of touch, smell and sound are as heightened as their sense of vision' (ibid.).

This emphasis on embodied experience is apparent in the various ways audiences are invited to engage with the mixed-media artworks inside individual cells or among corridors, to sharpen a sense of Wilde's direct and indirect influence on generations of artists. In one cell, thanks to Nan Goldin, *The Boy* is composed of a collage of numerous sensual pictures of the actor Clemens Schick, which appear to speak to Wilde's own obsession with Bosie, accompanied by a video interview with an elderly activist campaigning for a

Figure 5.1 Artangel's *Inside: Artists and Writers in Reading Prison* featuring Oscar Wilde's cell door in Jean-Michel Pancin's installation *In Memoriam*, Reading, UK (2016). Photographer: William Eckersley.

government apology for his homosexuality conviction seventy years previous. Next door, also by Goldin, a silent film of Wilde's play *Salomé* screens on a loop, while in another Jean Genet's film *Chant d'Amour* is viewable only through a peephole. In a different unit, in paintings by Dumas, the murdered gay Italian film director Pier Paolo Pasolini encounters his mother; and in another, also by Dumas, portraits of Wilde and Bosie icily look away from one another on a wall (Figure 5.2). These carefully positioned artworks jostle against other situational reminders of the past – worn surfaces and peeled paint, or graffitied text and drawings by former inmates that remind us of the long and recent history etched into the fabric of the building.

Many of the cells still contain bunk beds. In Steve McQueen's *Weight* the beds are draped with a gold-plated mosquito net, which afford them an incongruous glamour, while invoking, in contrast, his brutal depictions of republican incarceration in the film *Hunger*

Figure 5.2 Artangel's *Inside: Artists and Writers in Reading Prison* featuring Marlene Dumas's painting *Oscar Wilde*, Reading, UK (2016). Photographer: Marcus J. Leith.

(2008). Posters by Félix González-Torres, the Cuban-US artist who died of AIDS in 1996, are stacked in one of the landing wings, depicting birds in otherwise empty skies; his beaded curtains hanging across open cell entrances. Wolfgang Tillmans's distorted photographic portraits – *Separate System, Reading Prison* – were made from damaged mirrors once used by former inmates that the artist found in the prison.

While Wilde was forbidden to write anything apart from an occasional letter during his first year in prison, a new governor who joined Reading in 1896 afforded him enough paper to write *De Profundis* – a sprawling, embittered letter to Bosie. This text supplies inspiration for a number of writers who compose letters to people facing forced separation, which we can listen to being read aloud, weaving between the deeply personal and political. Danny Morrison imagines a final letter from Irish revolutionary Reginald Dunne, who was involved in the 1916 Easter Rising and held in Wandsworth Prison. Gillian Slovo writes to her mother, who was murdered by the South African secret service in Mozambique while in exile. Binyavanga Wainaina addresses his dead mother about the struggle to reveal his homosexuality. Inspired by Shakespeare's *The Winter's Tale*, Jeanette Winterson imagines a letter from Hermione to Perdita written during the sixteen years she is adopted, following her father's abandonment and her mother's presumed death. 'Why is the measure of love, loss?', the voice asks, in a formulation that reminds us that if so much of what we encounter in the prison is premised on experiences of painful loss, it is only because we can gauge them against the joys of love. Ai Weiwei writes to his son, in another cell, describing his eighty-one-day detention in China in 2011. Deborah Levy directs her message to Wilde himself, questioning what a man is and the motives of those who condemned him to imprisonment: 'Meanwhile, the old white men of politics, like an ancient crocodile, drags its thick tail across the 21st century. They are still with us, fragile but powerful, those who whisper, "I am not saying you are it, but you look like it." '

Water, like blood, runs through the arteries of Robert Gober's excavations. In *Treasure Chest*, a wooden box opens into a subterranean view of a stream rippling over stones, its banks held open by hands in surgical gloves. On an adjacent wall, titled *Waterfall*, the back of a suited torso is embedded with a similar watery view. Gober's apertures are highly evocative, suggesting everything from the narrow gaps of cells (keyholes, bars and windows), to chance escape routes, glory holes and bodily orifices. His objects are archaeological devices, which, in excavating the building, reveal its wild foundations and hidden bodies struggling to survive. They strike a religious note too, like an open tomb situated next to an elevated icon, whose wounds strive to bridge times and places, the living and dead, worlds primal and punitive.

The term 'dark tourism' is sometimes used to describe the draw of visitors to tragic sites, which through practices of museumization or entertainment, at worst risk commodifying, fetishizing and distancing suffering. In one sense, dark tourism resembles a secularized form of pilgrimage, and sites associated with Wilde have also been subject to this particular construction. While Hirschfeld was noting public recitations of Wilde's work in Cambridge, for example, the Hôtel D'Alsace in Paris where Wilde died, and Bagneaux where he was first buried, also became sites of pilgrimage. Robert H. Sherard, Wilde's first biographer, recalls his participation in pilgrimages to both sites in his memoir *Twenty Years in Paris*. The hotel even let out Wilde's apartment 'exactly as it was in [Wilde's] day' (1905: 455), with the same furniture, including the syringe used to inject morphine 'in the last months of [Wilde's] slow agony'(ibid.: 456). Quoting the landlord, Sherard claims that 'hardly a week passes but that some visitor from foreign lands comes to the hotel and asks to be shown the room where Oscar Wilde died' (ibid.).

Something of this darkness, and our appetite for it, undoubtedly structures Artangel's project too. But as Phillip R. Stone posits, commemoration and dark tourism sometimes intersect in more ambiguous, even productive ways: 'Contemporary memorialisation is played out at the intersection of dark tourism, where consumer experiences can catalyse sympathy for the victims or revulsion at the context', and 'provide reflectivity of both place and people' (2018: vii–xviii). So while Artangel's artwork at least flirts with the morbid curiosity we might have to witness Wilde's place of internment, in its spatio-temporal sensitive curation it invites us to think reflexively about the prison and those it contained, and the relationship between curtailment, punishment and artistic production.

Artangel's project fundamentally invites us to explore a foundational site in the punishment of homosexuality, which paved the way for its legalization in the twentieth century, and Wilde's own pardon in the twenty-first. We encounter the prison not only as a site of suffering, but also as a space for reflecting on issues of injustice, loss, isolation and longing, which extend beyond its primary functional context. It also becomes a scene for demonstrating how Wilde's work and death expanded the horizons of twentieth- and twenty-first-century queer activism and art across the world, transforming a space of isolation and punishment into a network of collaboration and resilience. In the spatialized orderings of time, and time's marks on physical space, Wilde's role as an organizing and disorganizing force is given as ever-present since the nineteenth century.

Saints, sinners and idols

With *The Oscar Wilde Temple*, artists David McDermott and Peter McGough construct a space of worship for honouring the life and legacy of Wilde. The project opened in New York in 2017 and in London in 2018, where I saw it, and is among the pair's most immersive artwork to date, developed over a twenty year period. Studio Voltaire is housed in a former Methodist Chapel, with a beamed roof and church windows, which make easy its transposition from gallery to temple. Indeed, the project's earlier iteration in New York, also took place in a church – the Russell Chapel, the Church of the Village. These particular sites amplify the sense that Wilde continues to grate against institutional orthodoxies, perhaps especially religiously constructed notions of sin, while elevating Wilde as our new rightful object of devotion. Inside the studio, at the top of the exhibition space, Wilde's luminescent form beams bright from an altar. From this position, he mirrors and displaces more familiar Christian iconography to become the patron Saint of marginalized and dispossessed lives, in further endorsement of his long-standing title of 'Saint Oscar'[5] (Figure 5.3).

Of course, a temple can be its own kind of prison, and even this one, decorated with William Morris-style floral paper, displays images of suffering and sacrifice. Wilde's prison writings reveal his own self-identification as a Christian martyr, and he seemingly converted to Catholicism on his deathbed. On the left wall of the

Figure 5.3 McDermott & McGough's *The Oscar Wilde Temple*, Studio Voltaire, London, UK (2018). Courtesy of the artist Peter McGough and Studio Voltaire. Photographer: Francis Ware.

temple hangs a series of twelve painted scenes from Wilde's life and trial, taking the form of stations of the cross. Smaller depictions of other historical LGBTQ+ pioneers and activists line the top walls, including Alan Turing and murdered US gay rights activist and community leader Harvey Milk. Featured too is Marsha P. Johnson, an African-American transwoman and activist involved in the Stonewall uprising, whose memory was erased in many accounts of the time, although revived by others, not least in light of the Black Lives Matter and Black Trans Lives Matter movements.[6] Also depicted is Sakia Gunn, a fifteen-year-old African American lesbian who was murdered in a homophobic attack in 2015. Other panels hanging on the walls carry text like protest banners: one reads 'QUEER'; another includes jumbled slurs including 'Mary', 'Homo', 'Pansy', 'Cocksucker'. In the entrance hall a panel lists: 'No homophobia, transphobia, bigotry, misogyny, racism, fascism, neo-fascism, white supremacy, anti-Semitism, anti-immigration, only love here'.

Operating mainly between New York and Dublin since the 1980s, McDermott & McGough are preoccupied with the past, especially Victorian subjects and the period's authentic design, architecture, materials and techniques. A key feature of the pair's work is their resistance to living in the present, preferring to inhabit the turn of the twentieth century instead, on account of the devastation wrought by the First World War. 'I've seen the future', they have often interchangeably said, 'and I'm not going'.[7]

McDermott & McGough have described their work as 'experimenting in time'[8] challenging ideas of linear chronology, often by investing in homoerotic aspects of the past. This approach resembles what Elizabeth Freeman elaborates as erotohistoriography—a mode of desirous historical investigation that 'indexes how queer relations complexly exceed the present' (2005: 59). But while the artists typically appeal to the past for comfort, with this project it is an unaccommodating destination, that both anticipates and is haunted by its violent future. Despite its persistent hostilities, the present emerges as an unusually welcome vantage point for McDermott & McGough.

The temple primarily functions as an installation of visual artworks made by the pair, which viewers are invited to freely roam around and interact with. You can even light a devotional candle, if you wish. In this, the piece is less structured and busier than the Artangel project. In addition to operating as a site of historical reflection, however, the temple also served as a centre for LGBTQ+ community events and ceremonies, the kind unavailable to many of its documented forbears. In its iteration in London, the temple was opened to communities for ceremonies, reading groups, meetings, educational visits and other special events, in particular serving the local LGBTQ+ communities of Clapham, Brixton and Wandsworth. Some of these occasions included a 'The Day of the Dead' drumming circle with the Radical Faeries of Albion; a 'Queer New Year' letter writing workshop with Kingston LGBT Forum; a wide-reaching engagement programme in partnership with national LGBT youth homelessness charity, The Albert Kennedy Trust; a faith gathering for LGBTQ+ people of colour with the House of Rainbow and a eulogy ceremony with artist Salote Tawale.

Whereas the Artangel project is sharply attuned to the aesthetic and affective experiences of sexuality, loneliness and isolation, McDermott & McGough's intervention is set on dignifying Wilde as a sacrificial hero. But as I indicated at the outset of this chapter, Wilde's status as hero goes through waves of complication. In *The Trials of Oscar Wilde* (which opened in St James's Theatre, London, before transferring to Trafalgar Studios in the West End in 2014), elaborate verbatim accounts of Wilde's incriminating trial were aired in a theatre, more extensive than those featured in Moisés Kaufman's earlier *Gross Indecency: The Three Trials of Oscar Wilde* (1997). Co-written by John O'Connor and Merlin Holland, Wilde's grandson (drawing on Holland's 2003 book, *Irish Peacock and Scarlet Marquess: The Real Trial of Oscar Wilde*), the play was based on transcripts at the Old Bailey, allowing Wilde's own words to be heard. In the same year, Antony Edmonds published *Oscar Wilde's Scandalous Summer: The 1894 Worthing Holiday and the Aftermath*, a book that accounted for the summer Wilde wrote *The Importance of Being Earnest*, and his turbulent relationship with Bosie.

Both of these works confirmed that not only did Wilde have sex with men, but that he solicited younger boys of a lower social class, and sometimes treated them unkindly, prompting Marcus Field in *The Independent* to call for a reassessment of Wilde's status in light of Operation Yewtree (2014).[9] Can we separate the man from the art, is a question many have asked in recent years, particularly in light of the #MeToo era. But with Wilde, the life and work so often collapse, separate and blur in multiple ways, such that the question seems especially difficult to resolve.

McDermott & McGough's project insists on elevating Wilde as an artist-martyr, by affording him the gravity of a beautifully designed installed temple, and by downplaying aspects of his sexuality, as others have done before, such as his dubious soliciting of young males of lower classes. As with Artangel's project, McDermott & McGough's installation reminds us of the enduring effect and legacy of Wilde on the present day. He is memorialized, alongside activists and victims of homophobia and transphobia, to saintly status – a figure we should not forget despite living in seemingly more accommodating circumstances. But Wilde also becomes the occasion for transforming space – changing a gallery into a temple, and a temple into a community venue – inviting those who are homeless or otherwise displaced and marginalized to come under its roof, albeit temporarily. Honouring Wilde's status as insider and outsider, the artists create a performative space that straddles artistic disciplines and functions, operating as a temple, a gallery and a community centre all at once.

In affording Wilde his own temple, rather than a prison, in one sense the project is faithful to McDermott & McGough's guiding conceit that our glory days are behind us. After all, temples tend to have one eye on the lived past, and another on the immortal future. In decorating the space with latter day activists and would-be martyrs, however, and by inviting communities in to view and use the space, McDermott & McGough's artwork makes Wilde a figure very much for the present. His abiding significance not only helps us make sense of the international landscape of contemporary queer politics and culture, but in a sense undoes the pair's signature turn of the century fixation. Here is a Wilde *of* the past and *for* the future, very much rooted in the here and now.

Public display

While installations by Artangel and McDermott & McGough are very much in dialogue with Wilde as a theatrical and literary figure, they echo and extend other site-specific renderings and memorializations. In the UK, for example, between 1995 and 2000 numerous events took place to commemorate Wilde's conviction for gross indecency in London and his death in Paris. These included the consecration of a window in Wilde's honour in Poets Corner, Westminster Abbey (1995), and the erection of Maggi Hambling's *A Conversation with Oscar Wilde* in Adelaide Street, London (1998), in which an eternally chatting and smoking Wilde appears to rise from a casket to entertain passersby. In Dublin, Wilde's embrace by the public imagination was best signalled by the erection of Danny Osborne's *Oscar Wilde Memorial Sculpture* is Merrion Square Dublin (1997). This work sees a smirking Wilde, reclining pompously on a rock, flanked by pillars supporting a nude model of his wife Constance Lloyd, and Dionysus, the Greek god of wine and drama, etched with quotes by Wilde in the script of writers including Seamus Heaney, John B. Keane and Michael D. Higgins, the country's current President.

These outdoor sculptures not only register Wilde as an important cultural figure, but materially solidify his reputation for posing and public display. There may be truth to this, and yet one of the most anguished passages from Wilde's prison writings – a letter to the Home Secretary dated 22 April 1897 – captures his despair at being exhibited following his sentencing. Standing cuffed at Clapham Junction station, he was mocked and jeered by passersby. Wilde recalls the event as being 'so utterly distressing', leaving him 'quite unable to undergo any similar exhibition to the public gaze' ([1897] 2013: 184). This very account inspired a commemorative rainbow plaque to be erected in the station in 2019, spearheaded by Studio Voltaire in association with Wandsworth LGBTQ+ community group.

Sited objects, such as these, can be seen to signal the more celebratory display of Wilde, and his sure embrace after nearly a century of uncertainty. They recuperate Wilde's shame, and perhaps ours too, by commemorating his life, death and work, and elevate him as a figure for all. Although static forms, even these have not been able to resist the sort of interactivity we expect of installation – Wilde's Dublin statue is a frequent stop for tourists to have their photographs taken; and his London incarnation, tucked away on the edges of Soho, is less the subject of pilgrimage than spontaneous engagement and vandalism – his cigarette having been repeatedly excised and replaced.

However, it is Wilde's grave at Père Lachaise cemetery (where he was reburied in 1909, following an initial pauper's burial in Bagneaux cemetery, on the outskirts of Paris), which perhaps tells the most dynamic story of how he has been sculpturally forgotten and remembered. Created by Jacob Epstein, and installed in 1914, the grave includes a sculpture bearing the inscription from *De Profundis*: 'And alien tears will fill for him/Pity's long-broken urn,/ For his mourners will be outcast men,/And outcasts always mourn'. Epstein's tomb was inspired by Assyrian guardian statues, and featured a Sphinx-like winged young man, arms outstretched as if in flight. According to Ellen Crowell, the sculpture's modernism jarred with other graves in the nineteenth-century cemetery, which led viewers to see it 'as future-rather than past-oriented, more modernist than Victorian, a monument to enlightened pride rather than retrograde shame' (2012). Many were also shocked by the figure's exposed genitals, not lest given people assumed the statue was a depiction of Wilde and/or his male lovers. Before Epstein had even finished his work on the statue, Parisian officials instructed that the figure's genitals be covered. The bronze modesty leaf did not last long, however, said to have been stolen by poets and artists from the Latin Quarter. Once the First World War began, the sculpture's nudity was not so much a priority, receding from public attention until the genitals were severed in 1961.

Wilde's grave became a focal point of queer pilgrimage in the latter part of the twentieth century, in particular in the wake of the AIDS crisis when public attitudes to homosexuality began to change. Giles Robertson, joint executor of the estate of Robert Ross (Wilde's literary executor and one-time lover, who was with him when he died), told Michael Pennington that since the 1950s the tomb had become known as a 'a place of pilgrimage to the homosexual community'. Adoration for Wilde was expressed in graffiti, he claimed, while suggesting that 'the extraordinarily polished, shiny quality of the angel's pendulous testicles', next to the 'dull, grainy texture of the rest of the tomb' was due to the 'continual touching, stroking and caressing by the hands of homosexual admirers in worship and reverence to those parts of Oscar Wilde for which they believe he was martyred' (Pennington 1987: 60–1).

Whether this diagnosis is true or not, graffiti and lipstick kisses on Wilde's tomb became more popular during the 1990s, to the extent that the oils eventually damaged the stone, requiring costly resurfacing.[10] In 2011, a glass barrier was erected around the tomb, paid for by Ireland's Office of Public Works, that treats it as an Irish monument overseas. Ultimately, Wilde's internment was chased posthumously by three more interments. In the final act, Wilde was not separated from his own desire, as he was in Reading Gaol, but somewhat ironically from the public's desire for him.

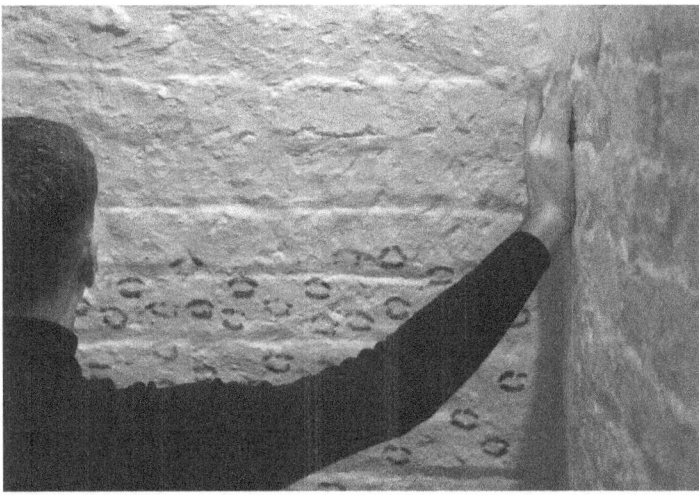

Figure 5.4 Francis Fay kisses a cell wall in Kilmainham Gaol, Dublin, Ireland, as part of his durational performance *Marking Time/A Love Letter* (2010). Photographer: Manu Di Marco.

These iconic Père Lachaise kisses were invoked as part of Francis Fay's 2010 durational performance *Marking Time/A Love Letter* for the Performance Art Live group exhibition *Right Here Right Now* in Dublin (Figure 5.4). Set in Kilmainham Gaol, Fay applied kisses to the walls of a cell for four hours, recalling both Wilde's commemorative tomb and his imprisonment, to the extent that it felt like Fay's gestures found a way to transfer the headstone kisses to the centre of Wilde's cell – not unlike how the Artangel project allowed artists to show their indebtedness to Wilde by exhibiting in his former prison. However, Kilmainham Gaol is best known for holding political prisoners of the 1916 Easter Rising (as did Reading Gaol), including Pádraig Pearse, Constance Markievicz and James Connolly. Fay's performance, in this context, can also be seen to locate Wilde's imprisonment within a history of Irish national(ist) politics.

Wilde's relationship to objecthood can of course be seen to both commemorate and commodify him – the former mode perhaps allowing for a greater deal of reflexivity and engagement than the latter. Observing Artangel and McDermott & McGough as operating in dialogue with the tradition of these other sited sculptures and performances, as well as Wilde's art and life, however, foregrounds an undisciplined if not a cross-disciplinary impulse at play, which is reflected both in the subversiveness of Wilde's life and work, and its refusal to be entrapped within a single moral interpretation or artistic form. In this way, these iterations continue to energize our understanding of Wilde in the present, and expand and qualify the histories, networks and urgencies of contemporary queer culture. We see Wilde migrate beyond theatrical and literary contexts to become a figure to be encountered and experienced, collaborated and interacted with. Wilde is liberated from internment as a figure of and for the past, defined only by theatrical and literary culture, or indeed his sexual crimes. Instead Wilde becomes the root context for viewing a plethora of activists, artists, victims, heroes and troublemakers in the present.

Wild(e) possessions

Commentators have long referred to the wildness of Wilde, in part because the homophonic resonance all too easily seemed to capture layers of the man's gender, sexual and artistic subversiveness,[11] and in part due to an effort to dehumanize him. Wilde was often seen as effeminate and unmanly in his early life, rather than homosexual, for instance, and as Alan Sinfield has argued, effeminacy and homosexuality really only began to cohere following Wilde's trials (1994). In *De Profundis*, Wilde registers a sense of his own primal alignment. Reflecting on his life before prison, Wilde likened his own sexual behaviour to 'feasting with panthers', a phrase which lent Richard Cumming (et al.'s) play its title (*Feasting with Panthers: A Play about Oscar Wilde*, 1987). In the same section, Wilde continues to claim his liaisons made him feel like a 'snake-charmer must feel when he lures the cobra to stir from the painted cloth or reed-basked that holds it, and makes it spread its hood at his bidding' (Wilde 2013: 136). This idea of wildness is countered by that produced in prison, which is given as a time of 'wild despair' (ibid.: 101). In the closing pages of the text, Wilde meditates on society and nature, civility and wildness, and looks forward to nature's landscapes making him 'whole' (ibid.: 159). 'Society, as we have constituted it', Wilde writes,

> will have no place for me, has none to offer; but Nature, whose sweet rains fall on unjust and just alike, will have clefts in the rocks where I may hide, and secret valleys in whose silence I may weep undisturbed. She will hang the night with stars so that I may walk abroad in the darkness without stumbling, and send the wind over my footprints so that none may track me to my hurt. (Wildie 2013: 158–9)

Here, we see Wilde's condition of detainment precipitate the more comforting fantasy of being dispossessed into a wild landscape.

Michèle Mendelssohn illuminates how Wilde's presumed transgressiveness was not only rooted in claims to his effeminacy, as well as in the disruptive force of his art, but also in ideas of race. Focusing on Wilde's American lecture tour of 1882, before the height of his success or infamy, Mendelssohn tracks the ways in which Wilde's Irishness was associated with a sort of simian primitivism, often popularized by *Punch* illustrations at the time, which led him to be compared to African Americans. For instance, numerous caricatures and posters of the period depict a black-skinned Wilde, or show him as an ape. A drawing from *The Washing Post* on 22 January 1882, for example, compares two images – one of an apparent man of Borneo holding a fruit and one of Wilde holding a sunflower, the symbol of aestheticism. The accompanying text reads:

> We present in close juxtaposition the pictures of Mr Wilde of England and a citizen of Borneo, who, so far as we have any record of him, is also Wild, and judging from the resemblance in feature, pose and occupation, undoubtedly akin. If Mr Darwin is right in

his theory, has not the climax of evolution been reached and are we not tending down the hill toward the aboriginal starting point again? (Mendelssohn 2018: 90–109)

Aligning Wilde with primitivism allowed some American commentators to mobilize racialized colonial stereotypes, in order to both compound racism towards African-Americans and to an extent Irish emigrants, and to disrupt any of the favourable attention that Wilde had won. In being used in this way, Wilde's wildness was constructed beyond word play, and was used to undermine and discredit him as an uncivil native, even inhuman, rather than as a knowing or sophisticated operator. Mendelssohn also proffers that Wilde's relationship with race was more complex than just being its victim – he had a Black servant during his American tour, his uncle had a plantation and in his comments and lectures he seemed to sympathize with the confederacy and aligned it with the Irish national cause. Indeed Wilde, and certainly his mother Speranza, in many ways saw the Irish as a superior Celtic race. Suffice to say, even though Wilde was deemed an unruly artistic force, and primitivized by British colonial discourse for his race and sexuality, he was no easy champion for the racially oppressed.

In a special issue of the *South Atlantic Quarterly*, Jack Halberstam and Tavia Nyong'o draw ideas of wildness and queerness into closer relation, suggesting links between constructions of wildness and queer theory's investment in the denaturalizing of civil culture. Parsing these elements in their editorial, they write: 'Wildness has certainly functioned as a foil to civilization, as the dumping ground for all that white settler colonialism has wanted to declare expired, unmanageable, undomesticated, and politically unruly … Like another problematical term – queer – wildness names, while rendering partially opaque, what hegemonic systems would interdict or push to the margins' (Halberstam and Nyong'o 2018: 453). To think about the queer and the wild, the editors contend, is to look at 'the expunged features of our own critical systems of making sense and order. It is time to rewild theory' (ibid.: 454).[12]

While Wilde does not feature in the same issue, he perhaps deserves special consideration, as a particularly dynamic figure for thinking about what is civil and central, unruly and marginal. As we have seen, claims to Wilde's wildness were more than an easy pun, premised on complex sexual, racial and artistic associations and formulations. Indeed, wild alignments appear to have chased Wilde throughout his life and since his death, as a way to try and name the impossibility of neatly categorizing him and his own unwillingness to be contained.

Mike Pearson, discussing his work with Cliff McLucas as co-artistic directors of the Welsh theatre company Brith Gof, describes site-specific performance as involving the interplay of the host (the site) and the ghost (the scenography brought to the site) (2012: 70). Certainly, the sited work examined in this chapter is designed to capture a sense of Wilde's spirit permeating the present. But this is not a civil, passive presence that complies with Wilde's established reputation, but a restless, disruptive spirit that recaptures and recontextualizes Wilde's work, life, legacy and influence for the contemporary moment. While flirting, perhaps inevitably, with deification, these works do so by displacing Wilde from explicitly theatrical and literary contexts where he has been perhaps most objectified since the latter part of the twentieth century, allowing his legacy to find form in repurposed sites and multi-media forms, in newly contextualized ways, for new audiences. This wilding of Wilde is a dispossessing gesture, that releases him from the shackles of architectural, institutional and cultural containment, so that his spirit can guide the present. Harnessing this wild spirit for queer culture more broadly, then, we might acknowledge the importance of recognizing the historical events, practices and figures that come before us, and the unlikely network of collaborators and inspirations that surround and follow them. While celebrating these queer cultural figures in the present, we should be careful not to sanctify them too much, as this is the gateway to hollow signalling. We ought to remodel historical practices to make them appropriate for our time, while also fashioning space for artistic responses and cultural experiences that do not easily fit into or recognize these histories, which appear to break from them, so that they can trace or inaugurate new patterns still. The wildness of Wilde not only reminds us of the radical, complex and often contradictory sexual and artistic practices and politics that undergird queer cultural history, but also of the importance of keeping room for similar modes and tensions in the present.

This might also mean continuing to forge artistic, social and political alliances with other aliens, outcasts and dispossessed wild things – as unlikely as the network of descendants tracked by Artangel and McDermott & McGough – nurturing queerness's promise to create space for frustrated, fluctuating, failed or emergent forms and identities, across gendered, sexual, classed and ethnic lines. This does not even necessarily mean replaying or building explicitly on Wilde and his work, as my examples discussed in this chapter did – to rewild(e) need not involve directly involve Wilde. Rather, it might involve tuning into a wild Wildean frequency to ensure something of his spirit persists in the production of queer culture.

Conclusion

The perceived importance of Wilde to queer culture has oscillated throughout the twentieth and twenty-first centuries, and this has been partly due to a deep-seated cultural shame at his treatment in the years surrounding his death, the challenges posed by the particularities of some of his actions and the difficulty of locating him within a specific artistic, cultural or political tradition. At a time when parts of the UK and Ireland were enjoying advances in queer recognition, whose historical backdrop could readily be forgotten, the practices under focus in this chapter remind us of the influence and significance of Wilde's work, life and legacy in the development of modern and contemporary LGBTQ+ culture, and of the urgency to keep alive the richness and complexity he introduces. Wilde's spirit, as memory and influence, disrupts and exceeds efforts to commodify and control him, allowing his life and legacy to help us understand the layers of queer history sedimenting under and holding up the present.

These works alert us to the necessity of maintaining a historical perspective on current advancements in queer history and culture, while continuing to mine its figures and practices, revising lineages and networks of inspiration and influence, as well as prompting ongoing aesthetic experimentation. Deploying strategies of installation, immersion and participation in particular, in their architectural and scenographic inventiveness they collapse over a century of temporal distinction to challenge any presumption that queer time and place belong only to the past or indeed the present. In embedding us in Wilde's past, and he in our present, they enact a double gesture that illuminates some new gaps and overlaps in queer history, but fundamentally view it as always stretching and unfurling, occupying the underlayer of the present, even while seeming buried in the past. They also nudge Wilde and contemporary queer culture towards a future in which queer history becomes the basis for engaging not only with questions of sexuality, but also with broader issues of social and cultural injustice, exclusion and dispossession, by inviting other artists, activists, audiences and subjectivities into the discursive and artistic remit largely inaugurated by Wilde. In these Wilde works, we witness queer culture's capacity to orientate us towards those times and contexts, even in the past, in which subjectivity, identity and artistic form are structures to be engaged and interrogated, rather than containers to be admired or bolstered, encouraging us to take ownership of queer history's ghosts, objects, sites and narratives, so that we might forge new capacious forms and modes for our times.

6

Grief's ricochet: Intermedial returns

In 2019, I was invited to deliver a lecture at a university based on my current research, and I took as my subject some of the ideas now included in Chapter 1 of this book. I discussed Dickie Beau's *Re-Member Me*, exploring the ways in which it recalled the life and work of Ian Charleson and recovered lost cultural histories of the AIDS crisis. In the questions that followed, someone in the back row raised their hand to ask: 'But who is this production for?' The question initially took me by surprise, as I had just spent forty minutes trying to communicate the subject matter's relevance and value, to an audience that I assumed would not need to be so strenuously persuaded. But I quickly had the suspicion that what the questioner was really saying was: 'This is not relevant to me.'

At the time, I recall emphasizing that Beau's work spoke directly to those affected by AIDS, as well as potentially other traumatic cultural histories and how they shape lives and art practices in the present. However, the question rattled around in my head, partly as wondering if I could have answered it better, but mostly in surprise that someone might approach theatre with the rather narrow question of whether it was for them or not. I have always felt that for privileged audiences such as researchers, it is our duty to appreciate what theatre is at least trying to do on its own terms, rather than expect it to speak to us in more direct, personal ways. Is queer theatre too niche, I wondered, for colleagues to believe it has any value to their lives or research. Or is this how homophobia surfaces in institutional spaces, I asked myself, as the seemingly benign doubt of relevance or significance?

In less than a year, in an unexpected twist, it appeared as if theatres around the world would try to settle the question. As the covid-19 coronavirus spread around the globe, and theatres adapted to quarantined modes of communication, a swathe of digitized queer performance was released online, or made specifically for virtual environments. While impossible to catalogue in its entirety here, some of the work I encountered included the musical adaptation of Alison Bechdel's *Fun Home* (Victory Gardens Theatre, Chicago, 2017/20), Taylor Mac's *Taylor Mac's Holiday Sauce … Pandemic!* (2020/21), or the more socially focused Queer House Party. As global lockdowns tentatively gave way to live or hybrid productions, this pattern continued with the staging or mediatization of theatre and performance focused on the early decades of the AIDS crisis and how it continues to shape and illuminate the present, including Larry Kramer's *The Normal Heart* (National Theatre, London, 2020), Jonathan Larson's *Rent* (online/Hope Mill Theatre Manchester, 2020/21) and the premiere of Phillip McMahon's *Once Before I Go* (Gate Theatre, Dublin, 2021), in which the central protagonist, who dies of AIDS, returns to haunt the final scene with a rousing musical routine. Written and performed by Jack Holden during the pandemic, *Cruise* (The Duchess Theatre, London, 2021) is structured as an odyssey through Soho, London, in the 1980s, tracking the effects of AIDS on the city and its people, from the perspective of the present crisis. In the installation *The Ward – Revisited* (The Fitzrovia Chapel, London, 2023), Gideon Mendel's wrenching documentation of the HIV/AIDS wards at the Middlesex Hospital, London, in 1993, and the afterlives of those who tended to the sick and dying, the impact of AIDS and its enduring grief are allowed to quiver unobtrusively next to the effects of the covid-19 pandemic, and the open question of how it will be recorded and remembered.[1] Queer performative art, in its preoccupation with the plague of AIDS, death, grief and social stigmatization, as this programming appeared to suggest, had a vital role to play in navigating the experience of the coronavirus pandemic, and the coronavirus pandemic had a part to play in reanimating queer histories and cultural archives.

This chapter takes as its focus the programming of queer theatre and performance as a response to the covid-19 pandemic. It addresses a number of productions made for live, mediatized and intermedial environments, in an apparent effort to mobilize and widely disseminate queer theatre and performance history to help reckon with the impact of covid-19, including a 2020 digital iteration of Belfast Ensemble's production of Mark Ravenhill's *Ten Plagues* (2011), and a mediatized (2020) and intermedial (2021) production of Split Britches's *Last Gasp*.[2] I explore how this programming performed two simultaneous gestures: in the first, it worked to recontextualize queer theatre and performance from being ostensibly forms of historical interest, about and for LGBTQ+ people, to being of urgent and widespread value in helping us to understand the pandemic and its effects; in the second, and perhaps less intentionally, it spoke to the sudden spike in violence against LGBTQ+ people reported during the pandemic, when covid-19 stirred memories of AIDS, and revived attempts to scapegoat the LGBTQ+ community as its wreckless vector. The chapter considers how, with this work, the losses of the queer past and pandemic present collided in a kind of emotional ricochet across digital and live forms, which exposed the grief felt, repressed and delayed that united the two discrete contexts. What is the effect of resituating queer theatre and performance in this way, this chapter asks, to pitch them as pivotal guides in navigating the pandemic present, by reaching into their own reservoirs of loss? Can queer theatre and performance history be mined to speak to an ostensibly non-queer subject of global concern, or highlight queer concerns where we thought there were none? Might the experience of covid-19 mark a turning point in the reanimation of queer culture and its theories, via the possibility of their extended transposition and application?

Transposing plague

Mark Ravenhill's *Ten Plagues* was first performed at the Traverse Theatre, Edinburgh, in 2011. A song cycle originally developed with composer Conor Mitchell, now artistic director of Belfast Ensemble, and performed by Marc Almond, *Ten Plagues* drew inspiration from plagues throughout history, including Biblical plagues, various histories of ancient and medieval plagues, Samuel Pepys' diary entries on plague (1660–9) and Albert Camus's novel *The Plague* (1947). Its primary inspiration, however, was Daniel Defoe's mock diary *A Journal of the Plague Year* (1722), which focuses on the effect of the Great Plague of London, which began in 1665. The central guide in Ravenhill's libretto leads us through generations of plague and its consequences, like an angel of death and resilience, evoking figures such as Virginia Woolf's *Orlando* (from the 1928 novel of the same title) and Shakespeare's *Hamlet*.

In 2018, the production was redeveloped for Belfast's queer festival Outburst Arts by Belfast Ensemble, which was established the previous year to focus on new approaches to music theatre. Following the coronavirus outbreak, during a lockdown, Belfast Ensemble created a digital version of the production to be disseminated online, which was released in May 2020. Belfast Ensemble's previous work includes *Abomination: A DUP Opera* (2019), which centred on one-time Democratic Unionist Party (DUP) Member of Parliament Iris Robinson's referring to homosexuality as an 'abomination', and its consequences; a series of events I wrote about for their theatrical power before the opera came into being (Walsh 2013). Certainly, the digital iteration of *Ten Plagues* not only absorbs and rearticulates the original live production for a pandemic climate, but it also invokes and extends the moral critique of *Abomination: A DUP Opera*.

Ravenhill does not mention AIDS explicitly in the cycle, although he has discussed and written about his own experience of living with HIV (2008). Belfast Ensemble's online production of *Ten Plagues,* directed by Nicky Larkin, locates the text more explicitly within this realm. The film opens with an introduction from the company's artistic director Conor Mitchell, who recalls his involvement in the original development of the piece, saying: 'When it was created, we imagined it as a parable of the AIDS pandemic in the 80s'. Reflecting on the cycle's preoccupation with illness, death and social isolation, Mitchell comments: 'I could never have imagined that those were the very environments that we could be filming this in today', primarily locating the digital intervention as a bridge between the coronavirus pandemic and AIDS.

Shot in a warehouse, the digital iteration of *Ten Plagues* is simple and faithful to the original stage production, featuring Matthew Cavan as the solo performer, who is flanked by Mitchell on the piano. Cavan is well-known in Northern Ireland for his drag act Cherrie Ontop, and a vocal campaigner for stamping out stigma against those with HIV, including himself. The camera focuses on Cavan's painted face, which figures him as a ghoulish cabaret emcee, possessed by the plagues of history, who haunts the present from plagues past, occasionally panning across the stage to reveal Mitchell. Behind them we see the exposed bricks of the back wall, over which are projected flickering lights and fleeting effects – clouds, raindrops, stained glass windows. While Cavan's vocals switch between tortured torch songs and operatic arias, the tone is predominantly wrenching and mournful; the sound of a lone man trying to make sense of the horrors he encounters (Figure 6.1).

In *Ten Plagues,* the songs' historical references are primarily anchored in the seventeenth century of its inspiration. For example, one song reveals that the subject saw a production of *Hamlet* – 'Tonight/I went to see/The player say/To die/To die, to sleep/To sleep/Perchance to dream' – before dreaming of being 'filled' with 'spittle, sweat and seed'. 'If death is one long dream/ Of you,' he sings, 'Then send me plague/And let me die' (Ravenhill 2011: 6). Here, in this sequence, Hamlet's dream precipitates the dream of its seventeenth-century spectator, who in turn appears

Figure 6.1 Belfast Ensemble's digital production of *Ten Plagues* (2022) featuring Matthew Cavan. Screengrab of the production's promotional video.

to dream of being infected with HIV. In another scene, someone enters the performer's room at night. He moves to kiss him, but is stopped by the visitor, who pulls up his shirt to reveal a tumour; 'Hard and round/A silver penny/Of contagion' (ibid.: 10). Indeed, in the promotional image for the original production, Almond is depicted holding a skull, Hamlet's iconic pose.

In an interview with Mark Fisher, ahead of the cycle's premier, Almond recalls hearing about AIDS for the first time in 1981, when he was visiting New York to record his debut album with Soft Cell. Almond observed the downtown arts scene diminish in the 1980s, with its affected neighbourhoods 'go very dark, desperate, fearful and unfriendly' (Fisher 2011). Friends Klaus Nomi, Freddie Mercury and Derek Jarman would later die of AIDS-related illness, eventually hardening Almonds's response to death, like the character in *Ten Plagues*, whose encounters with death take place alongside bouts of shopping. 'Whereas I used to get very affected by somebody dying', Almond says, 'now I feel a grief but I take it in my stride. That's a thing of getting older anyway; we're all on this conveyor belt and dropping off the end of it' (ibid.).

The story-telling singer in *Ten Plagues* likewise anticipates his own illness, by detecting swellings of the neck and groin. But he is unafraid of death, and imagines himself running through the streets towards the corpse pits, to be among his friends: 'My friends/I'm here/I choose/To be with you/Hold me close in your/Embrace/And then I'll throw myself/Into the pit/Happy with/The company I keep' (2011: 9). References to quarantine laws bridge the seventeenth century and the forced social isolation of the coronavirus pandemic. These, too, are a form of social death – 'how like death/This solitude' (ibid.: 19) – and the singer bends under the weight of the scale of sickness and decay: 'Too many gone/To mourn another/We all are plagued/Our hearts are gone/Our bodies live/We walking dead/ About the city now' (ibid.: 20–1).

Despite the illness that engulfs our guide, all is not death. We are reminded, repeatedly, that he is alive. For instance, when he likens himself to an Israelite navigating a biblical plague, the horrors are counterbalanced by the insistent refrain 'I live': 'I am as an/ Israelite when Ten plagues/Infect the land/ I live; I see/The waters flow with blood/I live/Frogs outnumber men/I live' (ibid.: 25). In these moments, the performer's voice is tinged with wonder that he survives against the odds, and guilt for having done so. Nonetheless, painful memories are briskly repressed, as a necessary means to continue living. Those who survive 'learn the new dance/Sing the new song (ibid.: 26).

As a song cycle saturated in the grief and longing of a lone figure, *Ten Plagues* evokes Franz Schubert's *Winterreise* (1827–8), in which a young man sets off on a journey through the snow to overcome his love. But it is perhaps more directly inspired by Kurt Weill's song cycle *The Seven Deadly Sins*, featuring a libretto by Bertolt Brecht.[3] Set in a version of the United States, Weill's 'sung ballet' focuses on Anna, a woman forced to make money for her cruel and greedy Louisiana family. In the course of the cycle, Anna visits different cities, where she is forced to grapple with each of the deadly sins. Weill made a career in Berlin during the 1920s, in particular via his collaborations with Brecht, especially *The Threepenny Opera*. Both Weill and Brecht left Berlin to escape the Nazi regime in the early 1930s, and the song cycle was first produced in June 1933 at Théâtre des Champs-Élysées, Paris. While *The Seven Deadly Sins* foremost functions as a critique of rising industrial capitalism, and to an extent biblical orthodoxy, it also exposes the moral corruption of the age, and the shadow of Nazism that surrounds its conditions of production. So while *Ten Plagues* is indeed narratively and thematically rooted in plagues, it is dramaturgically supported by a form devised to counterbalance and critique the effects of European industrialization, religious hypocrisy and fascism.

The last moments of the digitized *Ten Plagues* explicitly locate the production as an intervention into covid-19, by featuring quotes from world leaders flashing across the screen. From Nicola Sturgeon, First Minister of Scotland, we read: 'I stress this every day, but it is important – never think of these numbers as statistics. They represent individuals whose loss is a source of sorrow to many'. 'Be kind … we will get through this together, but only if we stick together. Be strong and be kind' comes from New Zealand Prime Minister Jacinda Ardern. Andrew Cuomo, Governor of New York from 2011 to 2021, is quoted as saying: 'And at the end of the day, my friends, even if it is a long day, and this is a long day, love wins. Always. And it will win again through this virus'. Cuomo's 'love wins' notably echoed the 'love wins' slogan used by many same-sex marriage campaigns around the world, thus linking the history of gay rights to that of the struggle to overcome covid-19.[4]

While there are numerous reasons to draw AIDS and the coronavirus pandemic into conversation, as this production insists, it is important to acknowledge that they also diverge at the level of social stigmatization and government response. Largely because when AIDS first emerged in gay communities in the 1980s, it was seen as a 'gay plague', as Ronald Regan's Republican administration referred to it, or latterly a problem concentrated in Africa, it took governments around the world years to fund medical research, the fruits of which not everyone has equal access to. A globally distributed vaccine for coronavirus, on the contrary, was developed in a matter of months. Those who lived through the initial period of HIV/AIDS stigmatization without medical support, in particular, might justifiably feel dismayed by the rapid response to the coronavirus pandemic, and in turn, the appeal to queer culture for steerage.

Marc Arthur argues that comparisons between the initial outbreak of AIDS in the 1980s and covid-19 are problematic 'because they often diminish the extent to which AIDS is still an ongoing pandemic' (2021: 20). This claim is arguably true of a lot of the social and political commentary that surrounded the coronavirus pandemic, which makes reference to the AIDS crisis as if it belonged to a finished and understood past from which we might now all dispassionately learn. But *Ten Plagues*, and productions such as those I mentioned at the outset of this chapter, counter this tendency, by enacting a temporal form in which historical plagues seep into one another, like the bleed of notes in Mitchell's melancholic refrains. Via these, we appreciate that we might experience both comfort and understanding in reading about plague against plague, illness against illness, death against death. But perhaps, for one plague to confidently guide another, we need to first feel that it has been adequately responded to, managed and controlled, if not safely consigned to the past.

Ultimately, however, Belfast Ensemble's digital production of *Ten Plagues* proved to be a powerful statement of the fact that we have much to learn from queer theatre and performance about HIV/AIDS, to help understand and process the coronavirus pandemic, and perhaps even other epidemics and pandemics to come. In its recontextualization and digital presentation, Ravenhill's text was infused with fresh energy and value, illustrating how aesthetic and dramaturgical innovation have the capacity to expand and reorient what are often seen as the narrow preoccupations and interventions of queer theatre and performance. In its thematic breadth and formal agility, *Ten Plagues* refuted any sense that queer theatre and performance are niche or relevant only to a marginal demographic. In it, queerness features as a mutable thread that haunts theatre history and cultural crises, as the mark not only of endangerment and death, but also of longevity, adaptability and survival.

Shared breath

Split Britches's *Last Gasp WFH* (Working from Home) was created during the first four months of lockdown in 2020, using the Zoom technology that suddenly became a feature of our daily communications. Directed by Lois Weaver, and performed by both Weaver and Peggy Shaw, it was later produced live at Barbican's The Pit in November 2021, as *Last Gasp: A Recalibration*, adapting its digital form for live presentation, while still operating in an intermedial register.

The Zoom iteration begins with Lois Weaver in a room in a London home which has been emptied of furniture, as if preparing to move. Surrounded by fading décor, and the sound of invisible bees frantically buzzing, Weaver moves her hands in counterpoint to her speech, as if she is playing an imaginary violin or conducting an orchestra. Wearing a black dress, Weaver speaks directly to the camera, to say: 'This is a very emotional moment for me, because twenty, thirty, forty years ago I bought this dress. Now you might ask the question – how did she know? How did she know that she could need this dress forty years later? I don't know'. Weaver's opening establishes her performance as a dialogue across time, and less a conversation in which the present reaches *back*, than one in which the past reaches *forward*. Like Ta-Nehisi Coates, whom she references, Weaver does not know how generations speak to each other across times, or how the first gasps of a career flow forward to the last.[5] But with her career-spanning garment, Weaver submits that every beginning is imprinted with the (inadvertent) preparation for its ending, every rehearsal a preparation for a curtain call.

Last Gasp does not fix its eye solely on the start of Split Britches's career in the 1980s, when it rose to fame as a leading experimental lesbian theatre company that explored butch-femme aesthetics, mainly via the respective presentations of Shaw and Weaver. Rather, it zigzags between the past and the present, the United States and London, leaping from Weaver's childhood memories of pretending to make supper on her family porch sixty-five years ago, to closet crooner Johnny Ray in the 1950s who inspired Shaw, along with a host of Black male singers including Hank Williams and Johnny Bragg, to Shaw's working with Hot Peaches troupe in the 1970s.

While Weaver is focused on finding a form to hold the past in the present, via rhythmic speech, repetitive movement and collaborative action, Shaw is more explicit about the frictions that have developed over time. In particular, Shaw bemoans the arguments between different queer generations, characterized by splintered identity categories and what she sees as the policing of language. Shaw claims she wears a 'word proof vest' so that she can say what she wants without being injured for it. Back when Shaw came of age, everyone was called 'gay', she tells us, 'everyone was a she. Even Ronald Regan'. More recently, when Shaw was participating in a long table discussion, a young woman took issue with her views, and told her to go away: 'You sound like some old conservative white man ... go away old lady, she said, if you can't keep up.' Shaw, now in her seventies, resists being told to feel ashamed for all the things she built her career on. 'How did this seventy-five year old, old school queer, start feeling ashamed to call myself all the things I had spent all my life time imagining. How did I end up on the other side just by coming to the table?'

Words trouble Shaw in other ways too. Since she had a stroke in 2011, the subject of her solo performance *RUFF* (2013), Shaw's memory has been compromised, and so Weaver speaks the script into an earpiece for her to recite.[6] But Shaw is past trying to hold onto language, she tells us; she is here to release the words that have been building up for seventy-five years. This will be her last show, Shaw informs the audience, and she sees it as an estate sale in which attendees 'might pick up something useful, or nostalgic, or old school', or just pull out a gun, 'and shoot me for something I just said'.

Weaver's investment in remembering as a tool for binding the past and present is threatened by Shaw's memory loss. 'What if we didn't know?', becomes Weaver's refrain, that anchors her as she navigates the absence of knowledge that comes with the fading of memory. 'What if we didn't know how to recover? How to shelter? How to restore? What if we didn't know how to repair?' For Weaver, the current risk is not just that she loses the capacity to interact with Shaw, or fails to store knowledge of their long relationship and career together, but to know how to respond to new crises as they emerge. Future action, Weaver's dilemma exposes, is dependent on the ability to recall past responses.

The performance's occasionally playful tone builds up the question of how to survive an emergency, an apocalypse, a loss. For Weaver, the most appropriate response is 'to recalibrate'. She insists on the basics, the setting of a table, even in the midst of rubble. Moving through a series of tableaux vivants, both Weaver and Shaw rehearse their responses around and under the table – hiding, curling, standing on one foot (Figure 6.2).

Dramatic momentum in the show is supplied by a mounting sense of time running out, which builds towards the last gasp of the show's title. On a narrative level, this pertains to time passing (in life and for the performance), memory loss and the impending end of their career following Shaw's insistence that this is her last production. The performance also finds impetus in the crises of breathing that supply the backdrop to this production. At one point, a window sticker in their home reveals a Black Lives Matter logo, whose catchphrase 'I can't breathe' draws on the last words of those killed under police chokehold in the United States, including

Figure 6.2 Peggy Shaw (left) and Lois Weaver (right) in *Last Gasp: A Recalibration*, The Pit, Barbican, London, UK (2021). Photographer: Naz Simsek.

George Floyd in 2020 and Eric Garner in 2014.[7] In the year of *Last Gasp*'s first production, which took place in the shadow of both respiratory and racial crises, breathing became a stage of medical and political struggle, affecting how we conducted our intimate and public lives. With this nod, Shaw's and Weaver's meditation on loss braids personal and queer culture into broader histories of gender and racial violence.

A concern for the relationship among queer performance, breathing and mortality is a more central concern of Martin O'Brien's work. O'Brien has aligned himself with zombies, the living dead, on account of surviving past his life expectancy due to Cystic Fibrosis. Programmed to run at intervals between 2020 and 2021, at the ICA, London, *The Last Breath Society (Coughing Coffin)* featured daily durational performances by O'Brien, alongside a series of commissioned video artworks by Franko B, Ansuman Biswas, Rocío Boliver, Noëmi Lakmaier, Lechedevirgen

Trimegisto, Joseph Morgan Schofield, Kira O'Reilly, Sheree Rose, Shabnam Shabazi and Nicholas Tee. In the performance, a masked O'Brien manoeuvres coffins, lying on them and in them, occasionally coughing and gasping for breath. The work suggests that for those with chronic respiratory conditions, and those who are otherwise medically and socially vulnerable, including some of the queer artists represented in the accompanying videos, playing with death and grappling for control over its containers and paraphernalia, might be the only refuge from the terrors of being alive.

But the labour of Shaw and Weaver is less focused on breathing than remembering. While Weaver discreetly strives to ensure Shaw receives her lines, the balance of work is not without its difficulties. Weaver submits that Shaw has won more awards because she is butch, despite their long collaboration, and that Shaw is selfish in ending her career, as it might end Weaver's too. Weaver likens their relationship to that of the mythological Echo and Narcissus, in which the former falls in love for the latter, but the latter only falls in love with himself.

'How do you know when someone is finished?', Weaver asks in the closing moments. 'I can't believe I have to know you forever', she tells Shaw, sometimes I wake up in the morning and wish that you would die'. 'At least I know I'm gonna die', Shaw replies. As the camera shows us around the emptied house, Shaw and Weaver start to appear translucent, like they are already becoming ghosts, while a recording of Shaw singing 'The First Time I Ever Saw Your Face' plays out their disappearance. The closing scene suggests that even in our dematerialization – as people, as theatre makers, as audiences in the once material realm – what is last and what is first are in a perpetual dance, until, as the song infers, even the end of time.

The live iteration of *Last Gasp* is not quite live. While Weaver performs most of the same material on stage, Shaw's portions of the recording are projected on its back wall. In the Zoom presentation of the performance, Weaver and Shaw share domestic space, and it is the audience that is separated from them. But this intermedial presentation amplifies Shaw's absence from both Weaver and the audience, and Shaw's commitment to not performing again. As Weaver tells Shaw's digital avatar: 'We didn't even do our final duet … I feel stuck between your absence and your presence'. Weaver is also aware that Shaw's material absence does not equal loss; that her charisma can transcend a digital divide: 'I'm still the only one showing up on stage and you're still the centre of attention'. Shaw is adamant that this is her last show, and Weaver claims that her refusal is 'a kind of death'. 'I just don't know how to survive this loss', Weaver tells her, to which Shaw returns Weaver's own advice – 'Well first you recalibrate'.

With this instruction, Shaw walks on stage, from the wings, for the final moments of the show, to rehearse how to die. She and Weaver move through a sequence of poses, as if preparing how to die, or at least to act like they are dying. Weaver's voice coaches: 'Try to take deep breaths during the death scene so you have some time before you need to breathe again. You can disguise it by gasping … just because you're no longer involved in the play's action doesn't mean that your work is over'. Beyond the technicalities of dying on stage, Weaver is adamant that Shaw's responsibilities exceed her wish to stop performing. Shaw's dream, on the other hand, is less to act than to become an object – her ashes made into a diamond ring or a phonograph record.

Feeling time

What both *Ten Plagues* and *Last Gasp* share in common is an appeal to time past and passing to help navigate the grief of the present, countering the risks of stigmatization, isolation and illness by drawing on live and mediatized forms of presentation. Moreover, queer history's repository of grief – felt, repressed and delayed – emerges as a critical resource to help shape and steer the rising and suspended grief of the pandemic present.

In 2020, the American Psychiatric Association announced that it would add Prolonged Grief Disorder to its revised *DSM-5* (*Diagnostic and Statistical Manual of Mental Disorders*), to be published in 2022. The condition was added to account for intense thoughts of and longing for the deceased, most of the day for at least a month, that significantly impair the griever's life. When announcing the addition, the American Psychiatric Association's President Vivian B. Pender said in a launch address: 'The circumstances in which we are living, with more than 675,000 deaths due to covid-19, may make prolonged grief disorder more prevalent' (Pender in American Psychiatric Association, 2021). 'Grief in these circumstances is normal', Pender claimed, 'but not at certain levels and not most of the day, nearly every day for months' (ibid.). In a pandemic that has so far lasted three years, and resulted in over six million deaths worldwide,[8] that mere months of grief might constitute a *prolonged* condition, rather than an entirely appropriate response, might seem to some like a rather stringent diagnosis.

Christopher M. Moreman and A. David Lewis contend that we increasingly use digital environments to mourn in public, in particular social media platforms. Users, they tell us, 'are growing more accustomed to extending their sentiments for traditional mourning into digital environments – perhaps even more intensely' (2014: 2). Death, dying, mourning and grieving are increasingly experienced by many, they suggest, 'as a hybrid between the physical and the digital' (2014: 2). For example, one popular social media account to have developed this past decade has been The AIDS Memorial (Instagram and Facebook), which is composed of personal stories and photographs of those lost to AIDS.

Our turn to digital platforms to mourn was particularly evident during the covid-19 pandemic, not only across social media platforms, but also via digital and mediatized theatre that grieved for the dead and lost ways of living, including live theatre and performance. Various data sets from around the world concur that 2020 experienced a significant increase in internet usage, with the use of video-calling applications doubling in the UK.[9] As I have argued elsewhere, mediatized theatre during the pandemic did not simply announce the death of theatre, 'but in many instances tried to keep it alive via rapid and radical adaptation, while still grieving for the ways it has been hurt, with the mourning of live arts, shared physical experience, and human life intertwined' (2021: 407). Barbara Fuchs uses to the term 'lockdown theater' to account for those digital productions that took place during the coronavirus pandemic, which she claims 'transcend geographic and financial barriers to engage new audiences, while offering much needed, though limited, support for artists' (2022: 2). In this, it extended the digital patterns observed by Moreman and Lewis, to take on a more global scale and significance.

Both *Ten Plagues* and *Last Gasp* participate in this digital mourning, but by filtering the pandemic present through longer histories of queer loss, preserving and disseminating the narratives via digital form. In *Ten Plagues*, this recontextualization primarily happens through an invocation of the AIDS crisis as it affected queer communities, refracted through a longer history of plagues, including the black death of the seventeenth century, and Weill's and Brecht's song cycle, ultimately proposing that fascism may be the most dangerous form of plague. The production looks to plagues past to help steer us through the present, finding sympathy in its melancholic score, and comfort in the repetitiveness of the conditions, thoughts, feelings and behaviours it documents. In *Last Gasp*, this appeal to queer cultural history takes the form of Split Britches's revisiting its own work, and the relationship between Weaver and Shaw, to orient us through the scale and layers of loss that defined the pandemic. Their digital modes of mediatization offset some of the constraints of social quarantine, demonstrating how queer performance and digital culture can conspire in the production and preservation of archives, and in the broadening of accessibility and audience reach. Abigail De Kosnik describes digital cultural content not associated with a physical museum, library, or archive, as 'rogue archives', suggesting that for many people the Internet itself is 'a giant archive' (2016: 2). Digital and mediatized theatre during the pandemic not only enabled contact under social quarantine, and the grieving of the dying and dead, but the creation of a rogue archive of loss that also recontextualized and adapted other historical documents.

Grief is not an isolated emotion, and frequently arrives flanked by feelings of isolation and anger. If these works in question can be seen to respond to pandemic grief, by invoking queer cultural history, they do so while simultaneously countering the attacks levelled against LGBTQ+ people that escalated during the pandemic. Reports of sexual orientation and transgender hate crimes recorded by UK police forces rose during the pandemic, peaking during the summer of 2021. As reported in *The Guardian*, from January to August 2021 at least 14,670 homophobic hate crime offences were recorded, compared with 11,841 during the same interval in 2020 and 10,817 in 2019. Also between January and August 2021, police recorded 2,129 transphobic offences, far exceeding the 1,606 offences in 2020 and 1,602 in 2019. The early figures reflect the high number of incidents throughout the previous decade, but the steep rise during the summer months correspond with the opening of the country after months of lockdowns. According to Leni Morris, chief executive of the LGBT anti-violence charity Galop, same-sex couples may have been more visible when out in public during the restrictions, and some individuals were blamed for the pandemic, 'because perpetrators thought the pandemic was an act of God – because of the existence of LGBT+ people – or because of the community's association with the last major pandemic in people's minds, and that's the HIV Aids pandemic' (Chao-Fong 2021). These broadly reflect patterns in other countries and across the internet too, which saw attacks on LGBT, Asian and Pacific Island people being justified on claims that they were blamed for covid-19.[10]

While the examples of queer theatre and performance considered in this chapter were primarily produced to comment on the social and cultural effects of covid-19, as if the lessons of queer cultural history had been learned and could therefore be shared, less anticipated was the concurrent revival of attacks against LGBTQ+ people, which demonstrated that queer history haunted the present as an unresolved presence. While the ghosts of queer culture's past were summoned to guide the present, it became clear that they were never quite put to rest, and that they might even need the coronavirus pandemic to assist in this process. As this book has attempted to demonstrate, however, assuaging ghosts never quite means eliminating them, but listening to their stories and quietening their voices through the ongoing practice of cultural enactment, memorialization and understanding. It is too simplistic to argue that each production only re-performs the past, by recycling and repurposing history for the present. Rather, both productions work at the intersection of the past and present, the virtual and the real, to innovate a form that is responsive to its new conditions of production.

While both productions appeal to the past for present illumination, it is equally true that they make claims for theatre's anticipatory function by presenting queer performance as already possessing a knowledge to be shared in future. In this, the productions not only turn to the past for tools to understand the present, but also reveal how its theatre and performance were always-already preparing them for a future yet to transpire.

Ernst Bloch's writing on hope has been taken up by José Esteban Muñoz and Jill Dolan to account for performance's role in imagining better worlds. In his first volume on hope, Bloch uses the term 'mediated anticipations' to refer to images, produced by the 'concrete imagination', that ferment the 'forward dream' of brighter futures ([1959] 1986: 197). These anticipating elements are not totally unanchored abstractions, Bloch insists, but components of material reality. Muñoz reads Bloch to propose that performative art, emerging around and after New York's Stonewall riots in 1969, carries the imprint of a utopia to come, and his approach is to conduct 'a backward glance that enacts a future vision' (2009: 4). Focusing on the event of live performance, Dolan accounts for utopian performatives as those acts that 'describe or capture fleeting intimations of a better world' (2005: 2).

While Bloch is primarily interested in hope, as the garden in which anticipation thrives, hope and anticipation cannot be exclusively bound together. Bloch also knows this, when he writes that 'fear too can of course anticipate' ([1959] 1986: 12). While this chapter primarily has sought to examine how *Ten Plagues* and *Last Gasp* revised and mined the past, it has simultaneously exposed how the past theatre and performance on which these productions are based can also be seen to have anticipated and prepared us for the loss that gave them their contemporary urgency, and even other losses yet unimagined. This is not necessarily an anticipation grounded in fear, but one tempered by a clear-eyed understanding of history, including queer culture's capacity for resilience and renewal in the face of extreme adversity. But in the understandable enthusiasm to harness anticipatory hope as a social and political propellant, queer performance theory and indeed contemporary culture might too rashly forget their capacity to produce, hold and nourish anticipatory loss, which is as important a guide as any excitable future. Hope, without due recognition of loss (among other necessary cautions), can only amount to a light-headed skip through the present, unprepared for the obstacles and hazards that will inevitably appear and reappear in the way.

The idea that grief, as a response to loss, might be anticipated psychologically largely comes to us from Erich Lindemann, who coined the phrase 'anticipatory grief' to describe pre-emptive responses to expected death or loss (1944). Others have since queried Lindemann's biomedical model, and the premise that grief can be experienced in anticipation at all, identifying a distinction between the rehearsal of grief and its event (Fulton Madden, &

Minichiello, 1996: 1357). But perhaps, following Judith Butler, grief's anticipation more rightly lies in the fact that a feeling of dispossession is a fundamental condition of being; or to put it another way, the subject is always a haunted house in search of its ghosts, much like theatre itself.

Butler proffers that while many people think grief is privatizing and therefore depoliticizing, it foregrounds the complex binds that tie us to one another. In the experience of grief, our dependency and ethical responsibility towards others are exposed, revealing a 'political community of a complex order' (2004b: 22). In grief, we realize our fundamental sociality – that this person who has been lost was holding something in me together all along. But we also encounter a sense of our fundamental dispossession – not only for what we have lost, but also in apprehending that this person could only ever have occupied a vacant space. 'If I do not always know what it is *in* another person that I have lost,' Butler writes, 'it may be that this sphere of dispossession is precisely the one that exposes my unknowingness, the unconscious imprint of my primary sociality' (ibid.: 28).

Acknowledging how grief animates our primary interdependency helps us to understand how it operates on an individual and relational level, as well as how it functions intergenerationally via the transmission of culture. In the examples discussed in this chapter, what we might once have thought of as queer grief is recontextualized to speak to a different cultural moment, enabling it to serve as balm and guide for a different context and era, while also creating space for unresolved grief from previous times to be expressed and tended to. While we typically approach grief as a response to something that is lost in the past, we might also think of it as something that is equally anticipated for the future by the past. Peggy Phelan has suggested that 'it may well be that theatre and performance respond to a psychic need to rehearse for loss, and especially for death' (1997: 3). In theatre and performance, I submit, we find a nuanced model of anticipatory grief, in which loss is rehearsed, anticipated and felt all at once, not only so that one historical plague might prepare us for another future one, but for non-identical ruptures too. This layering of temporality and experience is embedded in theatre's tragic roots, of course, in which the staging of death is both enacted in the present of performance, while simultaneously indexing historical and theatrical antecedents, and anticipating future events and productions. As Hans-Thies Lehmann contends, tragic theatre performs a 'displacement of reality', by dematerializing facts even as it presents them, which sends them 'into a strange, floating state' ([2014] 2016: 29). Tragic theatre is therefore a haunted theatre, Lehmann argues, insofar as 'ghosts awaken to life on the stage time and again – mere representations of human beings that, at the same time, are made of human material, signs that *are* what they evoke' (ibid.).

While Freud maintained that mourning was a process with an ending, and melancholia a kind of open-ended grief or soft yearning ([1917] 2001), as I described in Chapter 1, more contemporary psychologists and psychiatrists contest or supplement these ideas. Margaret Stroebe and Henk Schut (1999) challenge the idea of 'grief work', which maintains that loss must be confronted head-on, and overcome in stages. Instead, they have proposed a dual process model of grief, which proposes that grief is not linear, but rather that it oscillates between feelings of loss (focusing on the lost person, yearning, remembering) and restoration (distraction, doing new things, forging new identities and bonds). Theatre not only helps us deal with loss and restoration, but also with anticipation and sharing. However, pandemics, like other instances of large-scale death, prompt the question of how we grieve when mass death is the order of the day? How can we mourn when there is so much work to be done, tasks to be administered, political battles to be fought? How can we grieve, when like Mother Courage, we have to keep on tugging carts in the hope that life might stagger to its feet again?

In the flickering between present and past, life and death, the virtual and the real that *Ten Plagues* and *Last Gasp* present, we can detect elements of the spectral tragic of which Lehmann speaks, in dynamic interaction with queer performance modalities. These intervene the present by mining the past, and in the process demonstrate how even contextually queer narratives and experiences have the capacity to serve and anticipate broader application. The ricochets of grief find support in a supple form that bridges live and digital performance, and ensures that not only does the past possess the present, but that it can also be recontextualized, disseminated and dispossessed for current times and emergent futures.

Conclusion

Those who might think that queer theatre and performance are narrow in their preoccupations, or made only for a LGBTQ+ demographic, will not find their suspicions confirmed in *Ten Plagues* and *Last Gasp*. Both productions demonstrate how there is no such thing as exclusively queer content or form, but rather that even these are dependent on the absorption and remodelling of ideas and practices of wider reach. In a similar way, even as both productions focus on queer cultural history, they show how queer theatre and performance have the capacity to speak to wider concerns in the present, in particular the scale and layers of loss engendered by the coronavirus pandemic, while anticipating future applications, as yet unknown. Disseminated digitally in response to covid-19, the productions demonstrate how the queer past has the capacity to speak to the global present, finding in queer history and culture stories, experiences, aesthetics and dramaturgies uniquely qualified to speak to wider public concerns. This work, in turn, inevitably becomes imprinted by these new pandemic conditions, so that it can no longer be deemed to be solely for LGBTQ+ people, but for us all.

With this chapter I have aimed to highlight how covid-19 summoned queer theatre and performance history, to help process experiences of isolation, illness, death and stigmatization that defined the pandemic. The increase in hate crimes against LGBTQ+ people during this time demonstrated the past was not the past at all, but also that queer culture contained a rich, roguish archive of art, knowledge and feeling that could be raided to help navigate the current pandemic and its social effects. This turn to the queer past does not just represent queer theatre and performance naval-gazing into their own histories but demonstrates how they have never been just for those of us identifying as LGBTQ+, but for anyone willing to encounter them. As the examples considered in this chapter demonstrate, queer theatre and performance have never been solely for a minority audience, but rather they have always been rehearsing, even unwittingly, for a time when their heaving archives of grief, hurt and love might be dispossessed of lessons for all.

7

Epilogue: Shorelines of the dispossessed

David Hoyle has died on stage more than once. There was that time in 2000, for instance, when he killed off his alter-ego The Divine David in an ice rink in Streatham, London, and in 2022, when he left the stage at the end of his show *Ten Commandments* to have his eulogy, pre-scripted by a friend, read aloud by an audience member, before returning to enjoy one final round of applause.[1] 'Survived by a nest of rats and an avalanche of unpaid bills,' it went, 'is this how you honour a starburst? Nameless, unremembered, abandoned, demeaned, devalued, diminished … is this where you place your oracles?' Hoyle's work is concerned with death in other ways too: having performed in clubs and theatres since the 1980s, it has been imprinted by decades of queer culture, including the broadly homophobic climate of the 1980s and 1990s, and the effect of mass deaths due to AIDS. Across his anarchic cabaret and theatre performances, the recurring targets of Hoyle's searing critiques are the monarchy, the military-industrial complex, religious orthodoxy, fascists and political conservatives (and especially the Tories), all of whom he deems to be responsible for the ceaseless assault on minorities, and queer and working-class people in particular. The victims of these attacks are dispossessed by the institutions he dissects – shamed for their sexuality, immiserated by poverty, refused sanctuary, brutalized by systems of oppression, rendered an underclass, wilfully killed or let die. As Hoyle declaims in *Ten*

Commandments, with a Ukrainian flag billowing on a screen behind him in acknowledgement of Russia's concurrent invasion of the country: 'The only war that counts is class war.'

Directed by Mark Whitelaw, Hoyle takes the stage in *Ten Commandments* to deliver a new set of rules to live by, which might help rescue us from the crushing bleakness he identifies. Standing behind a makeshift pulpit, like a secular priest, Hoyle begins by screening footage of scrambling rats, to invoke his apparently infested Manchester flat, in order to urge us to resist the 'suicidal poverty' he sees as being mandated by the current Conservative government. Other commandments call for the disbandment of nuclear weapons and landfills, and an end to the destruction of the climate. The tenth commandment is reserved for the audience to conceive, which on the night I saw the production was: do not confuse social media with activism. From the dystopic present, marred by years of a pandemic and a new war led by Russia against Ukraine, Hoyle imagines a garden of Eden free from poverty, pollution, war and other forms of state-licensed violence.

Arguing for the value of art, Hoyle shows us an image of his favourite work: Théodore Géricault's *Le Radeau de la Méduse* (*The Raft of the Medusa*, 1818–19 (Figure 7.1). The Romantic French oil painting, now hanging in the Louvre, depicts the aftermath of the wreck of the naval frigate Méduse that ran aground off the coast of Mauritania on 2 July 1816. The ship formed part of a fleet carrying French officials to Senegal to assume control of the colony from the British. While approximately 147 people were put on the constructed raft depicted in the painting, all but fifteen died before their rescue, as a result of dehydration, starvation, illness and murder. Those who survived resorted to cannibalism to live. Géricault's painting captures a moment in this chaotic journey, in which the bodies of the living and the dead are tangled on a raft, with some groping each other for support, or as potential food. In the background, some survivors rise towards the sky, desperately searching for help. As Nina Athanassoglou-Kallmyer tells us,

Shorelines of the Dispossessed 187

Figure 7.1 Théodore Géricault, *Le Radeau de la Méduse* (1818–19), Musée du Louvre, Paris, France.

Géricault's 'genre noir' techniques of 'shock, terror, black humor, irony, and surreal fantasy' drew attention to the 'gruesome social realities of the day' (Athanassoglou-Kallmyer 1992: 617).

One of those who survived the disaster was Alexandre Corréard, who wrote about his ordeal. He blamed the government for the incompetent leadership of the Medusa, weak rescue efforts and neglect of the survivors. Corréard, like Géricault, was an abolitionist at a time when slavery was still an important feature of French imperialism. At a late stage in the painting of *The Raft of the Medusa*, Géricault added three Black figures to the raft, including one raised on the shoulders of his comrades, waving a cloth in the wind. In Géricault's painting, those who are most savagely dispossessed are most passionately moved in the pursuit of freedom.

According to Paul Virilio, as discussed in Chapter 4, technologies include the instruments of their potential extinction (Virilio 1999: 89). For Virilio, the shipwreck serves as a powerful image for how progress carries the tools of its own destruction, with every vessel shadowed by its capacity for sinkage. This idea is powerfully captured in Géricault's painting too, with the ship on the horizon and its wreck on the shore drawn in mutual recognition.

Although not mentioned by Hoyle on the night I attended his performance, *Raft of the Medusa* is also the name of a play by Joe Pintauro, which premiered in New York in 1991. Pintauro's play is set in a support group for people living with HIV/AIDS, including members of a diverse range of gender, sexual, ethnic and political positions – a motley crew adrift on a sea of illness, stigmatization and uncertainty. When it is discovered that one member is not infected with the virus, but an undercover reporter, the group turns on him for betraying their trust. Pintauro's play not only captures the sense of carnage and confusion during the initial outbreak of AIDS, but it also seems to suggest that shared trauma is necessary for deep understanding to emerge.

Hoyle, like Pintauro before him, is drawn to the savagery of the historical event, in which the survival of the dispossessed is dependent on the most extreme act of possession – the physical cannibalization of the other. This Hoyle reads as a fitting distillation of the class wars he rages against, in which migrants, refugees, the poor, and LGBTQ+ people are baited like animals. Hoyle is attracted to the warm light on the horizon of Géricault's painting, which illuminates a ship passing by, leading him to wryly wonder if he can see a Russian yacht on the skyline. 'Are we seeing another ship on the horizon coming to save us?', Hoyle asks the audience; 'No, it's just an oligarch sailing by'. In Hoyle's art history lesson, eating the other and being possessed by the other are distinct but perilously close practices. To be possessed by the other is to keep the other alive; to eat the other is to possess him solely for personal survival. Pitted against one another in unbearable circumstances, as we so frequently are within the LGBTQ+ umbrella, it often feels like we are being deliberately set-up to do the former (Figure 7.2).

Another ghost haunts Hoyle's performance too, in the form of David Wojnarowicz. In one segment, Hoyle recites the text in Wojnarowicz's *Untitled (One Day This Kid…)* (1990–1), while

Figure 7.2 David Hoyle speaking from a pulpit in *Ten Commandments*, Soho Theatre, London, UK (2022). Photographer: Holly Revell.

projecting an image of the artwork upstage. The piece features the artist as a smiling boy, surrounded by text that warns of his future. It is a grim litany of violence and dispossession, made worse by the cool collision of image and text, optimism and despair, the past and future: 'This kid will be faced with electro-shock, drugs, and conditioning therapies in laboratories tended by psychologists and research scientists. He will be subject to loss of home, civil rights, jobs, and all conceivable freedoms.' Wojnarowicz created the work not long before his own death of AIDS-related illness in the United States in 1992, during a time of wilful disregard for the lives of queer people. From the artwork's present, the future strains back to warn the child, while the child smiles obliviously towards the unknown. Here, the present is haunted by the past, but the past is also haunted by the future. For Hoyle, and Wojnarowicz before him, tuning into this layered temporal frequency, while affording it aesthetic space to expand and resound, is required to learn from history's hurts.

I think of Hoyle's commandments as *queer heirlooms* – wisdom accumulated over decades – from art, life and other people – and passed down through generations, including via this theatre performance. Hoyle is unique among the artists examined in this book, because he is keenly self-aware of his role as someone who delivers the past into the present, gathering and distributing personal insight with social and political analysis in often improvised, unpredictable ways throughout his prolific career. The past is inscribed on and in Hoyle's body and memories, which, like a shaman, he conjures and shares with his audiences. The social dispossession that preoccupies Hoyle is tempered via the riotous exchange of history, story, song and advice among his audiences. In performing the past, time passing and rehearsing his own death and comic resurrection, Hoyle routinely invites us to look obliquely on our own losses and fading lives, our known and unknown inheritances; to stand outside history and watch the arc of time bend, if only for a moment.

While José Esteban Muñoz has influentially claimed that 'queerness is primarily about futurity and hope' and therefore 'always in the horizon' (Muñoz 2009: 11), in Hoyle the horizon is a marker of inevitable disappointment, a dark joke whose duplicitous seductions waste our energy, dreams and time. Hoyle, like the other artists examined in this book, reminds us that the allure of the horizon must not distract us from also monitoring the shoreline, in order to identify and even salvage the flotsam and jetsam of history. In Derek Jarman's sculptures, made from found objects on the beach, we see this impulse take on a literal form, with lost toys, jewellery, tin cans and ky jelly assembled into a collage of things lost and found, time past and run ashore (e.g. *K.Y.*, 1998). But these differing emphases need not be thought of as oppositional stances – every skyline is another's shoreline, every future another's past, after all. When simultaneously viewed and accounted for, these braided perspectives contribute to a panoramic vision of queer cultural politics, which is not blinded by a forward-facing utopian impulse, but balanced by the ritualistic encounter with the dispossessed via acts of collective witnessing, remembrance and material reconfiguration.

There were times in researching the book when I wondered if queer theatre and performance's investment in the past, in particular the difficult past, suggested that there was little interesting left in contemporary culture to mine. Or, worse still, perhaps queer culture is too attached to a narrative of woundedness, too invested in its traumatic stories to generate new targets and passions.[2] Are we possessed by the difficult past, I asked myself, or is the difficult past our most valuable cultural inspiration and political currency? However, as I have endeavoured to demonstrate in this book, the aesthetics and dramaturgies of theatre and performance invariably disrupt linear time, by making the past present – not just in a metaphorical sense, but also in the very real way its figures and materials take centre stage as stimulus or representation. Contemporary queer theatre and performance exploit this formal tendency to reveal themselves not only to be *of* the past but also to be possessed *by* it – haunted by its ghosts, holding its losses, nursing its wounds, laden with its psychic and material remains, foreshadowing history's inevitable returns. But the book has also argued that these works represent an effort to take control of the past via representational strategies that escort it into the present for us to recognize and refashion psychically, emotionally and materially. If theatre and performance do not do this work for us and with us – if they do not possess and dispossess the past in the public spaces of culture – history's hurts will return in ever-more destructive ways.

In *Enduring Time*, Lisa Baraitser examines states of suspended temporality, in an attempt to understand 'how to continue when time has stopped' (Baraitser 2017: 5). Avoiding the language of rupture and disruption, which is typically used to track generative events in history, Baraitser apprehends in enduring times 'a quiet noticing that something remains, which is the permanent capacity to begin again' (ibid.: 188). I think of the possessed time of theatre and performance as enduring time, not in the sense of time as having stopped, but for its facility to hold history in the arms of an instant. By steering the past onto the shore of the present, and sharing its burdens with those gathered to collectively witness, remember and transform them, this artwork lightens the weight for successive generations to bear. From the remains of what has passed, and the spoils of what seems to be lost forever, we must forge new forms and rafts with which to transmit history, propelled by our enduring capacity to find the beginning in every apparent ending.

Notes

Introduction: Performing queer possession

1 The production is also profiled in the documentary *Before the Last Curtain Falls* (2014).
2 More information on current and recent legislation affecting LGBTQ people across the USA can be found on the ACLU (American Civil Liberties Union) (2022) website.
3 Section 28 affected England, Scotland and Wales, and bolstered the homophobia of the time, which was fuelled by anxieties concerning the transmission of HIV/AIDS. See Local Government Act 1988 (1988).
4 In the UK, the Home Office reported that hate crimes based on sexual orientation doubled between 2016 and 2017 (8,569 reported) and between 2020 and 2021 (17,135 reported). See Home Office (2021). A similar rising trend was reported by the FBI, with 20 per cent of all cases in 2020 pertaining to sexual orientation, and 2.7 per cent gender identity; the latter figure showing an increase on the previous year, the former a slight drop. See The United States Department of Justice (2020). Similarly, a Council of Europe Parliamentary Assembly report warned of an increase in hate speech, violence and hate crime against LGBTI people, communities and organizations across many member States of the Council of Europe. See Council of Europe Parliamentary Assembly (2022).
5 On 24 June 2022, the US Supreme Court overturned Roe v. Wade, the 1973 Supreme Court decision that affirmed the constitutional right to abortion, in a move that also appeared to threaten access to contraception and even the legitimacy of interracial and same-sex marriages, without codification in law.
6 A UCL Urban Laboratory study of queer venues in the UK revealed a drop of 44 per cent in UK nightclubs (2005–15), 35 per cent in

London grassroots venues (2007–16) and 25 per cent in UK pubs (2001–16). See Campkin and Marshall (2017). A similar study of gay bars closing in the United States suggested that they showed their largest five-year decline between 2012 and 2017, losing 18.6 per cent. See Mattson (2019). As recent as April 2022, Rash, a gay bar in New York, was deliberately set ablaze, and in 2016, Pulse, a gay nightclub in Orlando, Florida, was the scene of a mass shooting.
7 For data on hate crimes against LGBTQ+ people in Germany, see Bundesministerium des Innern und für Heimat Federal Ministry of the Interior and for Community (2021). The report tracks rises in a number of hate crimes, including new data for crimes against people on account of their gender identity.
8 The law was named after the code-breaker Alan Turing who was charged with gross indecency in 1952. In April 2022, the UK government agreed to ban conversion therapy for sexual orientation in England and Wales, but not for gender identity, effectively excluding transgender people.
9 The slogan 'It gets better' is taken from Dan Savage and Terry Miller's 'It Gets Better Project', which was set up in the United States in 2010 in response to the suicide of teenagers who were bullied for being gay or presumed to be. The slogan has since been widely circulated by celebrities and high profile politicians, including Barack Obama.
10 See 'possession' entry in the online *Merriam-Webster Dictionary*, https://www.merriam-webster.com/dictionary/possession (accessed 1 June 2022).

1 Channelling ghosts: The haunted present

1 While *Angels in America* and *The Inheritance* supply important context for this Chapter, I eschew focusing on them in further depth as they have enjoyed significant critical and commercial attention to date.
2 For a broader consideration of HIV and AIDS in contemporary theatre, see Campbell and Gindt (2018).

3 All *Re-Member Me* quotes are taken from the unpublished manuscript provided by Dickie Beau.
4 Icke's *Hamlet* played at the Almeida Theatre from February to April 2017 before transferring to the Harold Pinter Theatre in the West End in June. *Re-Member Me* was programmed for a number of nights between March and April of this initial run, taking place on the same set. It has since toured nationally and internationally, including to Under the Radar Festival in New York (2018), Melbourne International Arts Festival (2018) and Perth Festival (2019).
5 Eve Kosofsky Sedgwick (1990) suggests that in European thought, gossip has been devalued in its association with servants, effeminate and gay men, and all women. Less to do with the 'transmission of necessary news', Sedgwick argues, gossip can be concerned 'with the refinement of necessary skills for making, testing, and using unrationalized and provisional hypotheses about what *kinds of people* there are to be found in one's world'. See Sedgwick (1990: 23).
6 The act decriminalized sex between men over twenty-one in private. It affected England and Wales, but did not apply to the Armed Forces or Merchant Navy. Homosexual Acts were decriminalized in Scotland in 1980, taking effect in 1981 (under the Criminal Justice (Scotland) Act 1980) and in Northern Ireland in 1982 (under the Homosexual Offences (Northern Ireland) Order 1982).
7 In 2017, Public Health England (2017) reported a 21 per cent decrease in new diagnoses amongst gay and bisexual men, although acquisitions had been rising steadily since 2007.
8 The programme for Eyre's production recognizes this by featuring a three-page overview of actors who have played Hamlet throughout the play's history, from Richard Burbage to Jonathan Pryce.
9 Richard Eyre's *Hamlet* opened on 10 March 1989 and closed on 13 December of the same year. It opened with Daniel Day-Lewis in the title role, which was taken over by Jeremy Northam, then Charleson and then Northam again.
10 This information comes courtesy of the National Theatre Archive. In addition to the absence of photographic record, it was not common practice to record productions until the mid-1990s.
11 In his personal website, McKellen recalls how both he and Charleson were also involved in the Arts Lobby, founded in 1988 to contest

Section 28, by arguing it was an attack on culture as well as homosexuals. On 5 June 1988, one month after the law had been enacted, Charleson and McKellen participated in a protest gala at Piccadilly Theatre that provocatively featured work that could be seen to actively 'promote' homosexuality. Two weeks later, McKellen came out as a gay man on Radio 3 at the age of forty-nine. See 'Section 28/ The Arts Lobby', available online: http://www.mckellen.com/activism/section28.htm (accessed 1 June 2022).

12 See reviews from *The Guardian*, *Standard* and *Financial Times* in National Theatre Archive.

13 Davison's article includes a detailed analysis of Charleson's performance and quotes from the cast and crew whom he interviewed.

14 See 'contagion' entry in *Online Etymology Dictionary*, https://www.etymonline.com/search?q=contagion (accessed 1 June 2022).

15 Nicholas de Jongh's play *Plague Over England*, first staged in 2008, explores events surrounding Gielgud's arrest.

16 All *Written in Sand* quotes are taken from the unpublished manuscript provided by Karen Finley.

17 Quote taken from a promotional video for *Séances*. Available online: https://www.jaamil.com/performance (accessed 1 June 2022).

18 Legislation to allow for same-sex marriages in England, Wales and Scotland came into effect in 2014.

2 Muscle memories: Exe(o)rcising history

1 Both performances have had a number of iterations to date and have been widely documented via different media. I mainly draw on their London performances – *Milk & Blood* at Toynbee Studios (2015 and 2018) and *Becoming an Image* at National Theatre Studio (2013) as part of SPILL Festival – as well as other photographic, video and written documentation. For these performances, and others mentioned in the chapter, I include the year of first presentation.

2 In the online abstract to his article on physical culture and the Edwardian strongman George Hackenschmidt, Broderick D. V. Chow

(2015) aligns working through with working out, although the idea is not pursued in the article itself.

3   Brecht's partially written 'Life Story of the Boxer Samson-Körner,' his short story 'The Uppercut,' his planned novel on the 1921 Dempsey-Carpenter fight, 'Das renommee: Ein boxerroman,' and *Rise and Fall of the City of Mahagonny* also reveal an interest in boxing.

4   Other recent theatre works exploring boxing include Bryony Lavery's *Beautiful Burnout* (2010) and Charlotte Josephine's *Bitch Boxer* (2012), although this is not an exhaustive list.

5   In a previous publication, I explored these themes in relation to the aesthetics of abjection in Franko's performances, although I was much more attentive to the psychic texture of the work. See Walsh (2010).

6   Performance products sometimes become other artworks for Cassils. For example, a mound of clay (*After*) produced by *Becoming an Image* was exhibited as part of the artist's 2013 solo show at Ronald Feldman Fine Arts, New York; as was a concrete, resin and bronze mold (*The Resilience of the 20%*). A sound installation built around a clay mound incorporated sounds of the live performance (*Ghost*).

7   Anne Anlin Cheng (2011) also discusses the relationship between sweat and skin aesthetics in relation to the US-born French entertainer Josephine Baker in *Second Skin: Josephine Baker and the Modern Surface*.

8   I am referring here to the teary reunion of Ulay and Abramović in *The Artist is Present* at the Museum of Modern Art, New York, in 2010, which resulted in a viral internet video.

3   Re-enacting violence: Sharing responsibility

1   I focus on the production of *La Reprise* at Théâtre National, Wallonie-Bruxelles (2018) and *Burgerz* at Hackney Showroom, London (2018), including the published play text which I sometimes quote directly.

2   The IIPM was founded by Rau for the creation, distribution and documentation of his theatre productions, performance works and films. Since 2007, IIPM has realized over fifty theatre productions, films, books, exhibitions and actions.

3 Matthew Shepard was a gay student at the University of Wyoming who was beaten, tortured and left to die near Laramie on 6 October 1998. *The Laramie Project* was developed by Tectonic Theater Project in response to the murder, drawing on interviews conducted by the company with residents of the town, company members' own journal entries and news reports. The production inspired the film *The Laramie Project* (2002) and the theatre project *The Laramie Project: Ten Years Later* in (2009), which reflected on the intervening period.

4 Hannah Arendt originally reported on the trial for *The New Yorker*, which formed the basis of her fuller account in the 1963 book *Eichmann in Jerusalem: A Report on the Banality of Evil*.

5 See the section on 'Emotion Memory' in Stanislavski's *An Actor Prepares*, pp. 141-66.

6 For the translation from German into English, I rely on Hörnigk and Magshamrain (2006), p. 1.

7 In the Kierkegaard ([1843] 2009) edition used for reference in this chapter, the quote is given as: 'Repetition and recollection are the same movement, just in opposite directions, because what is recollected has always been and is thus repeated backwards, whereas genuine repetition is recollected forwards.' See 'Repetition' in *Repetition and Philosophical Crumbs*, p. 3.

8 Duckie is a collective of performance artists and a club night based at London's Royal Vauxhall Tavern. It opened in 1995 and ended its regular Saturday night residency in 2022. The Bishopsgate Institute, London, cares for the collections of Duckie and the Museum of Transology, as well as other archives.

9 The nineteen-point report also includes a list of action points for states to respond to. In order to read in full, see Council of Europe Parliamentary Assembly (2022).

4 Arresting objects: Transforming matters

1 The objectification of Black people is in part supported by their hypervisibility in certain public spaces. This is true of mainstream commercial theatres too, dominated by white middle-class audiences.

In a gesture to combat this experience, Harris introduced a Black Out performance as part of *'Daddy'* at the Almeida, which he inaugurated with *Slave Play*, which saw all the tickets for a performance reserved for Black-identifying audience members. Harris developed the idea because he felt it important for Black spectators to experience being in a theatre where the whole audience looks like them.

2 A gate featuring the same slogan was also stolen from Auschwitz in 2009.
3 See 'Dachau' entry in *United States Holocaust Memorial Museum*, https://encyclopedia.ushmm.org/content/en/article/dachau (accessed 1 June 2022).
4 For more on Hirschfeld, see Bauer (2017).
5 Paragraph 175 was a provision of the German Criminal Code from 1871 to 1994, which made homosexual acts between men a crime. It was revised in 1935 to introduce penal servitude and imprisonment for related crimes (175a) and outlaw bestiality (175b), thus associating it with homosexuality.
6 See 'Homosexual Prisoners in the Dachau Concentration Camp', https://www.comiteinternationaldachau.com/de/geschichten/454-homosexuelle-haeftlinge-im-konzentrationslager-dachau (accessed 1 June 2022).
7 For more on this contemporary political rhetoric and its historical resonances, see Walsh (2020).
8 The scheme rescued children from the encroachment of Nazis in Europe in the months leading up to the war, in order to rehome them in safer territories, including the UK.

5 Wilde spirits: Occupation and commemoration

1 The inscription on Wilde's tomb reads: 'And alien tears will fill for him/Pity's long-broken urn,/For his mourners will be outcast men,/And outcasts always mourn'.
2 See 'rewilding' entry in the online *Merriam-Webster Dictionary*, https://www.merriam-webster.com/dictionary/rewilding (accessed 1 June 2022).

3 I rely here on Heike Bauer's (2017) translations.
4 As per its logo on https://www.artangel.org.uk (accessed 1 June 2022).
5 For a discussion of Wilde's relationship to claims of sainthood see the chapter 'Saint Oscar' in Janes (2015: 133–54).
6 For example, Roland Emmerich's film *Stonewall* (2015) was widely critiqued for downplaying the role of trans and Black activists, including Johnson, while David France's *The Death and Life of Marsha P. Johnson* (2017) sought to rectify this narrative by placing her centre stage.
7 See also McGough's 2017 memoir.
8 Quoted on the artists' website, http://www.mcdermottandmcgough.com (accessed 1 June 2022).
9 Operation Yewtree was the name given to a British police investigation, launched in 2012, into sexual allegations, and in particular child sexual abuse, involving Jimmy Savile and other high-profile figures.
10 Ireland's Office of Public Works considers the tomb an Irish monument overseas and therefore has paid for its cleaning and the erection of the barrier.
11 Questions of Wilde's 'manliness' and racial category preceded interrogations of his sexuality, although all conspired to construct an image of aberrance.
12 Coming from a different position, but resonating with a similar theme, Alyson Campbell has made a case for the use of feral pedagogies for queer teaching within the academy, describing them as those that might exploit 'privileged position within the academy'. See Campbell (2019: 177).

6 Grief's ricochet: Intermedial returns

1 We can consider this theatre programming alongside the release of the Jonathan Larson biographical musical drama film *tick, tick … BOOM!* (2021) (which itself began as a rock monologue written by Larson), and the television drama *It's a Sin* (2021) which focused on the early years of AIDS in the UK.
2 The mediatized version, titled *Last Gasp WFH* (Working from Home), was created using Zoom in 2020. The live version, incorporating

mediatized elements (qualifying it as intermedial), was first presented at Barbican's The Pit in 2021 as *Last Gasp: A Recalibration*. I refer to the show as *Last Gasp* when discussing both or shared elements.
3 This was the last major collaboration between Weill and Brecht, whose most successful project was *The Threepenny Opera* which premiered in 1928 at Theater am Schiffbauerdamm, Berlin.
4 In June 2015, when the US Supreme Court extended the right to marry to same-sex couples, the slogan # LoveWins widely circulated widely across social media, including by President Obama in his announcement. The slogan also featured as part of other campaigns, including the Republic of Ireland (legalized in 2015), Taiwan (legalized in 2019) and Northern Ireland (legalized in 2020).
5 Coates's non-fiction book *Between the World and Me* (2015) undertakes a similar cross-generational conversation, insofar as it is written as a letter to the author's teenage son, in which he tries to speak about the experience being Black in the United States.
6 The published script of *Ruff* can be accessed in Shaw and Weaver (2018).
7 Floyd's death in 2020 sparked mass gatherings and protests around the world, which were striking for straddling and sometimes disrupting periods of social quarantine.
8 Covid-19 death toll. Available online: https://www.worldometers.info/coronavirus/coronavirus-death-toll/ (accessed 1 June 2022).
9 For example, see Ofcom (2020).
10 For more on these statistics, see Anti-Defamation League (ADL) (2020) and Movement Advancement Project (2020). See also endnote 4 in the book's introduction.

7 Epilogue: Shorelines of the dispossessed

1 *Ten Commandments* opened at The Lowry in Manchester before transferring to Soho Theatre, London in March 2022.
2 The attachment of minority identities to woundedness has been persuasively critiqued by Wendy Brown (1995).

References

Abraham, N., and M. Torok (1994), *The Shell and the Kernel: Renewals of Psychoanalysis*, Volume 1, ed., trans. with intro. N. T. Rand, Chicago: University of Chicago Press.

Abram, J. ([1996] 2018), *The Language of Winnicott: A Dictionary of Winnicott's Use of Words*, Abingdon: Routledge.

ACLU (American Civil Liberties Union) (2022), 'Legislation Affecting LGBTQ Rights Across the Country'. Available online: https://www.aclu.org/legislation-affecting-lgbtq-rights-across-country (accessed 1 June 2022).

Adebayo, M. ([2008] 2011), 'Muhammad Ali and Me', in *Mojisola Adebayo: Plays One*, London: Oberon Books.

Adebayo, M. and L. Goddard (2023), 'Introduction and Survey of Afriquia Plays,' in M. Adebayo and L. Goddard (eds), *Black British Queer Plays and Practitioners: An Anthology of Afriquia Theatre*, 1–20, London: Methuen Drama.

Ahmed, S. (2013), 'Changing Hands', *feministkilljoys* (blog), 28 August. Available online: feministkilljoys.com/2013/08/28/changing-hands/ (accessed 1 June 2022).

Ahmed, S. (2014), 'A Killjoy in Crisis', *feministkilljoys* (blog), 28 August. Available online: feministkilljoys.com/2014/08/28/a-killjoy-in-crisis/ (accessed 1 June 2022).

Alabanza, T. ([2018] 2021), *Burgerz*, London: Methuen Drama.

Als, H. ([2014] 2018), *White Girls*, London: Penguin Books.

Alston, A. (2016), *Beyond Immersive Theatre: Aesthetics, Politics and Productive Participation*, London: Palgrave Macmillan.

American Psychiatric Association (2013), *DSM-5 (Diagnostic and Statistical Manual of Mental Disorders)*, 5th edn, Washington, DC: American Psychiatric Association.

American Psychiatric Association (2021), 'APA Offers Tips for Understanding Prolonged Grief Disorder', 22 September. Available online: https://www.psychiatry.org/newsroom/news-releases/apa-off

ers-tips-for-understanding-prolonged-grief-disorder (accessed 1 June 2022).

American Psychiatric Association (2022), *DSM-5-TR (Diagnostic and Statistical Manual of Mental Disorders)*, 5th edn, Text Revision, Washington, DC: American Psychiatric Association.

Ansen, D. (1993), 'AIDS and the Arts: A Lost Generation', *Newsweek*, 17 January. Available online: http://europe.newsweek.com/lost-generation-192398?rm=eu (accessed 1 June 2022).

Anti-Defamation League (ADL) (2020), 'Coronavirus: Anti-Immigration, Xenophobia and Homophobia', 21 April. Available online: https://www.adl.org/blog/coronavirus-anti-immigration-xenophobia-and-homophobia (accessed 1 June 2022).

Arendt, H. (1963), *Eichmann in Jerusalem: A Report on the Banality of Evil*, New York: Viking Press.

Aristotle ([1895] 1907), *The Poetics of Aristotle*, 4th edn, ed. and trans. S. H. Butcher, London: Macmillan.

Arthur, M. (2021), 'Nostalgia and Chronicity: Two Temporalities in the Restaging of AIDS', *Theatre Journal*, 73 (1): 19–36.

Athanassoglou-Kallmyer, N. (1992), 'Géricault's Severed Heads and Limbs: The Politics and Aesthetics of the Scaffold', *Art Bulletin*, 74 (4): 599–618.

Baraitser, L. (2017), *Enduring Time*, London: Bloomsbury.

Bartlett, N. (1988), *Who Was That Man?: A Present for Mr Oscar Wilde*, London: Serpent's Tail.

Bartlett, N. (2000), *In Extremis*, London: Oberon Books.

Bauer, H. (2017), *The Hirschfeld Archives: Violence, Death, and Modern Queer Culture*, Philadelphia: Temple University Press.

Beau, D. (2016a), 'Lost in Trans' [production description]. Available online: http://dickiebeau.com/portfolio/lost-in-trans-2/ (accessed 1 June 2022).

Beau, D. (2016b), 'Re-Member Me' [production description]. Available online: http://dickiebeau.com/portfolio/re-member-me/ (accessed 1 June 2022).

Before the Last Curtain Falls (2014), [documentary] Dir. Thomas Wallner, Berlin: Gebrueder Beetz Filmproduktion.

Benedict, D. (1995), 'Good Night, Sweet Prince', *The Independent*, 6 January. Available online: https://www.independent.co.uk/arts-entert

ainment/theatre-good-night-sweet-prince-1566786.html (accessed 1 June 2022).

Benjamin, W. ([1935] 2007), 'The Work of Art in the Age of Mechanical Reproduction', in *Illuminations*, ed. H. Arendt, trans. H. Zohn, 217–51, New York: Schocken Books.

Bennett, A. ([2004] 2008), *The History Boys*, New York: Farrar, Straus and Giroux.

Berlant, L. (2011), *Cruel Optimism*, Durham: Duke University Press.

Berlant, L. (2012), *Desire/Love*, New York: Punctum Books.

Berlant, L., and L. Edelman (2014), *Sex, or the Unbearable*, Durham: Duke University Press.

Bhabha, H. K. (1991), '"Race", Time and the Revision of Modernity', *Oxford Literary Review*, 13 (1/2): 193–219.

Bion, W. R. ([1962] 2004), *Learning from Experience*, Lanham: Rowman & Littlefield.

Bion, W. R. (1967), *Second Thoughts: Selected Papers on Psycho-Analysis*, London: William Heinemann Medical Books.

Bishop, C. (2005), *Installation Art: A Critical History*, London: Tate Publishing.

Bloch, E. ([1959] 1986), *The Principle of Hope*, Volume One, trans. Neville Plaice, Stephen Plaice and Paul Knight, Cambridge, MA: MIT Press.

Boddy, K. (2008), *Boxing: A Cultural History*, London: Reaktion.

Brantley, B. (2014), 'A Raging Grief, Adamantly Diminished', *New York Times*, 14 October. Available online: https://www.nytimes.com/2014/10/16/theater/karen-finley-relives-the-aids-epidemic-in-written-in-sand.html (accessed 1 June 2022).

Braun, K. (2021), *Biopolitics and Historic Justice: Coming to Terms with the Injuries of Normality*, Bielefeld: Transcript Verlag.

Brecht, B. ([1927] 1994), 'In the Jungle of Cities', in J. Willett and R. Mannheim (eds), trans. G. Nellhaus, *Brecht Collected Plays: 1*, 117–78, London: Methuen Drama.

Brennan, T. (2004), *The Transmission of Affect*, Ithaca: Cornell University Press.

Breuer, J. ([1893-1895] 2001), 'Theoretical', in ed. and trans. J. Strachey, *The Standard Edition of the Complete Psychological Works of Sigmund Freud*, Volume II (1893-1895), 183-251, London: Vintage.

Brown, B. (1998), 'How to Do Things with Things (A Toy Story)', *Critical Inquiry*, 24 (4): 935–64.

Brown, B. (2006), 'Reification, Reanimation, and the American Uncanny', *Critical Inquiry*, 32 (2): 175–207.

Brown, W. (1995), *States of Injury: Power and Freedom in Late Modernity*, Princeton: Princeton University Press.

Bundesministerium des Innern und für Heimat [Federal Ministry of the Interior and for Community] (2021), 'Politisch motivierte Kriminalität im Jahr 2020' [Politically motivated crime in 2020]. Available online: https://www.bmi.bund.de/SharedDocs/downloads/DE/vero effentlichungen/2021/05/pmk-2020-bundesweite-fallzahlen.pdf?__b lob=publicationFile&v=4 (accessed 1 June 2022).

Bundestag (2017), 'Gesetz zur Strafrechtlichen Rehabilitierung der nach dem 8. Mai 1945 Wegen Einvernehmlicher Homosexueller Handlungen Verurteilten Personen und zur Änderung des Einkommensteuergesetze' [Act on the Criminal Rehabilitation of Persons Sentenced for Consensual Homosexual Acts after 8 May 1945]. Available online: https://www.bgbl.de/xaver/bgbl/text. xav?SID=&tf=xaver.component.Text_0&tocf=&qmf=&hlf=xaver. component.Hitlist_0&bk=bgbl&start=%2F%2F*%5B%40n ode_id%3D%27942966%27%5D&skin=pdf&tlevel=-2&noh ist=1&sinst=FD24EE8C (accessed 1 June 2022).

Butler, J. (1997), *The Psychic Life of Power: Theories of Subjection*, Stanford: Stanford University Press.

Butler, J. (2004a), *Undoing Gender*, New York: Routledge.

Butler, J. (2004b), *Precarious Life: The Powers of Mourning and Violence*, London: Verso.

Campbell, A., and D. Gindt, eds (2018), *Viral Dramaturgies: HIV and AIDS in Performance in the Twenty-First Century*, Cham: Palgrave Macmillan.

Campbell, A. (2019), 'Going feral: queerly de-domesticating the institution (and running wild)', in P. Eckersall and H. Grehan (eds), *The Routledge Companion to Theatre and Politics*, 177–80, Abingdon: Routledge.

Campkin, B., and L. Marshall (2017), 'LGBTQ+ Cultural Infrastructure in London: Night Venues, 2006–present', London: UCL Urban Laboratory. Available online: https://www.ucl.ac.uk/urban-lab/docs/ LGBTQ_cultural_infrastructure_in_London_nightlife_venues_2006 _to_the_present.pdf (accessed 1 June 2022).

Carlson, M. (2001), *The Haunted Stage: The Theatre as Memory Machine*, Ann Arbor: University of Michigan Press.

Caruth, C. (1995), 'Introduction', in C. Caruth (ed.), *Trauma: Explorations in Memory*, 3–12, Baltimore: The Johns Hopkins University Press.

Cassils (2013), *Becoming an Image* [promotional video]. Available online: www.youtube.com/watch?v=TzM8GTL2WGo (accessed 1 June 2022).

Centre for Disease Control (1995), 'Trends in AIDS Among Men Who Have Sex with Men – United States, 1989-1994'. 2 June. Available online: https://www.cdc.gov/mmwr/preview/mmwrhtml/00037153.htm (accessed 1 June 2022).

Chambers-Letson, J. (2018), *After the Party: A Manifesto for Queer of Color Life*, New York: New York University Press.

Chao-Fong, L. (2021), 'Recorded Homophobic Hate Crimes Soared in Pandemic, Figures Show', *The Guardian*, 3 December. Available online: https://www.theguardian.com/world/2021/dec/03/recorded-homophobic-hate-crimes-soared-in-pandemic-figures-show (accessed 1 June 2022).

Charcot, J.-M., and P. Richer (1887), *Les Démoniaques dans l'art*, Paris: Delahaye et Lecrosnier.

Cheng, A. A. (2011), *Second Skin: Josephine Baker and the Modern Surface*, Oxford: Oxford University Press.

Chow, B. D. V. (2015), 'A Professional Body: Remembering, Repeating, and Working Out Masculinities in *Fin-de-Siècle* Physical Culture', *Performance Research*, 20 (5): 30–41.

Chow, B. D. V. (2017), 'The Unlikely Origins of Fitness Culture Could Give Us a Different View on What It Is to Be a Man', *Conversation*, 1 December. Available online: scroll.in/article/860275/the-unlikely-origins-of-fitness-culture-could-give-us-a-different-view-on-what-it-is-to-be-a-man (accessed 1 June 2022).

Coates, T. (2015), *Between the World and Me*, New York: Spiegel & Grau.

Council of Europe Parliamentary Assembly (2022), 'Combating Rising Hate against LGBTI People in Europe'. Available online: https://pace.coe.int/en/files/29712/html?__cf_chl_jschl_tk__=wq4APxdHGXM8WNzzmWlk9ZZ7unktUWfj5R2YbnKmWHM-1643140463-0-gaNycGzNBv0 (accessed 1 June 2022).

Critchley, S., and J. Webster (2013), *The Hamlet Doctrine*, London: Verso.

Crowell, E. (2012), 'Oscar Wilde's Tomb: Silence and the Aesthetics of Queer Memorial', *BRANCH: Britain, Representation and Nineteenth-Century History*, November. Available online: http://www.branc hcollective.org/?ps_articles=ellen-crowell-oscar-wildes-tomb-sile nce-and-the-aesthetics-of-queer-memorial (accessed 1 June 2022).

Dant, T. (1999), *Material Culture in the Social World: Values, Activities, Lifestyles*, Buckingham: Open University Press.

Davison, R. A. (1999), 'The Readiness Was All: Ian Charleson and Richard Eyre's *Hamlet*', in L. Potter, and Arthur F. Kinney (eds), *Shakespeare: Text and Theater – Essays in Honor of Jay Halio*, 170–82, New Jersey: Associated University Presses.

De Jongh, N. (2009), *Plague Over England*, London: Samuel French.

De Kostnik, A. (2016), *Rogue Archives: Digital Cultural Memory and Media Fandom*, Cambridge, MA: MIT Press.

Dean, T. (2008), 'Breeding Culture: Barebacking, Bugchasing, Giftgiving', *Massachusetts Review*, 49 (1&2): 80–94.

Defoe, D. ([1772] 2003), *A Journal of the Plague Year*, ed. with intro. C. Wall, London: Penguin Books.

Derrida, J. ([1993] 2006), *Specters of Marx: The State of the Debt, the Work of Mourning and the New International*, trans. P. Kamuf, New York: Routledge Classics.

Di Benedetto, S. (2002), 'The Body as Fluid Dramaturgy: Live Art, Corporeality, and Perception', *Journal of Dramatic Criticism*, 14 (2): 4–15.

Diamond, E. (1995), 'The Shudder of Catharsis in Twentieth-Century Performance', in A. Parker and E. K. Sedgwick (eds), *Performativity and Performance*, 152–72, New York: Routledge.

Diaz, R. (2015), 'The Limits of *Bakla* and Gay: Feminist Readings of *My Husband's Lover*, Vice Ganda, and Charice Pempengco', *Signs*, 40 (3): 721–45.

Dolan, J. (2005), *Utopia in Performance: Finding Hope at the Theatre*, Ann Arbor: University of Michigan Press.

Dyer, R. (1997), *White*, Abingdon: Routledge.

Eagleton, T. (1989), *Saint Oscar*, Derry: Field Day.

Eagleton, T. (2003), *Sweet Violence: The Idea of the Tragic*, Oxford: Blackwell.

Edelman, L. (2004), *No Future: Queer Theory and the Death Drive*, Durham: Duke University Press.

Enelow, S. (2019), 'Sweating Tennessee Williams: Working Actors in *a Streetcar Named Desire* and *Portrait of a Madonna*', *Modern Drama*, 26 (2): 129–48.

Eng, D. L., and D. Kazanjian, eds (2003), *Loss: The Politics of Mourning*, Berkeley: University of California Press.

EU Agency for Fundamental Rights (2020), 'A Long Way to Go'. Available online: https://fra.europa.eu/sites/default/files/fra_uploads/fra-2020-lgbti-equality_en.pdf (accessed 1 June 2022).

Eyre, R. (2003), *National Service: Diary of a Decade at the National Theatre*, London: Bloomsbury Publishing.

Fairbairn. W. R. D. ([1952] 1994), *Psychoanalytic Studies of the Personality*, London: Routledge.

Faye, S. ([2021] 2022), *The Transgender Issue: An Argument for Justice*, London: Penguin Books.

Felman, S., and D. Laub (1992), *Testimony: Crises of Witnessing in Literature, Psychoanalysis, and History*, New York: Routledge.

Field, M. (2014), 'Is Oscar Wilde's Reputation due for Another Reassessment', *The Independent*, 5 October. Available online: https://www.independent.co.uk/arts-entertainment/theatre-dance/features/is-oscar-wilde-facing-a-retrial-9773718.html (accessed 1 June 2022).

Finley, K. ([1990] 2015), *Shock Treatment*, San Francisco: City Lights.

Fisher, M. (2011), 'Marc Almond: From Bedsit to Plague Pit', *The Guardian*, 18 July. Available online: https://www.theguardian.com/stage/2011/jul/18/marc-almond-interview-ten-plagues (accessed 1 June 2022).

Fisher, M. (2019), 'Making a Murder: True-Crime Stage Show Recreates a Shocking Killing', *The Guardian*, 9 July. Available online: https://www.theguardian.com/stage/2019/jul/09/milo-rau-true-crime-murder-edinburgh (accessed 1 June 2022).

Flashdance (1983) [film] Dir. Adrian Lyne, USA: PolyGram Pictures.

Florida House of Representatives (2022), 'HB 1557'. Available online: https://www.flsenate.gov/Session/Bill/2022/1557/BillText/er/PDF (accessed 1 June 2022).

Franko B (2015), 'Insignificant'. Available online: https://www.franko-b.com/Insignificant.html (accessed 1 June 2022).

Franko B (2016), 'Franko B interviewed by Jessica Greenall for artinliverpool.com', July. Available online: https://www.franko-b.com/Jessica_Greenall_interview.html (accessed 1 June 2022).

Freeman, E. (2005), 'Time Binds, or Erotohistoriogaphy,' *Social Text*, 23 (3–4): 57–68.

Freeman, E. (2010), *Time Binds: Queer Temporalities, Queer Histories*, Durham: Duke University Press.

Freud, S. ([1900] 2001), 'The Interpretation of Dreams' (part 1), in *The Standard Edition of the Complete Psychological Works of Sigmund Freud*, Volume IV (1900), ed. and trans. J. Strachey, London: Vintage.

Freud, S. ([1900] 2001), 'The Interpretation of Dreams' (part 2), in *The Standard Edition of The Complete Psychological Works of Sigmund Freud*, Volume V (1901–5), ed. and trans. J. Strachey, 339–627, London: Vintage.

Freud, S. ([1905] 2001), 'Three Essays on the Theory of Sexuality', in *The Standard Edition of the Complete Psychological Works of Sigmund Freud*, Volume XXI (1927–31), ed. and trans. J. Strachey, 123–245, London: Vintage.

Freud, S. ([1913] 2001), 'Totem and Taboo', in *The Standard Edition of the Complete Psychological Works of Sigmund Freud*, Volume XIII (1913–14), ed. and trans. J. Strachey, vii–162, London: Vintage.

Freud, S. ([1914] 2001), 'Remembering, Repeating, and Working-Through (Further Recommendations on the Technique of Psycho-Analysis II)', in *The Standard Edition of the Complete Psychological Works of Sigmund Freud*, Volume XII (1911–13), ed. and trans. J. Strachey, 145–56, London: Vintage.

Freud, S. ([1915] 2001), 'Repression', in *The Standard Edition of the Complete Psychological Works of Sigmund Freud*, Volume XIV (1914–16), ed. and trans. J. Strachey, 141–58, London: Vintage.

Freud, S. ([1917] 2001), 'Mourning and Melancholia', in *The Standard Edition of the Complete Psychological Works of Sigmund Freud*, Volume XIV (1914–16), ed. and trans. J. Strachey, 237–60, London: Vintage.

Freud, S. ([1919] 2001), 'The Uncanny', in *The Standard Edition of the Complete Psychological Works of Sigmund Freud*, Volume XVII (1917–19), ed. and trans. J. Strachey, 217–56, London: Vintage.

Freud, S. ([1920] 2001), 'Beyond the Pleasure Principle', in *The Standard Edition of the Complete Psychological Works of Sigmund Freud*, Volume XVIII (1920–2), ed. and trans. J. Strachey, 1–64, London: Vintage.

Freud, S. ([1923] 2001), 'The Ego and the Id', in *The Standard Edition of the Complete Psychological Works of Sigmund Freud*, Volume XIX (1923–5), ed. and trans. J. Strachey, 1–66, London: Vintage.

Freud, S. ([1924] 2001), 'The Dissolution of the Oedipus Complex', in *The Standard Edition of the Complete Psychological Works of Sigmund Freud*, Volume XIX (1923–5), ed. and trans. J. Strachey, 171–9, London: Vintage.

Freud, S. [1927] 2001), 'Fetishism', in *The Standard Edition of the Complete Psychological Works of Sigmund Freud*, Volume XXI (1927–31), ed. and trans. J. Strachey, 147–57, London: Vintage.

Freud, S. ([1930] 2001), 'Civilization and its Discontents', in *The Standard Edition of the Complete Psychological Works of Sigmund Freud*, Volume XXI (1927–31), ed. and trans. J. Strachey, 57–145, London: Vintage.

Frosh, S. (2013), *Hauntings: Psychoanalysis and Ghostly Transmissions*, Basingstoke: Palgrave Macmillan.

Fuchs, B. (2022), *Theater of Lockdown: Digital and Distanced Performance in a Time of Pandemic*, London: Methuen Drama.

Fulton, G., C. Madden, and V. Minichiello. (1996), 'The social construction of anticipatory grief', *Social Science & Medicine*, 43 (9): 1349–58.

Fuss, D. (1995), *Identification Papers*, New York: Routledge.

German Criminal Code. Available online: https://www.gesetze-im-internet.de/englisch_stgb/englisch_stgb.pdf (accessed 1 June 2022).

Gluhovic, M. (2020), *Theory for Theatre Studies: Memory*, London: Methuen Drama.

Goldman, D. (2017), 'From Spectating to Witnessing: Performance in the Here and Now', *Arts and International Affairs Journal*, 2 (2). Available online: https://theartsjournal.net/2017/07/19/from-spectating-to-witnessing-performance-in-the-here-and-now/ (accessed 1 June 2022).

Gordon, A. F. ([1997] 2008), *Ghostly Matters: Haunting and the Sociological Imagination*, Minneapolis: University of Minnesota Press.

Gurr, A. (1992), *The Shakespearean Stage 1574–1642*, 3rd edn, Cambridge: Cambridge University Press.

Halberstam, J. (2005), *In a Queer Time and Place: Transgender Bodies, Subcultural Lives*, New York: New York University Press.

Halberstam, J. (2018) 'Unbuilding Gender: Trans* Anarchitectures in and beyond the Work of Gordon Matta-Clark', *Places Journal*, October. Available online: placesjournal.org/article/unbuilding-gender/ (accessed 1 June 2022).

Halberstam, J., and T. Nyong'o (2018), 'Introduction: Theory in the Wild', *The South Atlantic Quarterly*, 117 (3): 456–64.

Harding, J. M. (2013), *The Ghosts of the Avant-Garde(s): Exorcising Experimental Theater and Performance*, Ann Arbor: University of Michigan Press.

Hare, D. (1998), *The Judas Kiss*, London: Faber and Faber.

Harker, R. (2010), 'HIV and AIDS Statistics'. Available online: http://www.nhshistory.net/aidsdata.pdf (accessed 1 June 2022).

Harney, S., and F. Moten (2013), *The Undercommons: Fugitive Planning & Black Study*, Wivenhoe: Minor Compositions.

Harris, J. O. (2022), '*Daddy*': *A Melodrama*, London: Nick Hern Books.

Hartman, S. (2002), 'The Time of Slavery', *The South Atlantic Quarterly*, 101 (4): 757–77.

Heddon, D. (2008), *Autobiography and Performance*, Basingstoke: Palgrave Macmillan.

Hegberg, N. J., J. P. Hayes, and S. M. Hayes (2019), 'Exercise Intervention in PTSD: A Narrative Review and Rationale for Implementation', *Frontiers in Psychiatry*, 10: 1–13.

Home Office (2021), 'Hate Crime, England and Wales, 2020 to 2021'. Available online: https://www.gov.uk/government/statistics/hate-crime-england-and-wales-2020-to-2021/hate-crime-engl and-and-wales-2020-to-2021#introduction (accessed 1 June 2022).

Hörnigk, F., and R. L. Magshamrain (2006), 'Müller's Memory Work', *New German Critique*, 98 (Summer): 1–14.

Hunger (2008), [film] Dir. Steve McQueen, Ireland and UK: Film 4 Production, Channel 4, Northern Ireland Screen, Broadcasting Commission of Ireland and Wales Creative IP Fund.

International Dachau Committee, 'Homosexual Prisoners in the Dachau Concentration Camp'. Available online: https://www.comiteinternat ionaldachau.com/en/stories/455-homosexual-prisoners-in-the-dac hau-concentration-camp (accessed 1 June 2022).

International Institute of Political Murder (IIPM) website. Available online: http://international-institute.de/en/about-iipm-2/ (accessed 1 June 2022).

It's a Sin (2021), [television series] Channel 4, 2021.

Janes, D. (2015), *Visions of Queer Martyrdom from John Henry Newman to Derek Jarman*, Chicago: University of Chicago Press.

Jones, A. (2015), 'Material Traces: Performativity, Artistic "Work," and New Concepts of Agency', *TDR*, 59 (3): 18–35.

Jones, J. (2013), 'Stolen, Looted, Lost and Burned', *The Guardian*, 4 September. Available online: https://www.theguardian.com/artanddesign/2003/sep/04/arttheft.art (accessed 1 June 2022).

Josephine, C. (2013), *Bitch Boxer*, London: Oberon Books.

Jung, C. G. ([1945] 1976), 'Marginalia on Contemporary Events', in *The Collected Works of C. J. Jung*, Volume 18, ed. and trans. G. Adler and R. F. C. Hull, 591–603, Princeton: Princeton University Press.

Kalb, J. (2011), *Great Lengths: Seven Works of Marathon Theater*, Ann Arbor: University of Michigan Press.

Kartsaki, E. (2017), *Repetition in Performance: Returns and Invisible Forces*, London: Palgrave Macmillan.

Khomami, N. (2021), 'Banksy Offers to Raise £10m to Buy Reading Prison for Art Centre', *The Guardian*, 5 December. Available online: https://www.theguardian.com/artanddesign/2021/dec/05/bansky-offers-to-raises-10m-to-buy-reading-prison-for-art-centre (accessed 1 June 2022).

Kierkegaard, S. ([1843] 2009), 'Repetition' in *Repetition and Philosophical Crumbs*, trans. M. G. Piety, 1–82, Oxford: Oxford University Press.

Kilroy, T. (1997), *The Secret Fall of Constance Wilde*, Meath: Gallery Books.

Kosoko, J. O. (2017), *Séancers* [promotional video]. Available online: https://www.jaamil.com/performance (accessed 1 June 2022).

Kushner, T. (1992), *Angels in America, Part One: Millennium Approaches*, New York: Theatre Communications Group.

Lavery, B. (2010), *Beautiful Burnout*, London: Faber and Faber.

Lehmann, H.-T. ([2014] 2016), *Tragedy and Dramatic Theatre*, trans. E. Butler, Abingdon: Routledge.

Lindemann, E. (1944), 'Symptomatology and Management of Acute Grief', *American Journal of Psychiatry*, 101: 141–8.

Local Government Act 1988 (1988). 'Local Government Act 1988: Chapter 9'. Available online: https://www.legislation.gov.uk/ukpga/1988/9/pdfs/ukpga_19880009_en.pdf (accessed 1 June 2022).

Lopez, M. (2018), *The Inheritance*, London: Faber and Faber.

Lorde, A. ([1984] 2019), *Sister Outsider*, London: Penguin Classics.

Luckhurst, M. (2014), 'Giving up the Ghost: The Actor's Body as Haunted House', in M. Luckhurst and E. Morin (eds), *Theatre and Ghosts: Materiality, Performance and Modernity*, 163–77, Basingstoke: Palgrave Macmillan.

Lugones, M. (2008), 'The Coloniality of Gender', *Words & Knowledges Otherwise*, 2 (2): 1–17. Available online: https://globalstudies.trinity.duke.edu/sites/globalstudies.trinity.duke.edu/files/documents/v2d2_Lugones.pdf (accessed 1 June 2022).

Maitland, J. C. ([1852] 1893), *The Doll and Her Friends; or, Memoirs of the Lady Seraphina*, New York: Brentano's.

Mamet, D. (2007), 'Ultimate Fighting: The Final Frontier', *The Guardian*, 30 September. Available online: www.theguardian.com/sport/2007/sep/30/features.sport4 (accessed 1 June 2022).

Marriot, D. (2010), 'On Racial Fetishism', *Qui Parle*, 18 (2): 215–48.

Mars R. (2022), *Forge* [programme note] (Unpublished).

Martin, C. (2013), *Theatre of the Real*, Basingstoke: Palgrave Macmillan.

Martin, C. (2021), 'Holding a Mirror Up to Theatre: Milo Rau's *La Reprise: Histoire(s) du théâtre (I)*', *TDR*, 65 (1): 54–61.

Marx, K. (1844 [1977]), 'Private Property and Communism,' in *Economic and Philosophic Manuscripts of 1844*,' trans. M. Milligan, 93–108, Moscow: Progress Publishers.

Marx, K., and F. Engels ([1848] 1955), *The Communist Manifesto*, ed. S. H. Beer, New York: Appleton-Century-Crofts.

Marx, K. ([1867] 1982), *Capital: A Critique of Political Economy*, Volume 1, trans. B. Fowkes, Harmondsworth: Penguin Books.

Mattson, G. (2019), 'Are Gay Bars Closing? Using Business Listings to Infer Rates of Gay Bar Closure in the United States, 1977–2019', *Socius: Sociological Research for a Dynamic World*, 5: 1–2. Available online: https://journals.sagepub.com/doi/pdf/10.1177/2378023119894832 (accessed 1 June 2022).

McGough, P. (2017), *I've Seen the Future and I'm Not Going: The Art Scene and Downtown New York in the 1980s*, New York: Pantheon.

McKellen, I. (1990), 'Ian Charleson: Tribute', *Ian McKellen Writings*. Available online: http://www.mckellen.com/writings/90charleson.htm (accessed 1 June 2022).

Mendelssohn, M. (2018), *Making Oscar Wilde*, Oxford: Oxford University Press.

Metzger, G. ([1960] 2019), 'Manifesto Auto-Destructive Art (Second Manifesto)', in *Gustav Metzger Writing*s, 66–7, ed. M. Copeland, Zürich: JRP Editions.

Milk & Blood (2001), [film] Dir. Franko B. Available online: https://vimeo.com/126307870 (accessed 1 June 2022).

Minamore, B. (2019), 'Damn, I'm Good at This!' Is Travis Alabanza the Future of Theatre?', *The Guardian*, 27 March. Available online: https://www.theguardian.com/stage/2019/mar/27/travis-alabanza-interview-future-theatre (accessed 1 June 2022).

Moreman, C. M., and A. D. Lewis, eds (2014), 'Introduction', in *Digital Death: Mortality and Beyond in the Online Age*, 1–6, Santa Barbara: Praeger.

Moten, F. (2003), *In the Break: The Aesthetics of the Black Radical Tradition*, Minneapolis: University of Minnesota Press.

Movement Advancement Project (2020), 'The Rise of Hate Crimes', 29 May. Available online https://lgbtmap.medium.com/education-action-during-covid-19-the-rise-of-hate-crimes-a261fd723c8a (accessed 1 June 2022).

Müller, H. ([1981] 1986–94), 'Ich glaube an Konflikt: Sonst glaube ich an nichts, Gespräch mit Sylvère Lotringer', in *Gesammelte Irrtümer: Interviews und Gespräche*, 3 vols., Frankfurt am Main: Verlag der Autoren.

Müller, H., and F. M. Raddatz (1991), *Jenseits der Nation: Heiner Müller im Gespräch mit Frank M. Raddatz*, Berlin: Rotbuch.

Muñoz, J. E. (2009), *Cruising Utopia: The Then and There of Queer Futurity*, New York: New York University Press.

Nadel, I. B. (2011), 'Boxing with Brecht: David Mamet and Bertolt Brecht', *Journal of Dramatic Theory and Criticism*, 26 (1): 103–24.

Nead, L. (2011), 'Stilling the Punch: Boxing, Violence and the Photographic Image', *Journal of Visual Culture*, 10 (3): 305–23.

Nyong'o, T. (2019), *Afro-Fabulations: The Queer Drama of Black Life*, New York: New York University Press.

Oates, J. C. ([1987] 1997), *On Boxing*, London: Bloomsbury Publishing.

Ofcom (2020), 'Online Nation: 2020 Summary Report', 24 June. Available online https://www.ofcom.org.uk/__data/assets/pdf_file/0028/196408/online-nation-2020-summary.pdf (accessed 1 June 2022).

Pappas-Kelley, J. (2019), *Solvent Form: Art and Destruction*, Manchester: Manchester University Press.

Pearson, M. (2012), 'Haunted House: Staging the Persians with the British Army', in *Performing Site-Specific Theatre: Politics, Place, Practice*, ed. A. Birch and J. Tompkins, 69–83, Basingstoke: Palgrave Macmillan.

Pennington, M. (1987), *An Angel for a Martyr: Jacob Epstein's Tomb for Oscar Wilde*, Reading: Whiteknights Press.
Pepys, S. (2003), *The Diaries of Samuel Pepys — A Selection*, ed. R. Latham, London: Penguin Books.
Phelan, P. (1993), *Unmarked: The Politics of Performance*, Abingdon: Routledge.
Phelan, P. (1997), *Mourning Sex: Performing Public Memories*, Abingdon: Routledge.
Phillips, A. (2016), 'On "Remembering, Repeating, and Working Through," Again', *Contemporary Psychoanalysis*, 52 (3): 375–82.
Pintaruo, J. (1992), *Raft of the Medusa*, New York: Dramatists Play Service.
Plath, S. ([1962] 1981), 'Daddy', in *Sylvia Plath: Collected Poems*, ed. T. Hughes, 222–4, London: Faber and Faber.
Policing and Crime Act 2017. Available online: https://www.legislation.gov.uk/ukpga/2017/3/contents/enacted/data.htm (accessed 1 June 2022).
Price, G. (2018), *Oscar Wilde and Contemporary Irish Drama: Learning to be Oscar's Contemporary*, London: Palgrave Macmillan.
Pryor, J. I. (2017), *Time Slips: Queer Temporalities, Contemporary Performance, and the Hole of History*, Evanston: Northwestern University Press.
Public Health England (2017), 'Towards Elimination of HIV Transmission, AIDS and HIV-Related Deaths in the UK'. Available online: https://assets.publishing.service.gov.uk/government/uploads/system/uploads/attachment_data/file/675809/Towards_elimination_of_HIV_transmission_AIDS_and_HIV_related_deaths_in_the_UK.pdf (accessed 1 June 2022).
Ramirez, M. (2015), *The Royale*, London: Oberon Books.
Rau, M., and Ensemble (2021), 'La Reprise: Histoire(s) du théâtre (I)', *TDR*, 65 (1): 41–53.
Ravenhill, M. (2008), 'My Near Death Period', *The Guardian*, 26 March. Available online: https://www.theguardian.com/stage/2008/mar/26/theatre (accessed 1 June 2022).
Ravenhill, M. (2011), *Ten Plagues* [with *The Coronation of Poppea*], London: Methuen Drama.
Rosenberg, T., S. D'Urso, and A. R. Winget (2021), 'Introduction: Queer and Trans Feminist Performance', in ed. T. Rosenberg, S. D'Urso,

and A. R. Winget (eds), *The Palgrave Handbook of Queer and Trans Feminisms in Contemporary Performance*, 1–23, Cham: Palgrave Macmillan.

Rycroft, C. ([1968] 1972), *A Critical Dictionary of Psychoanalysis*, Harmondsworth: Penguin Books.

Sackler, H. ([1967] 1968), *The Great White Hope*, New York: Samuel French.

Sanders, J. (2022), 'Stitch in Time', *ARTFORUM*. Available online: https://www.artforum.com/print/202206/jasmine-sanders-on-black-dolls-88608 (accessed 1 June 2022).

Schneider, R. (2011), *Performing Remains: Art and War in Times of Theatrical Reenactment*, Abingdon: Routledge.

Sedgwick, E. K. (1990), *Epistemology of the Closet*, Berkeley and Los Angeles: University of California Press.

Sexual Offences Act 1967. Available online: http://www.legislation.gov.uk/ukpga/1967/60/pdfs/ukpga_19670060_en.pdf (accessed 1 June 2022).

Shakespeare, W. (2006), *Hamlet*, A. Thompson and N. Taylor (eds), London: Arden Shakespeare.

Shaw, P. ([1993] 2011), 'You're Just Like My Father', in J. Dolan (ed.), *Menopausal Gentleman: The Solo Performances of Peggy Shaw*, 47–64, Ann Arbor: University of Michigan Press.

Shaw, P., and Weaver, L. (2018), 'Ruff', *PAJ: A Journal of Performance and Art*, 40 (2): 108–32.

Sherard, R. H. (1905), *Twenty Years in Paris: Being Some Recollections of a Literary Life*, Philadelphia: George W. Jacobs.

Sherman, M. ([1979] 2004), 'Bent', in *Martin Sherman: Plays 1*, 51–142, London: Bloomsbury Methuen Drama.

Shnayerson, M. (2013), 'One by One', *Vanity Fair*, 21 August. Available online: http://www.vanityfair.com/culture/1987/03/devastation-of-aids-1980s (accessed 1 June 2022).

Silverstone, C. (2011), *Shakespeare, Trauma and Contemporary Performance*, Abingdon: Routledge.

Sinfield, A. (1994), *The Wilde Century: Oscar Wilde, Effeminacy and the Queer Moment*, New York: Columbia University Press.

Sofer, A. (2016), 'Getting on with Things: The Currency of Objects in Theatre and Performance Studies (Review Essay)', *Theatre Journal*, 68 (4): 673–84.

Stanislavski, C. ([1936] 2013), *An Actor Prepares*, trans. E. R. Hapgood, London: Bloomsbury.

Stone, P.R., ed. (2018), *The Palgrave Handbook of Dark Tourism Studies*, London: Palgrave Macmillan, 2018.

Stonewall (2015), [film] Dir. Roland Emmerich, Los Angeles, CA: Centropolis Entertainment.

Stonewall (2017), 'LGBT in Britain: Trans Report'. Available online: https://www.stonewall.org.uk/system/files/lgbt_in_britain_-_trans_report_final.pdf (accessed 1 June 2022).

Stroebe, M., and Schut, H. (1999), 'The Dual Process Model of Coping with Bereavement: Rationale and Description', *Death Studies*, 23 (3): 197–224.

Tatchell, P. (2017), 'Sexual Offences Act 1967: Reform and Repression'. Available online: http://www.petertatchellfoundation.org/sexual-offences-act-1967-reform-and-repression/ (accessed 1 June 2022).

Taylor, R. R. (1974), *The Word in Stone: The Role of Architecture in the Nationalist Socialist Ideology*, Berkeley: University of California Press.

The Death and Life of Marsha P. Johnson (2017), [film] Dir. David France, New York: Public Square Films.

The United States Department of Justice (2020), 'Hate Crime Statistics'. Available online: https://www.justice.gov/hatecrimes/hate-crime-statistics (accessed 1 June 2022).

Theweleit, K. ([1977] 1987), *Male Fantasies: Women, Floods, Bodies, History*, Volume 1, trans. S. Conway in collaboration with E. Carter and C. Turner, Minneapolis: University of Minnesota Press.

Thompson, M.G. (1994), *The Truth about Freud's Technique: The Encounter with the Real*, New York: New York University Press.

Tick, tick ... BOOM! (2021), [film] Dir. Lin-Manuel Miranda, Beverly Hills, CA: 5000 Broadway Productions and Imagine Entertainment.

Travers Smith, H. ([1924] 2003), *Oscar Wilde from Purgatory*. Available online: https://gutenberg.net.au/ebooks03/0301181.txt (accessed 1 June 2022).

Traversi, D. A. (1956), *An Approach to Shakespeare*, 2nd edn, New York: Doubleday.

Trouillot, M. (1995), *Silencing the Past: Power and the Production of History*, Boston: Beacon Press.

Turkle, S. (2007), 'Introduction: The Things That Matter', in S. Turkle (ed.), *Evocative Objects: Things We think With*, 3-11, Cambridge, MA: MIT Press.

United States Holocaust Memorial Museum, 'Dachau'. Available online: https://encyclopedia.ushmm.org/content/en/article/dachau (accessed 1 June 2022).

Van der Kolk, B. ([2014] 2015), *The Body Keeps the Score: Brain, Mind, and Body in the Healing of Trauma*, New York: Penguin Books.

Virilio, P. ([1996] 1999), *Politics of the Very Worst*, interview by P. Petit, ed. S Lotringer, trans. M. Cavaliere, New York: Semiotext(e).

Walsh, F. (2010), *Male Trouble: Masculinity and the Performance of Crisis*, Basingstoke: Palgrave Macmillan.

Walsh, F. (2013), 'Saving Ulster From Sodomy and Hysteria: Sexual and Political Performance in Northern Ireland,' *Contemporary Theatre Review*, 23 (3): 291–301.

Walsh, F. (2016), *Queer Performance and Contemporary Ireland: Dissent and Disorientation*, Basingstoke: Palgrave Macmillan.

Walsh, F, ed. (2020), *Theatres of Contagion: Transmitting Early Modern to Contemporary Performance*, London: Methuen Drama.

Walsh, F. (2020), 'Pathogenic Performativity: Urban Contagion and Fascist Affect', in K. E. Shepherd-Barr (ed.), *The Cambridge Companion to Theatre and Science*, 101–15, Cambridge: Cambridge University Press.

Walsh, F. (2021), 'Grief Machines: Transhumanist Theatre, Digital Performance, Pandemic Time', *Theatre Journal*, 73 (3): 391–407.

Walshe, E. (2011), *Oscar's Shadow: Wilde, Homosexuality and Modern Ireland*, Cork: Cork University Press.

Wardi, D. (1992), *Memorial Candles: Children of the Holocaust*, Abingdon: Routledge.

White, G. (2013), *Audience Participation in Theatre: Aesthetics of the Invitation*, Basingstoke: Palgrave Macmillan.

Williams, R. (2010), *Sucker Punch*, London: Methuen Drama.

Wilde, O. ([1897] 2013), *De Profundis and Other Prison Writings*, London: Penguin Classics.

Winnicott, D. W. ([1965] 2018), *The Maturational Processes and the Facilitating Environment*, Abingdon: Routledge.

Winnicott. D. W. ([1971] 2005), *Playing and Reality*, Abingdon: Routledge Classics.

Wolynn, M. (2016), *It Didn't Start with You: How Inherited Family Trauma Shapes Who We are and How to End the Cycle*, New York: Viking.

Index

Note: Emboldened pages indicate figures

Abbey Theatre, Dublin 136–7
Abraham, Nicolas 19, 54
Abram, Jan 114
Abramović, Marina
   The Artist is Present 80, 197 n.8
   (*see also* Ulay)
   Breathing in, Breathing Out 80
Acconci, Vito (*Seedbed*) 80
Act on the Criminal Rehabilitation of Persons Sentenced for Consensual Homosexual Acts after 8 May 1945 4
ACT UP 46, 119
Adebayo, Mojisola 112
   Muhammad Ali and Me 62–3
Adelphi Theatre, London 38
Adjibi, Tom 88–**9**, 93
Ahmed, Sara 81–2
AIDS Garden Chicago 6
Alabanza, Travis 26, 86, 96–106
   Burgerz 26, 86, 96–106
   Overflow 97
   Stories of a Queer Brown Muddy Kid 96–7
Albert Kennedy Trust 148
Almeida Theatre, London 27, 33, 37, **40**, 43, **113**
Almond, Marc 164, 166
Als, Hilton 112
American Psychiatric Association 176
Antin, Eleanor (*Carving: A Traditional Sculpture*) 69
antiretroviral treatment 36
Arbus, Diane 109

archive 8, 12, 15, 17, 23, 26, 34, 70, 163, 177–8, 184, 195 n.10, 196 n.12, 198 n.8
Ardern, Jacinda 168
Arendt, Hannah 90, 198 n.4
   the banality of evil 90
arresting objects 108 (*see also* Chapter 4)
Artangel 27, 132, 137–45, 148–50, 153–4, 158
   Inside – Artists and Writers in Reading Prison 27 (*see also* Chapter 5)
Athanassoglou-Kallmyer, Nina 186–7
Athey, Ron (*Four Scenes in a Harsh Life*) 80

bakla (or baklâ) 102
Ball, Hugo 13
Bang, Claes 108
Banksy 125, 131
   Girl with a Balloon 125
   Love is in the Bin 125
Baraitser, Lisa 192
Barbican, London 6, 47, **49**, 97, 170, **173**
Bartlett, Neil 135–6, 139
   In Extremis 136
   Who Was That Man? 135
Basquiat, Jean-Michel 109
Bauer, Heike 134–5
BBC 35, 131
Beale, Simon Russell 36–7
Beau, Dickie 5, 24, 26, 32–46, 50–7, 85, 161

¡Showmanism! 34
Blackouts: Twilights of the Idols 34
Camera Lucida 34
Lost in Trans 34
Re-Member Me 24, 26, 85, 161 (*see also* Chapter 1)
Bechdel, Alison (*Fun Home*) 162
Beit Ha'am 90
Belfast Ensemble 28, 163–5, 169–70 (*see also* Chapter 6)
 Abomination: A DUP Opera 164
 Ten Plagues 28, 163–70, 175, 177, 180, 183
Benjamin, Walter 11, 128
Bennett, Alan (*The History Boys*) 123
Bertish, Suzanne 39
Beuys, Joseph 63–4
 Boxing Match for Direct Democracy 64
 Organization for Direct Democracy through Referendum 63
Bhabha, Homi K. 11–12
Bion, Wilfred R. 25, 29, 115
 container-contained 25, 115
Bishop, Claire 140
Biswas, Ansuman 173
Black Cap, London 97
Bloch, Ernst 179–80
Boliver, Rocío 174
Book of Exodus 66
Bosie (Lord Alfred Douglas) 139–40, 142–3, 149
Bowery, Leigh (*Tell Them I've Gone to Papua New Guinea*) 6
Branagh, Kenneth 36
Brantley, Ben 51
Braun, Kathrin 117–18
Brecht, Bertolt 11–12, 62, 88, 93, 105, 167–8, 177
 In the Jungle of Cities 62
Brennan, Teresa (transmission of affect) 24
Breuer, Josef 17

Burke, Kathy 136
Butler, Judith 20, 48, 181

Cabaret Voltaire, Zurich 13
Calder, Alexander 109
Cameron, David 119
Camus, Albert (*The Plague*) 164
Carlson, Marvin 31, 39, 57
Caruth, Cathy 53–4
Cassils 26, 60, 61, 64–5, 69–75, 77–83, 126
 Becoming an Image 26, 59–60, 69–75, 77–83, 196 n.1, 197 n.6 (*see also* Chapter 2)
 Cuts: A Traditional Sculpture 69
 Inextinguishable Fire 69
 Tiresias 69
catharsis 49, 88, 90
Cavan, Matthew (Cherrie Ontop) 165–**6**
Chambers-Letson, Joshua 12, 100
channelling 8, 23, 25–6, 32–3, 56, 86 (*see also* Chapter 1)
Charcot, Jean-Martin 17
Charleson, Ian 33–5, 37–9, 42–3, 45–6, 54, 161, 195–6 n.11
Chow, Broderick D. V. 74
Clarke, Michael (*Michael Clarke: Cosmic Dancer*) 6
Coates, Ta-Nehisi 1, 170
commodification 127, 132–3
 art as commodity 107–9
 commodity fetishism 108, 124–5
 of people 15, 107–9, 127
 of suffering 107, 144
 of Wilde 132–3, 153, 159
Connolly, James 153
contagion 34, 40–2, 55, 166
Council of Europe 103, 193 n.4, 198 n.9
Covid-19 1, 28, 162–3, 168–9, 176, 178–9, 183–4
Craven, Arthur (Fabian Lloyd) 63
Criminal Law Amendment Act 1885 4, 133

Critchley, Simon 43
Crowell, Ellen 151
Cummings, Alan 36
Cuomo, Andrew 168

D'Urso, Sandra 101
Dachau 27, 107, 116–19, 123
Dada 13, 63
Dant, Tim 124
dark tourism 144–5
Davidson, Gordon 55
Day-Lewis, Daniel 36–7
De Kosnik, Abigail 178
De Laet, Andrea 1, **2**
Dean, Tim 55
Defoe, Daniel (*A Journal of the Plague Year*) 164
Derrida, Jacques 15–16, 52
Di Benedetto, Stephen 68
Diamond, Elin 49
digital theatre 8, 178
   intermedial theatre and performance 8, 23, 28, 163, 170, 175 (*see also* Chapter 6)
   mediatization 28, 34, 39, **40**, 43, 163–6, 169–70, 175–8, 183
   and performance 183
dispossession (to dispossess; the dispossessed) 10, 18–25, 29–30, 42, 100, 105–7, 116, 131–2, 139, 146, 155, 157–9, 181, 183–5, 187–92
   return of the dispossessed 20, 30
Dolan, Jill 87, 179–80
dolls 109–13, 115, 127
Dolz, Sonia Herman (*Yo Soy Asi*) 1
Don't Say Gay Bill (HB 1557) 3
Dowden, Hester (Hester Traverse Smith) 32
Dreamgirls 97
Dryden, John 91
DSM-5 (*Diagnostic and Statistical Manual of Mental Disorders*) 75, 176
Dublin Theatre Festival 5

Duchess Theatre, London 162
Duckie 97, 198 n.8
Dumas, Marlene 140, 142
Dutroux, Marc 87
Dyer, Richard 73–4

Eagleton, Terry 90
   Saint Oscar 136
Easter Rising (1916) 143, 153
Echo and Narcissus 34, 174
Edelman, Lee 9–10, 21, 30
Edgy Women Festival, Montreal 71
Edmonds, Antony 149
Eichmann, Adolf 90
Enelow, Shonni 81
Eng, David L. 53, 57
Enlightenment 90
exe(o)rcise 26, 60, 74, 80, 82, 86
   (*see also* Chapter 2)
Eyre, Richard 33, 36, 38

Facebook 176
Fairbairn, W. Ronald D. 115
   bizarre objects 115
Fay, Francis (*Marking Time/A Love Letter*) 153
Faye, Shon 99–100
Felman, Soshana 23
Femminiello 102
Fiennes, Ralph 36, 139
Finley, Karen 26, 36, 46–57
   Momentro Mori 47
   Written in Sand 26, 32, 46–57
   (*see also* Chapter 1)
First World War 63, 147, 152
Fisher, Mark 91, 93–4, 166
Fitzrovia Chapel, London 6, 162
Flanagan, Bob 70
Flashdance 121
Flintoff, Beth (*Oscar Wilde on Trial*) 139
Floyd, George 173, 201 n.7
Forster, E. M. 31
Franko B 26, 59–61, 64–8, 74–5, 77–83, 173

I'm Not Your Babe 66
Mama I Can't Sing 66
Milk & Blood (film) 66
Milk & Blood (performance) 26, 59–60, 64–9, 196 n.1
Oh Lover Boy 66
Freeman, Elizabeth 10–12, 56, 95, 147
chrononormative 11
erotohistoriography 11, 56, 147
Freud, Sigmund 17–21, 26, 42, 52–3, 60, 75–6, 113, 124, 182
and melancholia 53, 182
and mourning 53, 76, 182
return of the repressed 20
unheimlich 52
working through 8, 23, 26, 60, 68, 75–8, 82–3 (*see also* Chapter 2)
Frosh, Stephen 16–17, 19, 51, 54
Fuchs, Barbara 177
Fuss, Diana 18

Galop (LGBT anti-violence charity) 178
Garland, Judy 34
Garner, Eric 173
Gay Britannia 35
Gay Sweatshop 45
general antagonism 22
Genet, Jean (*Chant d'Amour*) 142
Géricault, Théodore (*Le Radeau de la Méduse* [*The Raft of the Medusa*]) 186–8
Gibson, Mel 36
Gielgud, John 36–7, 45, 54
GLBT Historical Society Museum, San Francisco 6
Gluhovic, Milija 76–7
Gober, Robert (*Treasure Chest*) 144
Godard, Jean-Luc 87
Goddard, Lynette 112
Goldin, Nan (*The Boy*) 140–2
González-Torres, Félix 143
Gordon, Avery F. 16–17

Great Plague of London 41, 164
grief 5, 7, 18, 22, 25, 28, 31, 42, 48, 51, 53, 121, 162–3, 166–7, 175–6, 178, 180–4 (*see also* Chapter 6)
anticipatory grief 180–2
grief work 182
(*see also* Freud, mourning)

Halberstam, Jack 71, 74, 139, 156
Hambling, Maggi (*A Conversation with Oscar Wilde*) 150
Harding, James M. 13
Hare, David (*The Judas Kiss*) 136
Haring, Keith (*Keith Haring*) 7
Harney, Stefano 21–2
Harris, Jeremy O. 27, 107–10, 113, 116
'Daddy': A Melodrama 27, 107–16, 125, 127–9 (*see also* Chapter 4)
Slave Play 108
Hartman, Saidiya 54, 100
Heddon, Deirdre 77
Hill, E. J. Hill (*O Captor, My Captor*) 64
Hirschfeld, Magnus 134–5, 144
Hitler, Adolf 117, 119
HIV/AIDS 4, 6, 10, 26, 31, 33, 35–8, 41–5, 47–8, 50, 52, 55–6, 92, 135–7, 143, 152, 161–6, 168–9, 176–8, 185, 188, 190
Hockney, David (*Portrait of an Artist (Pool with Two Figures)*) 35
Holden, Jack (*Cruise*) 162
Holland, Merlin 148
Holland, Vyvyan 134
Holocaust 90, 116, 119, 122–3, 127
Hoyle, David (The Divine David) 185–91
Diamond 35
Ten Commandments 185–90

Humphreys, Jonathan 139
Humphreys, Laud 70
Hunter, Kathryn 139

Instagram 176
installation 6, 8, 27, 47, 66, 108,
    116, 119–22, 132, 137–41,
    148–51, 159, 162
Institut für Sexualwissenschaft (the
    Institute for Sexual Science)
    117

Jarfi, Ihsane 26, 85, 87–96, 102,
    104
Jarman, Derek 6–7, 97, 166, 191
    Derek Jarman Protest! 6–7
    Jubilee 97
Jarrett, Terique 109, **113**
Johnson, Jack 62–3
Johnson, Marsha P. 147
Jones, Amelia 71–2
Joyce, James 32

Kalb, Jonathan (marathon theater)
    139
Kartsaki, Eirini 106
Kaufman, Moisés 87, 148
    *Gross Indecency: The Three Trials
    of Oscar Wilde* 148
    The Laramie Project 87–8
Kazanjian, David 53, 57
Kearns, Michael 70
Kierkegaard, Søren 94–6, 198 n.7
Kilmainham Gaol 153
Kilroy, Thomas (*The Secret Fall of
    Constance Wilde*) 136
Kimbook, Ioanna 109
kinship 35, 55–6
Kjartansson, Ragnar 139
    Me and My Mother 80
Kleeb, Josef 66
Kosoko, Jaamil Olawale (*Séancers*)
    26, 50
Kramer, Larry (*The Normal Heart*)
    162

Kushner, Tony (*Angels in America*)
    31, 35, 45, 55

La MaMa La Galleria, New York 47
Lakmaier, Noëmi 173
Larkin, Nicky 165
Larson, Jonathan (*Rent*) 162,
    200 n.1
Latham brothers 61
Latour, Bruno 72
Laub, Dori 23
Lehmann, Hans-Thies 93, 182–3
les ballets C de la B 1
    *Gardenia/Gardenia — 10 Years
    Later* 1–5
Levy, Deborah 143
Lewis, A. David 176–7
Leysen, Johan 85–6, 91
LGB Alliance 4
Liao, Li (*Attacking the Boxer from
    Behind Is Forbidden*) 64
Lichtenstein, Roy 109
Lindemann, Erich 180 (*see
    also* grief)
Local Government Act 1988
    (Section 28) 3, 44
Lopez, Matthew (*The Inheritance*)
    31, 35
Lorde, Audre 81
Lotringer, Sylvère 94
Luckhurst, Mary 32
Lugones, Maria 101
Lyric Theatre (Hammersmith) 97

Mac Liammóir, Micheál (*The
    Importance of Being Oscar*)
    135
Mac, Taylor (*Taylor Mac's Holiday
    Sauce ... Pandemic!*) 162
Mamet, David (*Speed-the-Plow*) 62
Mark Taper Forum, Los Angeles 55
Markievicz, Constance 153
Marriot, David 124
Mars, Rachel 27, 107, 116, 119–24
    Forge 27, 108, 116–25, 127–9

Martin, Carol 88, 90, 93
Marx, Karl 15, 124, 132
McCrea, John 109
McDermott & McGough (*The Oscar Wilde Temple*) 27, 132, 145–50, 154, 158
McGinty, Thom 136
McMahon, Phillip (*Once Before I Go*) 162
McQueen, Steve (*Hunger; Weight*) 142
melodrama 110
memory 15, 20, 25, 31, 33, 35, 37, 47, 57, 60–1, 77, 91, 123, 147, 159, 171–2
  commemoration 6, 8, 15, 23, 27–8, 31, 35, 45, 47, 107, 119, 121, 123–5, 127–8, 132–3, 144, 150–1, 153 (*see also* Chapter 5)
  memory industry (Schneider) 95
  remembrance 24–6, 34–6, 52–3, 57, 76–7, 191
Mendel, Gideon (*The Ward – Revisited*) 162
Mendelssohn, Michèle 155–6
Mercury, Freddie 51, 166
mesmerism 32
Metzger, Gustav (auto-destructive art) 126–7
Milk, Harvey 147
Minamore, Bridget 101–2
Mitchell, Conor 164–5, 169
Monroe, Marilyn 34
Moreman, Christopher 176–7
Morris, Leni 178
Moten, Fred 19, 21–2
Mullen, Dinah 119
Müller, Heiner 93–4
  necrophilia 94
Muñoz, José Esteban 10, 179–80, 190
Muybridge, Eadweard 61

National Theatre, London 33, 35, 37–8, 69, 136, 162

Nead, Lynda 68
Nebenzahl, Paul 48, 51
Newsweek 55
NHS (National Health Service) 36
Nicholls, Jacqueline 122–3
Nomi, Klaus 92, 166
Norris, David 136
Northam, Jeremy 36–7, 195 n.9
NOT OVER: 25 Years of Visual AIDS 47
Nottage, Lynne (*Sweat*) 80
NTGent, Belgium **2**, 86
Nyong'o, Tavia 12, 156

O'Connor, John 148
O'Brien, Martin (*The Last Breath Society (Coughing Coffin)*) 173–4
O'Keeffe, Georgia 109
O'Reilly, Kira 174
O'Toole, Peter 36
Oates, Joyce Carol 68
objectification 198–9 n.1 (*see also* commodification)
Office of Public Works (Ireland) 152
Old Bailey, London 138, 148
ONE National Gay & Lesbian Archives 70
Operation Yewtree 149, 200 n.9
Osborne, Danny (*Oscar Wilde Memorial Sculpture*) 150
Out and About! Archiving LGBTQ+ history at Bishopsgate Institute 6, 97

Pancin, Jean-Michel (*In Memoriam*) 140
pandemic 162–5, 167–9, 176–9, 182–4, 186 (*see also* Covid-19; HIV/AIDS)
Pappas-Kelley, Jarad 125–6
Pasolini, Pier Paolo 142
Peake, Maxine 139
Pearse, Pádraig 153
Pennington, Michael 36, 152

Index

Pepys, Samuel 164
Phelan, Peggy 12, 181
Phillips, Adam 76
Pintauro, Joe 188
Pitié-Salpêtrière, Paris 17
Platel, Alain 1
Plath, Sylvia 116
possession
 ghosts/ghosting 131–2, 157, 159, 174, 179, 181–2, 188, 191
 haunting 5, 7–8, 13–17, 19, 23, 26, 28, 31, 39, 43, 51–2, 54, 56, 92, 94, 106, 137, 147, 162, 165, 170, 179, 181–2, 188, 190–1
 hauntology 15 (Derrida)
 occupation 7–8, 14, 16–17, 20, 23, 25–9, 34, 40, 50, 52, 54, 57, 108, 113, 121, 132 (*see also* Chapter 5)
 ownership 15, 23–4, 52, 86, 95, 112, 132, 159
PrEP (pre-exposure prophylaxis) 10, 36, 55
Pride 35
Pryce, Jonathan 36
Pryor, Jacyln I. 12
psychic crypts 19
PTSD (posttraumatic stress disorder) 75, 78
pugilism 59, 61, 64, 78, 82–3
 pugilistic performance 26–7, 60–9, 78–9, 81–3 (*see also* Chapter 2)
Purcell, Henry 91–2
 'The Cold Song' 91–2

Queer Britain (museum) 6
queer conduit 26, 33
queer heirlooms 190
Queer House Party 162

Rainsford, Jenny 109
Ramirez, Marco (*The Royale*) 62–3
Rau, Milo 85–8, 90–7, 104, 106
 120 Days Of Sodom 87
 The Congo Tribunal 87
 Five Easy Pieces 87
 IIPM (International Institute of Political Murder) 86, 197 n.2
 La Reprise: Histoire(s) du théâtre (I) 26, 85–97 (*see also* Chapter 3)
Ravenhill, Mark (*Ten Plagues*) 28, 163–5, 169 (*see also* Chapter 6)
re-enactment 22, 27, 49, 88, 95, 102, 105–6 (*see also* Chapter 3)
Reading Prison (Gaol) 27, 131, 137 (*see also* Artangel)
recollection 8, 23, 48, 50–1, 57, 85–6, 80, 90, 94–7, 105
Rector, Enoch J. 61
Rees, Roger 36–7
repetition 11, 55, 65, 76, 91, 94–7, 106, 198 n.2
 to repeat 21–2, 53, 75–6, 91, 94, 103, 105–6, 112, 119
replay 8, 23, 86, 88, 95, 97, 102, 104–6, 158
reproduction 8, 23, 27, 56, 107, 116, 120, 122, 124, 127–8, 129
rewild(e)ing 28, 133, 156–8
Rickman, Alan 36–7
Robinson, Iris 164
Roe v Wade 3, 193 n.5
Rose, Sheree 70, 174
Rosenberg, Tiina 101
Russell Chapel, the Church of the Village, New York 146
Rycroft, Charles 76
Rylance, Mark 37

Sackler, Howard (*The Great White Hope*) 62
Sadler's Wells Theatre, London 1
Saint Katherine of Alexandria 66
same-sex marriage 3, 10, 55, 132, 168
 Marriage Equality (Ireland) 137

Schick, Clemens 140
Schneemann, Carolee (*Interior Scroll*) 80
Schneider, Rebecca 11, 95–6
Schofield, Joseph Morgan 174
Schubert, Franz (*Winterreise*) 167
Schut, Henk 182
Schwules Museum, Berlin 6
séance 33, 37
   performance-as 26, 31
   theatre-as 46, 50, 86
Second World War 127
Self, Tschabalala 109
Serrano, Andres 66, 80
   Milk, Blood 66
   Piss Christ 80
Sexual Offences Act 1967 34–5, 43–5
Shabazi, Shabnam 174
Shakespeare, William 39, 41
   Hamlet 15–16, 24–5, 32–3, 36–43, 45–6, 54, 85, 94, 96, 164–6
   The Winter's Tale 143
   Shaw, Peggy 63, 170–5, 177 (*see also* Split Britches)
   RUFF 177
   You're Just Like My Father 63
Shepard, Sam (*Fool for Love*) 37
Sherard, Robert H. 144
Sherman, Cindy 109
Sherman, Martin (*Bent*) 38, 118
Shiraga, Kazuo (*Challenging Mud*) 70
Shnayerson, Michael 41
Sissay, Lemn 139
Slinger, Jonathan 37
Slovo, Gillian 143
Smith, Patti 139
Sofer, Andrew 113
somatic practices 78
SPILL Festival 47, 70, 196 n.1
spiritualism 32
Split Britches 28, 163, 170–1, 177
   Last Gasp 28, 163, 170–5, 177, 180, 183

Stanislavski, Constantin 91
Stonewall (LGBT rights charity) 4, 38, 45, 98
Stonewall (riots) 147, 180
Streisand, Barbara 37
Stroebe, Margaret 182
Sturgeon, Nicola 168
sweat (perspiration) 41, 45, 59, 65, 68–9, 71–4, 79–82, 165, 197 n.7

Tate Britain, London 35, 140
Tate Liverpool 7
Taymor, Danya 109
Tectonic Theater Project 87, 198 n.3
Tee, Nicholas 174
Testbed, Leeds 107, 119–**20**
Tiresias 34
   Tiresias (Cassils) 69
The Aids Memorial 176
Théâtre des Champs-Élysées, Paris 168
Théâtre National, Wallonie-Bruxelles 87, **89**
Theweleit, Klaus 79
Thompson, M. Guy 76
Tillmans, Wolfgang (*Separate System, Reading Prison*) 143
Tóibín, Colm 139
Torok, Maria 19, 54
Toynbee Hall, London 65, **67**, 196 n.1
trans (transgender) 4, 97–101, 104, 147
trauma 8, 12–13, 17–19, 22–3, 25–7, 53–5, 60, 64, 68, 75–8, 82–3, 86, 107, 112, 119, 123, 161, 188, 191
Traverse Theatre, Edinburgh 164
Trimegisto, Lechedevirgen 173–4
Trouillot, Michel-Rolph 14
tumah 122

Turing, Alan 133, 147, 194 n.8
  Turing Law (Policing and Crime
    Act 2017) 4, 133
Turkle, Sherry 125

Ulay 80, 197 n.8 (*see also*
  Abramović)
undercommons 21–2

Van der Kolk, Bessel 78
Van Durme, Vanessa 1
Van Laecke, Frank 1
Virilio, Paul 126, 187

Walshe, Eibhear 136
Wardi, Dina 119
Weaver, Lois 170–5, 177 (*see also*
  Split Britches)
Webster, Jamieson 43
Weill, Kurt 167–8, 177
  The Seven Deadly Sins 167–8
  (*see also* Brecht)
Weiwei, Ai 143
Whishaw, Ben 37, 139
White, Gareth 104
Whitelaw, Mark 186
Whyte, Sharlene 109
Wilde, Oscar 24–8, 32, 63, 131–59
  The Ballad of Reading Gaol 134
  De Profundis 136, 139, 143,
    151, 154
  An Ideal Husband 136
  Lady Windermere's Fan 136
  The Picture of Dorian Gray 136
  Salomé 136, 142
  A Woman of No Importance
    136
Williams, Roy (*Sucker Punch*) 62
Williams, Tennessee 37, 81
  (*Cat on a Hot Tin Roof*) 37
Wilson, Ricky 51
Winget, Anna Renée 101
Winnicott, Donald W. 114–15
witnessing (to witness or bear
  witness) 23–4, 43, 52, 60, 68,
  71, 73, 75–7, 82, 86, 105–6,
  122, 145, 159, 191–2
Wojnarowicz, David (*Untitled (One
  Day This Kid…)*) 188–90
Wolynn, Mark 77–8
Woolf, Virginia (*Orlando*) 164
working out (to work out) 8, 23, 26,
  63–4, 60, 74, 76–9, 81–2

Yeats, W. B. 32
Young Vic, London 35

Zsarday 97

www.ingramcontent.com/pod-product-compliance
Lightning Source LLC
Chambersburg PA
CBHW071828300426
44116CB00009B/1483